ZOMBIE FILES

Gangs, Drugs, Politics and Voodoo under the Mandate of the United Nations

A confession about true events

by Max Kail

CHAPTER 1

My Country, my Rules

Haiti, Port au Prince, October 2007

Niko and I were moving slowly in our armored UN Toyota Land Cruiser through the intense traffic of downtown Port au Prince when our supervisor Gus called on my duty cell. The call went through and didn't cut off once for the entire five minutes. It was almost painful to concentrate on what he said since I just waited for the call to drop. He passed on information from a local source about five lynched dead bodies in Fontamara 47. In my mind I registered the excellent connection; wow the cell phones had really improved. A functional cell phone network was a positive change in the country, lynched dead bodies, on the contrary, were still a regular event in Port au Prince, Haiti's capital. Lynching was the only form of justice by which the Haitian population could be sure that criminals faced consequences, immediate and deadly ones. The number 5 was unusual though, one or two lynched bandits were typical, but five bandits should have had enough firepower to safely get away from the angry population. Gus was suspicious and sent us to check it out.

We all were in Haiti as United Nations Security Officers deployed with the United Nations Peacekeeping Operation (DPKO) mission named MINUSTAH that was established to stabilize the country after a civil conflict resulted in the departure of President Aristide. Gus was the Regional Security Officer, RSO in charge of the West Department including the Haitian capital. My colleagues, Niko and Abuelo, worked together with me in the Patrol Unit. We were the eyes and ears for the RSO in the field, the streets of Port au Prince. We were already headed in the direction where the five lynched bodies were found on our way to a weekly security meeting in the Martissant area. Niko was checking his guns and equipment, it was his automatic reflex with a task ahead, everything was in order and ready. Abuelo was already closer to the location with our second vehicle. Martissant had some terrible gang-controlled neighborhoods, three shooters were better than two.

We all had experience in different conflict zones with different cultures in our former military and UN careers, and none of us was going to judge the vigilante justice of the people; we just wanted to see what happened and if there was something more significant to the story. Most of the area in Martissant and Fontamara were shanty towns that grew like 'Favelas' into the hills above the Bay of Port au Prince with minimal access roads. Abuelo found the incident scene first and told us on the phone we had to see for ourselves. We called our Latin American friend and colleague "grandfather" in Spanish because he was the oldest one, he was over 50 and claimed the wisdom of the eldest. Whatever we still wanted to do, he had already done. Like the three generations of bulls standing on top of the hill looking down on the cows in the grass field and the youngest bull says: "let's run down and have sex with all the cows." Father bull answers: "Son, we go down slowly, stay relaxed and select the most beautiful cow". The the grandfather bull just says:" Shhhh, shut up both of you. They didn't see us yet, let's just go back the other side of the hill, so we have our

3

peace." Abuelo was a grandfather bull. But he seemed uncomfortable on the phone, even though I was sure I was mistaken, he wouldn't have entered a gang stronghold without our back up, and I couldn't imagine anything else making him uncomfortable. Maybe it was his hearing aid, Abuelo lost most of his hearing in an ambush in Iraq, and the hearing aid didn't work well in an open area with background noises. Our heavy-duty armored car was powerful enough to move its 4 tons up the mountain over the gravel and rocks. It was a great car and perfect for Port au Prince since 70 percent of the roads had no layer of asphalt or concrete anymore and were in terrible condition.

We parked the car next to Abuelo's vehicle close to the first dead body, we saw a Haitian National Police (HNP) pick-up parked 20 meters past the dead body. The body was covered by a plastic sheet, the first time I had seen this in Haiti. It was an unusual scene; nobody bothered covering dead bandits. The HNP pick-up was like most of their vehicles, completely banged up and looked like it had seen 20 years of hard service, even though it was more likely a contribution of some donor country within the last 4 years. I noticed the HNP vehicle had the left rear tire removed, and stones were placed under the axle to keep the rim in the air. A flat tire, no wonder with these roads. The bad roads made tire repair a popular and necessary business, and the Haitians were very good at it. On main roads, every few hundred meters was a pile of old tires that indicated a tire repair shop. A bucket of water, some form of a screwdriver and a simple hand pump was all they needed. Unfortunately, this crime scene was far away from the main road. We were surprised seeing police before us in such a location. HNP wouldn't have wasted their fuel or risk damaging their vehicle on this road, they would have come on the trucks of the blue helmets, the UN military contingent in the area. These police officers had made it all the way up here alone. There were two police officers in front and at least two more on the back seats because I saw two barrels of high-powered rifles sticking out of the open windows. Four more were sitting on a bench installed in the middle of the cargo area in the back. The four police officers on the back had old M14 rifles. I didn't know any of them and didn't believe they were from any Commissariat in the area. We visited the Commissariats frequently because of security issues and maintained good relations with the HNP officers there. There was no reaction from them to our arrival. We usually were welcomed by Haitian police officers and observed them be very proactive and professional around us. These guys just remained inside and on the vehicle.

We linked up with Abuelo, and he told us that five bodies in total were laying around 40 meters from each other. "And they don't look happy that we are here." His dark sunglasses didn't give away what he was looking at, but it was pretty evident to Niko and me. He was right, the HNP officers gave me a chill, even in this heat they made the hair on my neck stand up. They were not the trustworthy looking type, they reminded me of the 'zero tolerance' policy enforcers under former President Aristide that I had come across a few times. They killed everybody who was found without authorization on the street after dark or was perceived to be in opposition to Aristide's policies. I am sure it was not a specific method for Aristide, and none of the Haitian regimes before were more tolerant, Aristide was just the latest Haitian leader who applied the method. Over time I got an eye for these killers, they all had a ghost-like look, lifeless eyes. As if their own life got less and less with each life they took. I was right on the phone, 'Abuelo' didn't feel comfortable. Police on the scene before us and plastic covers for lynched bandits, something was not right. Also, it didn't look like the HNP officers were engaged a criminal investigation, they did not move from their vehicle. Standing around and watching them wasn't an option either but since we didn't want to leave the area, we had to act as if we were in charge. It helped us that we didn't look like the usual UN guys, they had no idea who we were. We all were in full body armor and besides our Glock 19 pistols we had our MP5 Submachine gun hanging on a sling. Our experience in Haiti showed us that being dressed like US mercenaries got us more respect from the gangs, HNP officers, and Haitians in general.

Niko had his camera out already and we passed four dead bodies until we reached the fifth body around 140 meters away. All five bodies were in the open area on or next to the dirt road near the simple brick houses. The population was still gathered around their homes. They were standing and watching. The lynching of bandits was common in Haiti, it wouldn't have kept the people from their normal routine and they would let the bodies rot in the sun. Once we removed the plastic sheet, we knew it was not the population that killed them. The body would have been chopped up by machetes or smashed by stones and burned. This young man was shot with one bullet in the mouth. To shoot somebody through the mouth in Haiti was usually the punishment for a snitch, somebody who talked to the wrong people about the wrong things. He was at the end of the dirt road and was closest to the brick buildings, one building was just three meters away, and the door was open. Nobody seemed to be inside, the people kept a distance from us. It was not a gang-controlled area, why had nobody approached us? Since Haitians had more trust and hope that we could help, they were always very helpful to us foreigners, but not today, they didn't want to talk. I looked at the door of the building close to the dead body. It was a thin metal door and had a significant dent in the center, like from a human body that slammed into it to force it open. The dead young man had been taken out of this home and was most likely the first to die.

His hands were not tied, they didn't need to if he was the first to die. They just held him down with their body weight, their knees on his chest. At least two men, he surely had trouble breathing until the bullet ended it. He was face up and must have seen his executioner. All five bodies were young men and had been shot in the mouth. The other four bodies had their hands tied behind the back, but at least one or two persons must have held them down to make sure they didn't escape. The other four victims must have heard the first shot and knew what was coming shot by shot until each of them met their executioner. I looked at all the lifeless bodies and the thick streams of blood flowings downhill. It was like their souls were still standing next to their bodies looking at me. All five looked like they were taken out of their beds, out of different homes. There were in shorts and t-shirts.

None of them had the usual gang tattoos. They didn't look like the typical gang members of a territorial gang in the area like in Grande Ravine or Ti-Bwa. These would have stayed together in one house. If they had criminal affiliations, it was related to a different area and a different form of crime, not the usual armed robbery or inter-gang violence. They lived here, most likely with their families. But if they were taken out of their family homes, where were the families? Where were the crying mothers next to their lifeless sons? I looked around, and the faces around me seemed frightened and shocked. It was not a gang stronghold, the dead bodies were not bandits who came here to do evil, evil came for them.

I was never a criminal investigator and had no idea how long these bodies might have been dead. I could only try to imagine what happened. Life started early in Haiti, with the first light of day at around 05:00. The victims must have been asleep when evil arrived. City power was rare and up here nonexistent, it was a dark night because of the new moon. The killers must have arrived here at least one or two hours before first light. There must have been multiple killers with somebody identifying the houses of their victims. At least two or three men entered each house and brought them out. I calculated a team of a minimum of 12 to 15 killers. There must have been one man who was the executioner, and he wanted to kill each of them, one after the other. Maybe he had even a message for them before he ended their lives. They didn't tie the hands of the first victim because he was the first to die and the shooter was right there when he was brought out of his home. They just forced him to lay still with their body weight on him until the executioner pulled the trigger. The others must have heard the first shot and knew they would be next. They must have tried everything to get away and at least 2 people held each of them down. Five bullets and no shells, most likely a revolver that did not eject the rounds. Looking at the wounds, a .38- caliber revolver fit the profile. The police were still officially armed with 38 revolvers. Niko took pictures of each victim, just in case one of our informants could recognize one. He came from the police car and just told me to check out the blood of the first victim.

There was now a second HNP vehicle parked next to our cars. Five HNP officers brought the missing tire, and they started remounting it. Amazing, not just that the police were before us at the scene, they even came all the way up here with two vehicles. Also, the second vehicle didn't seem to belong to any police station in the area. These HNP officers didn't approach us either. When I realized what Niko wanted me to see, I knew why. I missed it when I first passed the HNP vehicle. The young man who was killed on the road left blood across the dirt road downhill. There were no tire tracks of the HNP vehicle with the flat tire through the blood, there was no way around, and the police wouldn't have cared about a bloody tire. The HNP vehicle was there already when the young man's blood was spilled over the dirt road. Now it made all sense, and I knew why the population was not approaching us or moved on with their regular routine. The killers were still here. The mothers were looking at their son's killers and couldn't do anything. These HNP officers didn't come to investigate a crime, they were the criminals. I felt the police officers knew we realized what was going on but on their faces was just this cold look claiming, my country my rules.

I asked Niko if he got the HNP vehicles and HNP guys with his camera and he just nodded, of course he had. These five young men must have seriously pissed off some big shot with a lot of power and muscle, two HNP vehicles with at least 13 HNP officers was a dangerous kill squad. This was not the doing of a street gang; this was serious business related to Senators or other public officials, and we couldn't do anything about it. Anybody talking to us would have been another corpse shot through the mouth. We were heading out. Niko and I were heading to our joint security meeting in Martissant that was held every Friday in an empty 'high-school' building just above the market in the area. It was the focal point of the three main gang strongholds who were fighting over control and money from the market. The UN blue helmets of the Sri Lanka Battalion hosted the meeting under the leadership of MINUSTAH Civil Affairs Section. Our Civil Affairs and Human Rights representatives were experienced specialists, the finest examples of smart, well educated, enthusiastic liberals with a revolutionary spirit of social justice like Martin Luther King. That should have made them the natural enemies of any person with a military mindset. But, despite our military backgrounds, Niko, Abuelo and I had excellent working relations with them.

Upon arrival, we joined our Italian Civil Affairs colleague and Andrea Loi Valenzuela, our Chilean Human Rights Investigator. Andrea had just received a call from a trusted source about the execution of five young men in Fontamara 47 this morning. "Are you talking about these guys?" asked Niko when he showed them the pictures on his camera. We briefed them and agreed that Andrea would bring it up in the meeting without our details from the incident scene. The Inspector responsible for the area in the meeting had no idea about it but was going to visit the location after the meeting together with the UN Police and the commander of the Sri Lanka Battalion. Our colleagues from Civil Affairs and Human Rights had the mandate to follow up such issues and they could handle such cases without drawing attention to us. The last time we let them handle a case, it caused an international scandal, and more than a hundred soldiers of the Sri Lanka Battalion in Martissant were repatriated because of sexual misconduct. After the meeting, we contacted all our informants in the area to get a background story on the killing in Fontamara 47 and planned to visit the incident location again in the coming week. Civil Affairs and Human Rights couldn't get any details about the killings and our informants in the area came up completely empty. Five executions like this and we didn't get anything. Our confidential informants, 'CIs' did not even hear about it. The only lead was the HNP vehicles. They belonged to the commissariat of Jacmel, the regional capital of the South East Department more than 3 hours' drive from the incident.

Niko and I went back to Fontamara 47. The dead bodies were gone, the blood was washed away. We expected to be more successful, we always were, especially in the more impoverished areas. The people within the population were our best sources. But not here, we couldn't get anybody to talk to us. People were just standing and looking at us. There was a lady inside the house that I expected to be the home of the first victim. She could have been his mother. When I asked her if she knew the young men, she started crying, and an old man held her and told me to go away. I tried once more and asked them if the young man had recently been in Jacmel. I could see in both of their eyes that I hit on something. I could see the lady would have liked to talk, but the sadness in her face told me, not my country and their rules, the rules of the people in charge, the people above the law. They just went inside the small house and closed the door. It was still deformed with the dent in the center and didn't close very well.

I gave a few people little papers with my cell phone number and was hoping to receive a call, maybe this way somebody would feel safe enough to talk. It was late in the afternoon when we drove down from Fontamara and I looked at the beautiful blue and green Caribbean Sea. Most of the time I forgot that we were working on a Caribbean island and that this place was once called 'The pearl of the Antilles.' It was an incredible view. Niko said: "What a shame, they have no trust at all in MINUSTAH." That they didn't point at the killers when we came up was not a surprise, but that none of the people said anything to the HNP officer in charge who came with UN police and a platoon of UN soldiers, even though the killers had gone, was mind-blowingly sad. All the UN military troops in the country and we still couldn't provide them the fundamental right of personal security, at least so they could sleep safely at night.

I learned years later that in 2008, one of the killers, Jerry Enderson, an HNP officer from Jacmel was arrested for involvement with a kidnapping gang in lower Delmas, Port au Prince. He was also known to be an executioner for Senators who controlled the cocaine planes and marihuana shipments arriving on the Southeast coast of Haiti, the brother's Lambert and Senator Edwin Zenny. We never learned the reason why these young men had to die, but the fact that no one dared give information about it showed us who had the real power in the country - elected Haitian officials above the law.

Niko and I had both more than ten years in service already as civilian UN staff and knew the complexities of peacekeeping operations. I was former military but never a blue helmet, a military peacekeeper. I joined the civilian part of the United Nations directly after a few years of a very different kind of military service. I joined the army at 17 years of age. I was dropped from school, the school claiming I did not have enough hours of attendance to evaluate me. Apparently, being present at all sporting events was not enough. I was actually a victim of my time because if the world wide web had existed already, I could have finished the new school the same way I did my master's degree 20 years later, online. Since I always wanted to jump out of airplanes, I joined the mandatory military service and then the special forces as a professional soldier. I was more successful since the army focused more on physical education, special forces was a very small unit at the time and had nothing to do with the high speed, high tech combat machines from today who rescue hostages and capture wanted international war criminals or terrorists. We did not free hostages, we trained to take a hostage, a general of a foreign army for example. We prepared to operate in small groups undercover and blow up something that could bring a substantial conventional army to a halt without much contact and guidance from our command structure. It was called subversive, today we would have just said, terrorists. I adapted very well to this independent, rebellious mindset which was perfect for our operations but not so much for standard duty in the caserne. Like in my first school, life in the caserne with its strict hierarchy and I did not project a successful future.

I was selected for an educational program that provided me with my military salary and a civilian income as a student at an academy for security services. I was transferred to an administrative company in the capital and had to come once a month to sign the attendance sheet. It was like my time in my other school except that they didn't expect me to be there. The training at the security academy was very much learning by doing. We were only two, my partner came from the electronic surveillance part of the military counter intelligence. We bugged telephone lines of real targets, observed their daily routine, read their mail and sometimes checked their garbage or followed them to neighboring countries. We had no official credentials for such 'studies,' and many of the things would have brought us serious jail time had we been caught. Often these were the least of our worries since some of our targets had security details from foreign services. There was almost no supervision, we got the name and an idea of what was important to know and figured out a way to get it. We were very successful; we were smart enough to get it done and stupid enough to do it. Anyway, it was paradise, we had a double salary and were young free and single. When it came to an end for political reasons, there was no way I could get back into the uniform and the caserne.

Via some different assignments, I ended up as a Security Officer with the United Nations. I felt so proud of joining the real good guys and was amazed by the stories of my colleagues who served all over the world. I thought I was going to change the world. Here I was now, in the Caribbean. I looked over the beautiful bay of Port au Prince and the different blue and green shades of the Caribbean Sea. When I arrived in Haiti, I knew I was not going to change the world, but I was convinced I was going to change Haiti. I thought:" No ethnic conflict, no religious conflict, I will be actually part of a successful mission here."

CHAPTER 2

Chimères, the Monsters of Darkness

Haiti, Port au Prince April 2005,

"No 'chimères' here, you can leave it here." The man with a badge dressed in some sort of uniform told me to leave my 120-liter military 'Rucksack' on the floor next to the exit door of the International Airport in Port au Prince. I was wondering if the badge was real, but the person at least pretended well. The room was like the rest of the small airport terminal, full of people shouting and screaming. Some might have screamed at me. I must have missed my comrade Niko who told me he would be waiting for me inside the airport upon arrival. We knew each other from the previous mission, he was actually the one recommending me to the Chief Security Officer of MINUSTAH. I looked for him as soon as I stepped on the tarmac from the aircraft. I needed a second to overcome the humid heat which hit me like a hammer, especially after flying business class from Miami to Port au Prince. The business class was fully booked with rich Haitians who all knew and greeted each other like family. They seemed like very nice people. Before I walked down the tarmac, I saw to the left a line of people with carry-on bags pushing out of a door marked as 'Départ,' like a snake they moved slowly closer to the plane. I thought it was a bit early since I was one of the first disembarking the fully occupied Boing 737 of American Airlines. While I was going down the steps at least five men ran up already with black plastic bags. Actually, some of the crew members started collecting the garbage when the plane stopped. They were eager to get ready for take-off again. It was a short walk; the nose of the plane almost touched the airport terminal. The heat didn't stop inside, no air-conditioning, no electricity and no windows. There were no clear markings for immigration, but I saw a big opening into another room with more light. I held my blue United Nations Passport in front of me like the Bible and moved toward the light.

I learned in the middle east, never complicate things at border crossings by asking questions. It was essential to pretend to know exactly where to go and what to do until somebody said stop. I either took a short cut or passed immigration and customs without realizing it because I was already at the luggage claim. Nobody stamped or even asked for my passport. The luggage claim was a small corner with a hole in the wall through which bags were thrown. I saw two persons in civilian clothes stacking them next to the wall, it might have been their job or they were just proactive passengers waiting for their bags like me. The sweat on their faces suggested they didn't do it voluntarily. Once my bag was thrown in, I realized that I was just around the corner from the exit. Still no Niko. I wanted to return and was stopped by the man with the badge. I couldn't go back with the luggage. He didn't care about me, but the luggage had to stay, he was very firm about it. My first encounter with either Haitian authorities, or a scam, somebody who preyed on stupid new foreigners and was going to steal my bag.

I looked around and just saw chaos, I was convinced that no way my bag would be safe here. Outside the exit doors, it looked even more chaotic, almost frightening. There was a small fence that seemed to prevent an angry crowd of people from storming the airport. I had all my documents and money with me in my pants, so I figured my rucksack was collateral damage and went back into the luggage claim area. I found Niko and my untouched backpack. I was looking for the man with the badge to thank him but couldn't find him. Nobody paid attention to my bag. At least there was no terrorist threat in the country.

Niko had his UN vehicle parked close to the exit, a white Toyota 4Runner with a black UN logo on it. Haitians called it 'Machine un', Creole for vehicle one. In the car, Niko handed me his Glock 19 pistol in case of security issues on the way and briefed me on the situation. He was not surprised my rucksack was untouched because thieves captured in 'normal' public areas had very short trials. Anybody caught stealing an egg in the market was lynched on the spot. It was common Haitian justice executed by anybody, including women and children. The death sentence was carried out with machetes, stones, ropes, or gasoline, whatever was available. Once a friend intercepted an older man who wanted to attack a young man lying on the floor with a machete. He shot in the air to stop the man from committing a murder in front of him and told the man to drop the machete, which he did. Immediately, the around 12-year-old daughter picked up the machete intending to complete her father's work. The young man managed to get away in the confusion, but the anger of the daughter and father turned against my friend and other bystanders joined in. He got back in his car and took off with one more experience, don't mess with Haitian vigilante justice. But the man with the badge at the airport referred to 'chimères.' Niko explained to me, this was more than just a thief, it was Creole for a demon of darkness. It was the term used for the gangs, the militias from the slums of Port au Prince loyal to President Aristide. That sounded interesting, things seemed to be different in Haiti.

I got a hint how much different when I was introduced to the MINUSTAH Chief of Security. Bertrand Bourgain was sitting behind his computer in a very small room at the temporary MINUSTAH headquarters on the premises of the United Nations Development Program (UNDP) in Bourdon. His new office in the future MINUSTAH headquarters in the Christopher Hotel located a few hundred meters from UNDP was still under construction. He was using his index fingers to type and was talking, or rather cursing in French at the screen. It looked like he wanted to poke the recipient in the eye with each strike. Chuck, a UN 'old-timer' with several years as a UN Military Police Officer and now as a civilian DPKO Security, brought me in and waited for a moment to interrupt Bertrand. It looked like bad timing to me since the guy seemed to be really pissed off at somebody. It must have been the send button which he pressed underlining the stroke with "Fuck off." He turned to us and laughed," these people, fuck the UN, they all just blah blah blah, but I tell them to fuck off because I have a lot of work." Chuck tried to make an introduction, but Bertrand Bourgain continued:" You are the new one, good very good, you are recommended by good people. Just do your job, no blah blah and never forget this is a dangerous place…". He was looking for something under his desk and grabbed a brown leather briefcase, opened it and pulled out a Glock 19 pistole. He pointed the gun at an imaginary target at the wall frightening close to my head and said: "But if you are not ready to shoot and kill somebody, you are in the wrong place and better go home again." It was a relief for me that he didn't seem to expect a response because he was back at his computer screen and poking his fingers in his eyes again. I hesitated for a second because intuitively I wanted to salute him before leaving his office. There was a reason his nickname was

'Mad Max' when he commanded the rapid response company of the '2nd Rep.', the elite parachute regiment of the French Foreign Legion. He could be an amusing tall version of Louis de Funès when he talked at times, but in action, he was fearless and a great leader. Many called him crazy, but he was a warrior and a leader with a great heart.

Chuck stepped out and I followed. He said:" Don't worry, he is crazy and believes he is still a military commander. Many Officers in Security are new in the system. They don't know what it means to be a civilian. They do things UN Security is not supposed to do. But you know the system, we don't have to do shit." Chuck referred to our entitlements and benefits as a civilian staff member of the United Nations that provided us with an excellent salary, medical insurance and job security with long term contracts. But depending on the interpretation of these entitlements, it could enable us not to work at all. We were Security Officers of the Field Service category and in charge of the Safety and Security of the civilian component of the DPKO missions. In my previous missions, armed physical protection of UN staff was limited to UN premises except for protective details. In Haiti, things seemed to work differently.

The Chief's and Chuck's comments made me curious how different. Chuck brought me to the Christopher Hotel, the future MINUSTAH headquarters that was not yet ready to be fully occupied. It was also located in Bourdon just a few minutes away from the UNDP premises. Most of the Security Units had already moved in. The location was a nightmare, a dead-end street without secondary exits and minimal parking space. The UN HQ was supposed to a few hundred staff members with a hundred vehicles but no space to park. The Engineering Section declared it was not feasible because of the high cost of meeting Security Section requirements. The hotel had not been operational for several years, and was so deteriorated that significant efforts were still in progress to reach a minimum standard. According to the contract, the landlord should have provided electricity and water plus the refurbishing. Needless to say, our Engineering Section ended up fixing it and rented two large generators and one water truck which was permanently delivering water. I do not believe that these expenses of more than 20 000 USD per month were ever deducted from the ridiculously high monthly rent of 80 000 USD for the main MINUSTAH HQ building.

The building was chosen by Hocine Medili, the PDSRSG, Principal Deputy Special Representative Secretary General of MINUSTAH, the second in charge of the mission at the time, against the recommendation of Engineering and Security. He must have had a personal interest in this choice since he knew Haiti and the Hotel owner from previous missions. He had a reputation of pushing problems and responsibilities down to lower levels and then threatening subordinates' jobs if they did not comply. He insisted on the location, and it was then up to Engineering and Security to make it happen and provide the necessary paperwork to justify it. But the good news was that there was a restaurant serving breakfast and lunch buffet on the same floor as reception. Like the hotel, except for the amount they charged us, it was far from international standards. We called it the 'typhoid kitchen.' It was late lunchtime when I arrived, and many Security Officers were gathered in groups around the entrance and reception area next to the restaurant. I felt like the new inmate in the prison yard when in the movies the different groups or gangs were checking out the new guy to see if he was wearing any colors. On the balcony overlooking an empty swimming pool towards the back of the hotel was standing a short, slim man with reddish hair and pale skin. The tattoos on his lower arms were blue ink tattoos, not the expensive type. He was talking with a tall, slim man with blond hair who had a lighter and a pack of red Marlboro in his hand. The smaller one had a box of cigarettes in his shirt pocket. I saw something in common and knew where to smoke. They looked like military types, bar fight material, my type of guys. I walked over there to have a cigarette and get out of the spotlight. Without knowing, I had just chosen the colors I would be wearing.

They introduced themselves as Angus and John Taylor. Angus or just Gus was a Scotsman, with a heavy accent and the tattoos, he was the Regional Security Officer (RSO) in charge of all security matters for the West Department including the capital, Port au Prince. The other man was a Canadian, John Taylor from the Security Intelligence Unit, SICU. John and Gus were the two Security Officers Bertrand Bourgain relied on to keep all staff members safe. Despite the deployment of almost 8000 UN Military troops in the whole country, the countryside in Haiti had no severe security problem, but the capital, Port au Prince and its outskirts did. Vast territories of the metropolitan area were controlled by criminal gangs, paramilitary or militias and the Haitian National Police was outnumbered and outgunned. MINUSTAH military troops were positioned around these gang or militia strongholds and engaged in heavy gun battles daily. The Haitian National Police could not even protect themselves from criminal or paramilitary elements, so anybody on the street or in their residence was on their own. Port au Prince was like the wild west, without law and order. The perfect place for private security contractors. I believed Gus' brother described it best when he told me: "In my first two weeks in Haiti, I fired more rounds in shootouts with gangs than in 15 years with the British Military". He was a security contractor for the recently established cell phone company 'Comcell' with headquarters located on Martin Luther King Avenue facing Bel Air, a heavily armed 'chimères' stronghold.

Nothing was as feared as the 'chimères.' It seemed almost every Haitian I talked to in Port au Prince had a violent experience personally or within the family with the monsters of darkness. The 'chimères' were the curse President Aristide brought on anybody challenging his authority and even when Aristide's authority was gone after he left in 2004 the curse continued to haunt his opponents. Their favorite form of punishment was to burn somebody alive using a gasoline-soaked tire around the victim's neck. I still came across many necklaced dead bodies in 2005 and no question it creeped me out. The lifeless bodies were deep fried in upright unnatural positions, and their gestures and faces still showed the terrible pain. During morning patrols we discovered several mutilated dead bodies who must have felt terrible pain until death brought them relief and peace. At least these tortured bodies looked relieved, but not necklaced victims. The expression of pain in their face was infinite as though their soul was trapped inside the burnt body. The Haitians called it 'Pére Lebrun', named after a tire producer who advertised his tires on posters with a young boy looking through a tire. Where British humor was dark, Haitian humor was pitch black.

The 'chimères' were the youth and the children from the slums of Port au Prince. Aristide gave them hope and began to organize them as a priest in the St. Jean Bosco church in downtown Port au Prince. At the time, the slums were expanding daily with Haitians from the countryside looking for a job. In 1986 he founded an orphanage for 300 of these children that became the home to the most feared 'chimères' leaders of 2003. In 1985, Aristide stated in interviews that his role was to preach and organize; the solution to end social unfairness between the classes was revolution. He was a proponent of 'liberation theology' and was expelled in 1988 from the Salesian Order for his political activities and incitement of violence and hatred. But the impoverished masses in the slums along the seaside from Martissant in southern Port au Prince to Cite Soleil in the north of the capital waited for such a revolution. It was the perfect breeding ground for his political movement. The biggest and most dangerous slum of all was Cité Soleil. In 1957, 53 houses were built for workers of the Haitian American Sugar Company, HASCO. At the time this village was called

Cité Simone, after the wife of Dictator Francois Duvalier. HASCO closed its operation in 1987, and 3400 employees in Port au Prince and up to 40,000 sugar cane workers in the provinces lost their jobs. The old rusty steam locomotive parked in the ruins of HASCO close to Cité Soleil is to this day a contemporary witness of a better time. I was stunned when I saw it for the first time and realized that there was once a railway system in Haiti. What started with 53 houses, when former farm workers came to the capital to look for work, grew to be one of the biggest slums in the Northern Hemisphere, but all they found was garbage from the wealthier Haitians. The population in the hills of Port au Prince dumped their garbage in 'ravines,' dry river beds. The flash-floods during heavy Caribbean thunderstorms washed it all down the ravines that ended in the canals of the slums along the sea. These canals were already blocked off, and every rain flooded the homes of the poorest in the country.

I wonder if this gave Aristide the idea to call his political movement 'Lavalas,' flash-flood in Creole. It was like H.G. Wells 'Time Machine' where the 'Morlocks' living under-ground came out at night to eat the 'Elois' who enjoyed life on the surface. Aristide transformed the socio-economic suffering into a political force, the 'chimères' became his muscle in his last years as President. Aristide zombified them. He was their spiritual father, and their source of energy was the power of Voodoo and its feared black magic. Their love for Aristide and will to die for him was unbroken even after Aristide was forced out of office. They continued to fight the enemies of their leader, the foreign occupation force, the blue helmets of the MINUSTAH mission.

Gus and James Kfouri, a retired New York cop had to find out on their own. They had the task to identify potential locations for UN offices. Never having been to Port au Prince, they drove around looking for possible future office spaces for MINUSTAH. They drove on main roads until either the way became impassable or checkpoints with heavily armed Haitians indicated a gang or militia-controlled territory. The Haitian version of 'heavily armed' were light infantry weapons, mostly handguns and assault rifles, some quite old but still deadly. The 'chimères' controlled large portions, mostly the slums. The rest of Port au Prince was controlled by either the HNP or the Ex-Fadh, former Haitian military members who fought against Aristide and remained in some neighborhoods of Port au Prince. These Ex-Fadh did not pose a threat to MINUSTAH staff members in 2004, but the 'chimères' did. They were younger and 'trigger happy,' they had the tendency to shoot at anything related to MINUSTAH. Jim told me how often they made a wrong turn and looked into the surprised faces of these monsters of darkness. They could see them looking at each other and questioning what they should do with these crazy 'blancs' while Gus and Jim tried to turn around as fast as possible. Gus and Jim kept a picture of Aristide in the car. They held the picture up and gave the zombies a friendly "heyyy," thumbs up, or shouted: "Vive Aristide." This picture saved me as well many times in the years to come. But Jim was convinced that Voodoo saved them. These gang members must have thought these crazy 'blancs' were possessed by a voodoo spirit. For them, it was the only rational explanation for these 'blancs' to do something that stupid.

The first time I saw a spirit possessed person was at a Thursday night concert of the famous Voodoo band RAM at the Oloffson Hotel. They were calling one or more spirits with their Voodoo drums until some persons started to act unnaturally fast and hectic, just crazy. They got possessed until at some point they fell on the floor. For me it looked like a complete act, a show but I learned over the years there was nothing about acting when it came to Voodoo and the Haitian mind. No Haitian disrespected Voodoo, even though they might have been faithful members of the Catholic church, Voodoo was always there as well. Anything out of the ordinary, crazy behavior of a person or even an animal was usually attributed to Voodoo spirits.

Gus and Jim defined green, yellow and red zones according to the threat level in the metropolitan area of Port au Prince. Even though the green zone was considered relatively secure, the high potential of violent demonstrations, criminal incidents with armed bandits and general stupidity of naive and inexperienced UN personnel was still a significant challenge for the Security Section. Based on Gus and Jim's experience on patrols, the Security Patrol and Emergency Response Unit was created. The main task was to monitor the security situation in the capital, gather information about criminal gangs to support the guys working with John Taylor and respond to any emergency of UN employees. There were hundreds newly arrived UN civilian staff members driving around on the bad roads of the Haitian capital, getting lost or trapped in the crossfire between criminal gangs, surrounded by violent demonstrators or being attacked in their residences at night. Something had to compensate for the absence of Haitian law enforcement. As perfectly logical as the creation of such a Security Unit was to Bertrand and Gus, so absolutely unheard of was it in the UN system. The Patrol Unit operated like a national police unit, we rushed through traffic with sirens and blue emergency lights and had added Heckler & Koch MP 5 Submachine guns and shotguns to our Glock pistols. Haiti did not have the threat level of the Middle East, Africa or Afghanistan. The Patrol Unit had two armored vehicles with sirens and blue lights and didn't stop for anything. Still, to be shot at was no fun, so needless to say, it needed Security Officers who were willing or crazy enough to do it. There was a constant underlying discussion within the Security Section about the justification of what Gus' boys were doing in the gang territories and if it was covered by UN insurance. But at the time nobody would have dared to argue with Bertrand about it. As long he was the Chief of Security the safety and security of UN civilian staff in Haiti was our responsibility in or outside UN premises and justified the use of force if necessary. The Patrol and Emergency Response Unit was created to protect UN staff members from the 'chimères,' the monsters of darkness.

CHAPTER 3

Colombian Cocaine Cartels and a Haitian Coup d'Etat

Haiti, Port au Prince, April 2005

I didn't know much about the recent history of Haiti but was told that a violent rebellion forced President Aristide into exile. I just assumed that the United Nations deployed peacekeeping forces in Haiti because of a long, bloody conflict. Port au Prince reminded me of Beirut after the civil war, most of the metropolitan area looked destroyed. But a closer look didn't suggest that the source of destruction was a result of mortar impacts or bomb craters like in other conflict zones. Port au Prince was actually still a conflict zone, the capital was controlled by different armed groups. The 'chimères' controlled the slums, and the Ex-Army guys and Haitian National Police controlled portions of the wealthier parts of the Port au Prince. When I asked about the firepower of the armed groups involved in this conflict, I was surprised to hear that they didn't have any heavy weaponry, no rocket launchers, no tanks, not even a heavy machine gun. Conflict – light, a diet civil war. It was not just a light civil war, a coup d'état in Haiti was usually a very short event. Port au Prince just looked like a battleground of a long brutal armed conflict but was actually just the result of governments that did not invest in the country or maintain the infrastructure. I understood that since an Interim Government took over in February 2004, functional state institutions seized to exist. But the extent of deterioration and destruction I saw in the Haitian capital must have been a process over the at least past 15 years. The lower sections of the metropolitan area were one colossal garbage dump, roads were washed out and partially impassable, and electric poles were broken. I heard many times Haitians calling their country either a failed state or a narco-state. I could see for myself Haiti definitely looked like a failed state, but not like a narco-state in which I would have expected a flourishing business place with fancy roads and skyscrapers. A Haitian told me in the first few weeks, Haiti was all about perception versus reality. If I wanted to figure out what was going on in Haiti, I needed to be clear about what was the reality and what was perception. I also needed to know about the history, at least the recent past, when Aristide became President.

Aristide carried the hope of the majority of the Haitian population for social equality when he was inaugurated as President for only 9 months in 1991. A military coup-d'état led by General Raul Cedras and Lieutenant Colonel Michel Francois in 1991 exiled Aristide to the United States and removed his government under Prime Minister Rene Preval. Aristide claimed that the underlying cause for the coup was his intention to end the drug trafficking operation under Lieutenant Colonel Michel Francois, the head of the Military Intelligence and Secret Police. But people around Lt. Col. Michel Francois argued that Aristide didn't want to end the drug trafficking operation, he just wanted to end the cooperation with the Medellin Cartel under Pablo Escobar and make a new alliance with the Cali Cartel. Even though Pablo Escobar was already under heavy pressure by the Colombian Armed Forces and 'Los Pepes,' Michel Francois remained loyal to his friend, Pablo Escobar, and removed Aristide from power. While Aristide was in exile, demonstrations and street violence prevented new Presidential elections and kept Aristide officially the elected President. A wave of boat people from Haiti to the United States emerged and was a significant factor in the Clinton Administration decision to return Aristide to Haiti in 1994. Aristide's return was not expected to be welcomed by all Haitians. What 300 US Marines achieved in 1915 during the first US occupation of Haiti was ensured by 20,000 US troops in 1994 during operation 'Uphold Democracy.' Lt. Col Michel Francois together with General Cedras left Haiti, it was now their turn to go into exile. Aristide was back in Haiti. Pablo Escobar had been killed a few months earlier, the Cali cartel was the new power in Colombia and became the new partner of the Haitian government. Two young brothers, Jaques and Hector Ketant from Southern Haiti facilitated the switch to the new Colombian cartel and maintained the logistic part of the Haitian cocaine operation for years to come. The return of Aristide to Haiti brought an immediate halt to the refugee crisis. It showed how effective refugee masses or boat people could influence the internal and external policies of affected countries. Aristide was often described to me as an anarchist, but it seemed he was quite a strategist and long-term planner and his 'chimères' ensured that he could remain and return as the President of Haiti.

He returned with a United Nations Mission in his suitcase, named UNMIH, and blue helmets replaced US troops in the country. The mission's mandate was to modernize the Haitian Army and create a new Haitian National Police, the HNP. Once back in office he disbanded the Haitian Army, the FADH. Every FADH soldier became an Ex-Fadh overnight and lost all legal status, benefits and pension entitlements. Aristide was not convinced his efforts to infiltrate the army with his followers was sufficient to prevent future coup d'états and preferred to deal with thousands of enemies stripped of their legal status. Since he had UN military troops in the country, he could wait until the new Haitian Police Force was established with loyal officers. Lieutenant General Michel Francois alias 'Sweet Micky' was exiled to Honduras via the Dominican Republic and was charged in absentia by the US for exporting 33 tons of cocaine to the United States. It was estimated that the annual amount of cocaine was close to 50 tons and growing. Where Pablo Escobar had three warehouses in Haiti, the Cali cartel had hundreds. Aristide inherited the system in place to control and monitor the drug trade even though this system was accused of serious human rights violations against his own supporters. Youri Latorture was one, a young military officer who worked directly under Michel Francois in military intelligence and was known for his brutality against the 'chimères.' But his knowledge and contacts with the Colombian import-export operation made his services necessary to the National Palace. Aristide also kept the Ketant brothers, Jaques and Hector, in charge of the logistics. They provided transit through Haiti to the United States and facilitated distribution in Florida and New York via their extended Family members. The newly established Haitian National Police became the armed force representing Aristide and replaced the multinational force under a United Nations mandate after the successful election of Aristide's friend and political ally Rene Preval in 1996. The Haitian constitution of 1987 forbids two consecutive terms as President. Aristide was eligible to run for President again in 2000.

His victory in the Presidential elections in 2000 was no longer based on the hope of the majority of the Haitians. It was based on the dark force of his 'chimères' controlling the heavily populated slums of Port au Prince which provided the number of voters needed. He also lost his trust in most of his high-ranking Haitian National Police officers who wanted to renegotiate the arrangement with the Colombian Cali cartel and replace Aristide as the head of state. In fear of another coup d'état, Aristide ordered arrest warrants for the suspected traitors who fled across the border to the Dominican Republic. His 'chimères' made him President and became his most trusted security force for his last years in office. Just a few loyal HNP officers remained in his inner circle. The period from 2000 to 2004 was marked by the terror of the 'chimères' and the growing frustration within the private sector and the population. In 2003 many suspects close to Aristide were arrested and extradited to the United States on drug trafficking charges. Millions of US dollars were seized in their personal bank accounts, Forbes magazine even estimated Aristide's wealth at 800 million US dollars. Haiti did not gain from the cocaine business as it was claimed by loyal Aristide supporters, even one of his former bodyguards I talked to years later.

I was working a high-profile kidnapping case and was hoping to get key information from an ex-HNP officer who was protecting Aristide in 2003, he insisted Aristide was never involved in drug trafficking. The Ex-HNP was dead serious, I tried to clarify the statement that he never witnessed anything about drug trafficking when he was on Aristide's detail. He rolled his eyes and smiled: "Everybody was dealing with drugs, but not Aristide, he just told the drug dealers, one plane for you, the next plane for the country, one for you one for the country and so on." He referred to the planes landing with cocaine on Haitian soil and Aristide only made sure that the drug traffickers paid their fair share to 'the country.' Jaques Ketant stated in his trial in 2003 that he paid 500 000 US dollars for each cocaine plane landing in Haiti to Aristide. This explained Aristide's estimated fortune but not that he was not involved in drug trafficking. According to his former bodyguard, Aristide never actively moved drugs, people did it for him. It was Aristide's law, and he was above it. It blew my mind to hear the interpretation of law and justification for Aristide's innocence from a former police officer, but I wasn't surprised. If there was no action, there was no crime, the same principle was applied to money laundering. The concept of criminal intent and action by maintaining a supermarket which never had customers but had millions of dollars according to its official books was unknown in Haiti. Maybe since the official books were not maintained for Haitian authorities, they were used to justify bank accounts and villas in Florida to the US authorities.

I started to understand that drug trafficking played an essential role in Haitian politics; unfortunately, the money resulting from it was not invested in the country. I also realized that Haiti was not destroyed by civil conflict; the governmental institutions just didn't stop the destruction over several years. I started wondering by what justification were blue helmets deployed in Haiti since UN military components were usually very costly and deployed in real war zones. The yearly budget for MINUSTAH was beyond 500 million US dollars. The calculation and justification behind such huge mission budgets were that the destruction of a country's economy during a long civil war was still much more expensive than a peacekeeping force. But the conflict in Haiti was not a long civil war, most violent confrontations were very short and outside the capital. The first big city 'conquered' by the 'rebels' was Gonaives in February 2004 a few days before Aristide left the country. Conquered in Haitian terms was taking over the police stations in the city, which was not a real challenge since the support for Aristide in Gonaives was very limited. There were no heavily armed war parties that had to be separated in a peace agreement, these gangs or militias were illegal armed groups with small infantry arms, and most of these groups were gathered in or around Port au Prince. The rest of the country was very quiet, and almost no violent incidents were reported. What was our justification for being in Haiti?

I was told the HNP couldn't deal with the 'chimères.' The HNP in 2005 was just a small portion of the original force established in the last UN mission in 1996. In 2000 many high ranking HNP officers lost the trust of Aristide to oversee the control and protection of the Haitian cocaine operation and went into exile to the Dominican Republic. In 2004 many of the HNP officers who remained with Aristide were either arrested after his departure for drug trafficking or were dismissed from the force for irregularities. The loss of HNP officers in clashes with 'chimères' or the Ex-Fadh reduced it to the force it was in 2005. MINUSTAH was a great deal for Haiti. Haiti as a member of the United Nations paid a yearly contribution of less than 10 000 US dollars. For this contribution, it received a UN military force of 7000 soldiers, more than 1000 UN police officers, helicopters, vehicles, and many civilian staff members. Thousands of UN personnel were deployed in the country living and spending money in Haiti. All international investment left years ago because of the insane percentage Aristide was demanding. It seemed Aristide did not just ask the drug dealers for a very high share for the country, but any other business as well. The insecurity and nonexistent infrastructure in the country kept international investment away. The plan sounded simple, MINUSTAH provided security and foreign aid paid Haitian businesses to build up the infrastructure. This was an excellent deal for Haitian business. They did not have to maintain the MINUSTAH Force with tax money, and now they were paid to rebuild the Haitian infrastructure which was not maintained because they didn't pay taxes before either. Destruction of Haitian infrastructure was a risk-free long-term investment. And without competition from international companies due to the insecurity, the bidding process for these construction contracts could remain within the Haitian business families. I started to understand why it was said that such contracts were overpriced and didn't have a great reputation for implementation.

Gus was the first who warned me about doing business in Haiti and told me what happened to Jim and him on his patrols when they were searching for UN offices and camps for UN Military troops. Gus and Jim stopped at anything suitable. They also stopped at a hotel close to the National Palace. The hotel, like most functional and operational hotels in Haiti, was without guests. When Gus and Jim visited the hotel on their patrol, the owner came to welcome them. When he knew about their mission, he excused himself for a minute, went to his office and came back with a box. He put it in front of them on the table and told them that there were 100,000 US dollars inside and it would be his appreciation to them if they could grant security clearance for his hotel to become a future UN facility. Gus and Jim were stunned, and the owner explained to them that this was not an insult, this was how business was done in Haiti. Besides the immoral aspect of the offer, Gus and Jim could not sell out the safety of UN staff members since the area was too dangerous at the time to be considered as a UN location. Gus told me this story shortly after my arrival as a lesson to be aware of such methods, it was easy to get owned in Port au Prince.

Haiti looked like a failed state, but the number of expensive SUV limousines driving around in Port au Prince suggested Haiti was working pretty well for some people. Maybe for these people, Haiti was actually a perfectly functioning narco-state, not a failed state. But in the end, we all came here to change things to the better for the majority of the Haitians who lived in misery and insecurity. Once our UN military forces finished the criminal gangs, the country could start rebuilding and recovering. The MINUSTAH military was deployed with an aggressive mandate which enabled them to conduct military operations. The Interim government depended on the UN Military and their actions, since the existing force of Haitian National Police did not have the strength to keep any government in place. Therefore, our Military Forces had little political interference in their operations against illegal armed groups. But since these armed groups operated in highly populated areas, there was a very high probability of civilian casualties. Neither UN Police nor UN Military had the local experience, time or means to establish an intelligence network essential for successful operations. The central intelligence was provided directly from the acting Director General of the Haitian National Police to the MINUSTAH Forces. He never revealed his source of information, but it seemed to be very accurate.

CHAPTER 4
Zombie Hunters and the Men in the Shadow

Haiti, Port au Prince, May 2005

Three gang leaders of armed groups were identified as the root of all evil. They outgunned and outnumbered the Haitian National Police according to the highest-ranking Haitian police officer, Leon Charles. One of these gang leaders, 'Ravix,' was a holdover from the resistance against Aristide but refused to hand over his gang's weapons to HNP. He became an ally of the other gangs against their common enemies, the Haitian National Police and MINUSTAH. Remissainthe Ravix and his followers were the main controlling force around Route Frères between the police Academy and Petion Ville where many of our international staff members lived in private residences. They accepted International UN staff members residing within their territory. Ravix was an impressive man, especially when he received somebody in his office and banged a considerable machete on the table. Gus and John Taylor were sitting across from Ravix looking at the machete and trying hard to keep a straight face. We always had a good laugh in the years to come when we tried to imagine how their poker faces looked But Gus and John negotiated safe passage and authorization for UN staff members to reside in their territory and Ravix respected this agreement till his death.

The second root of all evil was Jean-Anthony René, alias 'Grenn Sonnen', ringing bells in Creole. He controlled a large portion of the area around Delmas 33 which was the main road leading from the airport to the UN Headquarters in Bourdon. Between 2001 and 2004 he operated in this area as a 'chimère' attached to the police Commissariat of Delmas 33 and led a kill squad against any critics of Aristide's politics and policies. The third root of all evil was a ghost, a myth. Not just a 'chimère,' the leader of the zombies in Cité Soleil, alias 'Dread Wilme.' He ruled over the biggest slum of Port au Prince and was the most challenging target. The UN Military forces surrounded the gang territories of Cité Soleil and his stronghold with checkpoints to isolate their power. Grenn Sonnen and Ravix were the first priority. The Director General of the Haitian National Police, Leon Charles, stated publicly the three gang leaders as the priority targets, especially Grenn Sonnen who had recently attacked the house of a high-ranking police officer and killed the bodyguard of the Minister of Justice in an ambush on his convoy. The Director General of the HNP initiated the creation of a joint intelligence unit with Haitian and UN Police Officers and was hoping that it would become a useful tool in future operations. For the time being the chief of police had to continue relying on his personal sources.

Ten days later on Saturday 9. April 2005, I had completed my check-in and was sitting in Sierra Base, the Security Communication Center. The Communication Center was the lifeline for all staff members traveling in Port au Prince and the West Department. Every staff member was issued with a radio since the frequent shootings and demonstrations on main roads in the green zones required temporary movement restrictions for specific areas. The cell phone network was deplorable in the country, and the walkie talkie was a reliable tool for staff members to receive and transmit messages in case of emergency. The national staff members, the assigned radio operators, were running the show in Sierra Base. They were fluent in Spanish, English, French, and Creole and did a great job. Still, there was an international Security Officer present to take responsibility for any decision, which most of the time was calling 'Sierra-Papa,' Port au Prince RSO Gus. It was part of the induction training for Security Officers to spend some days in Sierra Base. It was Saturday, and there was little radio traffic to expect on Channel 2, the Security Channel. But something was going on, the Sierra Charly call signs of John Taylor were communicating short cryptic messages. 'All set', 'ready', 'eyes on'. The 'Sierra Charlies' of SICU, the Security Information Coordination Unit, were busy. Also, Sierra Papa 1,2 and 3, the call signs of the Patrol Unit were involved. SP1 called SP:" Phase 1 completed". The duty cell-phone of Sierra Base was ringing. It showed Sierra Papa, I prepared myself for the heavy Scottish accent of Gus. I understood he wanted us to send an immediate travel restriction for all staff members in the area of Delmas 33. It didn't take long for the radio operator to draft one and was just about to transmit it to the civilian radio channel # 3 when we heard heavy gunfire on Channel 2. SP1 asked SP if the travel restriction was coming. Sierra Unit, Sierra 1, the chief called Sierra Papa on the radio requesting an update on results as soon as possible.

I learned afterward that SICU had intel on a meeting of Ravix and Grenn Sonnen in one of Sonnen's safe-houses in Delmas 33. Brazilian UN troops stood by with HNP until the confidential contact of SICU confirmed their presence. Ravix was shot and killed on the spot with six of his 'soldiers.' 'Grenn Sonnen'; escaped with injuries. SICU was tracking already the preferred nurse used by his gang for medical attention in the past and sent an informant to confirm his hideout. A similar set up followed the next day on Sunday and was the end of the Grenn Sonnen and five of his gang members. The operations were celebrated as a huge success since many weapons and ammunition were seized in the safe house. Also, many HNP uniforms were found which were used for kidnappings and other criminal operations. Grenn Sonnen and Ravix operated in residential areas where access was not so difficult, the third target 'Dread Wilme' in Cite Soleil was a different story, he lived in Zombie land.

There were several highly populated and highly polluted Port au Prince slums along the sea-side like Village de Dieu, Cité L'Eternell or Fort Dimanche, but none had an estimated population of more than 300 000 inhabitants. Nobody knew exactly how many people lived in Cité Soleil, but it was the most prominent congestion of metal roofs along canals full of human waste. Just a few international organizations had agreements with the gang leaders and were granted access to provide limited educational and medical programs. As neglected and disadvantaged their population was, they became important and influential in times when masses or popular movements were needed. When it came to demonstrations or elections, every politician turned into a caring friend of Cite Soleil, and a handful of gang leaders controlling these masses came in very handy. In general, demonstrations in Haiti were usually an organized event financed by a few individuals or a political entity to support a political agenda or goal. 'Lavalas' demonstrations at the time were by far the biggest mobilizations, not necessarily for the reason of popularity but for the support of criminal gangs controlling highly populated areas. One gang leader and his order to mobilize provided a few thousand demonstrators. It was also cost effective since the organizer had to pay only the gang leader instead of each individual demonstrator.

Even more important than providing demonstrators was the control of the gangs over the potential voters in such highly populated areas. Aristide didn't need a majority of Haitian voters to win in 2000. He just needed Cité Soleil and the other 'Lavalas' strongholds to cast their vote in his favor and at the same time make sure voters in the rest of Port au Prince were too scared to vote. Either the voters outside Port au Prince were ignored, or the election material didn't arrive in the capital in its original version. The system worked well, and until today the votes of these poor neighborhoods are used and abused by Politicians and their financial backers as the deciding factor. Dread Wilme was not the only gang leader in Cite Soleil, but the most notorious. For most of the Haitians, Cité Soleil was a place where only monsters lived, and 'Dread' was the lord of darkness. He was known to cut out the heart of captured enemies and eat them. Bit dramatic I thought, but I was told that this 'cannibalism' was a part of Voodoo black magic, the witchcraft. A powerful dark spirit protected 'Dread Wilme' from bullets but demanded a sacrifice or frequent sacrifices. The sacrifice could be the death of an enemy and eating his heart helped to gain the life force of his enemy. I wondered if there was any vegetarian gang leader. Could it also work with a cucumber? The Voodoo spirit was even physically present in the form of a small teddy bear which 'Dread' had hanging around his neck. This made him indestructible to a full metal jacket. I started to realize that Voodoo was more than the sticking needles in little dolls in a cartoon and I kept my 'non-believer' comments on these stories to myself. The Haitians who told me these stories took them very seriously. My friend Franz was right when he told me:" It doesn't matter if I believe in it, the fact that every Haitian believes in it made it very powerful."

He was very interested in Haitian art, which was often related to the spiritual aspect of Voodoo. When he bought a painting, he was always warned about the possible negative and positive effects of its spiritual force. Voodoo was much about knowledge of plants and powders, it could have healing power, but also evil poisoning force. I witnessed many times the influence it had on the Haitians. I saw it as similar to 'placebo effect,' when a person is given a sugar pill, believes it is medicine and is healed. The human mind was potent and could do great things if there was no doubt in it. There was a strong fear of the black magic force in Voodoo within the population. Obviously, stories of 'Dread Wilme' cutting out hearts and having them for lunch had its impact. 'Dread's' background reminded me a little bit of the child soldiers' life in Africa, except that instead of a refugee camp he was recruited and indoctrinated in an orphanage. Like many children in the capital but especially Cité Soleil, he grew up without parents or a home. Nobody knew at what point they became orphans; some were just given away by the parents. Dread Wilme found shelter and a home in 'Fanmi Selavi,' Creole for 'Family is live,' the orphanage Aristide founded in 1986. Together with 300 other orphans, he grew into the radical arm of the 'Lavalas' movement.

The orphanage had the special attention of Danny Toussaint. He was a founding Lavalas member, the bodyguard of Aristide and officer in the Haitian Army. There were unconfirmed reports of him teaching the orphans the handling of firearms and basic guerilla warfare tactics. It wasn't far-fetched since the teachings of Urban Guerilla Warfare of the Brazilian Carlos Marighella were not just prevalent within Colombian drug cartels and guerrilla groups, but among their Haitian counterparts as well. It could also explain the successful use of ambush strategies countering joint HNP/MINUSTAH operations with simple but effective technics such as anti-tank trenches and Molotov Cocktail traps. Dread Wilme, the orphan was today the most wanted zombie on the island, but nobody knew what he looked like. Neither HNP nor MINUSTAH had a photo of him. I knew John Taylor and Gus were working on it and I was watching and learning, as the Hebrew saying goes, stealing with eyes and ears. John Taylor and Gus started to fill me in more and more and even took me to confidential meetings. Some of these meetings would be in a small bar in Petion

Ville, depending on traffic 10 to 50 minutes away from the Christopher Hotel. I stayed close to the entrance. John Taylor sat down on a table with 4 men in the shadow, big dangerous looking people, at least what I could see in the dark. I saw their heads turning towards me the first time to check me out. I knew I was a prospect, and Gus and JT were testing if I could keep things to myself. Discretion was a very rare skillset within the United Nations.

One day JT introduced me to the men in the shadows. They still looked dangerous but had a great sense of humor. They had just come from SONAPI, an industrial complex very close to Cité Soleil. They met a CI, a confidential informant, who told them he could get a photo of 'Dread Wilme.' It was hanging on Dread Wilme's fridge. I was confused but didn't want to interrupt with stupid questions. John asked if he wasn't afraid somebody would realize the photo was missing. It took me some time to understand. The story was that these guys had a contact in Cité Soleil who could enter 'Dread Wilme's house, go to the fridge and take off a photo of 'Dread Wilme' stuck to the fridge with a magnet like in any other normal kitchen. I didn't know what was more surprising or crazy to me, that the heart-eating monster had a fridge, or that somebody was so crazy to steal a photo of 'Dread' from his fridge. My next thought was if people in Cité Soleil had electricity, did the fridge actually work or was it more a status symbol. I couldn't imagine the living conditions in Cité Soleil, but I knew the living conditions of the man working at my house. He stayed over-night in a small dark, humid cockroach-infested little hole in the back yard of the house next to the generator, without a fridge. I had to stop my mind and focus. They were all excited and couldn't believe he did it. Me neither, if this guy was eating the hearts of his enemies, what did he do to traitors?

The contact really did it, he took the photo and brought it to the men in the shadow. But there was nowhere a scanner to find or a camera. They had to drive almost back to Petion Ville to scan it at a friend's business and then returned it back to the CI. I couldn't imagine the CI walking back after a few hours and just placing the photo back on the fridge. Did he make it back in time, John asked? They didn't know yet. He would generally contact them in a couple of days if 'Dread' didn't have him for lunch already. The price to risk his life, or a terrible death, was 100 USD, this was how much he was asking for. They handed a paper to JT.

"In the middle is Dread," the white one of the men in the shadow said. John Taylor was looking at a photo of three men in front of a pick-up truck. The man in the middle was in military camouflage and had an Uzi submachine gun in his hand. It was the first photo of Dread Wilme in the hands of the Zombie Hunters. John Taylor was concerned about the Confidential Informant because he expected to receive aerial photos of Cité Soleil soon from the UN helicopter and was hoping their CI could identify the house with the fridge. They agreed to set up a meeting at the beginning of next week with the CI if he was still alive then. The guys in the shadow left. John Taylor and I were heading to Boucan Grégoire, a Bar and Restaurant further up in Petion Ville to meet up with Gus.

The bar was outside the restaurant area under a roof but separated from the street by a huge wall. Gus was sitting at one of the small tables together with a skinny white guy. He looked American, and his funny black pack told me he carried a gun. He could have been related to a US Agency, he introduced himself as Tommy Dutch. John gave both a short summary of the meeting. They knew the shadow warriors. John gave them the photo and mentioned that he will receive an electronic version via email. Tommy Dutch stepped aside for a phone call. Gus gave them an update on the aerial photos and said that the UN helicopter crew from the Chilean contingent with their Augusta Bell 212 were ready to operate by Friday. The meeting went off subject, and we were drinking beer while I was listening and sometimes asking questions. I just took a sip from the prestige bottle when heavily armed Haitians came into the bar area. Four Haitians in black cloths with a badge hanging on their chest spread out in the open bar area, one going into the restaurant area with his T-65, an export version of the famous US M-16 assault rifle. Gus, J.T. and Tommy Dutch seemed very relaxed about it, so I sat back on the high chair. A man in proper Haitian Police Uniform entered shielded by three men in suits with pistols in their hands. It was the phone call Tommy Dutch made earlier, he set up a meeting with Leon Charles, the HNP Director General. Gus, J.T. and Tommy Dutch went inside with him. I watched the funny pack of Tommy Dutch and the photo of Dread Wilme.

Gus told me afterwards that they just asked him to request MINUSTAH support for an operation in Cité Soleil based on credible intelligence information. Neither MINUSTAH nor the Chief of Police needed need to know from where the intel was coming from. I was confused, it seemed very complicated if our manager could do the same. But JT and Gus did not want to draw too much attention to themselves, Tommy Dutch or the men in the shadow. Gus explained to me later that, once the UN Military was involved officially, he could coordinate directly with the troops. The chief of HNP did not need to know what 'Dread Wilme' looked like, he didn't even need to know that a photo existed. The HNP was not expected to actively participate in any operation in Cité Soleil. The official books also required that the MINUSTAH action be requested by the Haitian National Police. In the official version, the HNP was of course leading any operation. Gus further told me that in Haiti, the key to success was the absolute control over information and who had it. I stayed on this evening, like many other evenings to learn more with Tommy Dutch. When things didn't go so well, and most of us thought Haiti was lost, he found a way to point out something positive. He compared development in Haiti with the 'Evolution,' slow but unstoppable. These meetings became regular security briefings with different security entities including the men in the shadow. Our colleague and friend Franz usually joined later and was my ride home.

Franz had already a few years more than me in the field. At the time he was going through his divorce process, and he always told me: "Watch me carefully, I live your future." He was the type of person who could be captured by a warrior tribe in the jungle or in the middle of Somaliland and sentenced to death. He would manage to trade himself free, challenge their best hunter and sit at the right of the King at the official feast the week after. We lived together in a house in Route Frères. Even after Ravix's death, the area was still a hostile place. Several houses got attacked during nights, and only firepower kept assailants away. Once the shooting started at one location, it spread like wildfire, on the one hand to alert the neighborhood and on the other letting the 'bad guys' know that there were weapons in the house. Franz and I adapted very well to this situation and started shooting on the way home from the bar and usually continued at home. Our roommates Christian and Edgardo needed some time to get used to it though. Some nights, our bursts of automatic gunfire at midnight gave them a harsh wake-up.

Dread Wilme also had a harsh wake-up when the Peruvian Special Forces of MINUSTAH reached his house in Bois Neuf undetected and tossed a few hand grenades through his door and windows before dawn on 6 July 2005. It was the heart of Cite Soleil, and an undetected approach seemed impossible. He felt safe in his house. The UN leadership wanted to avoid a massacre which ruled out a massive MINUSTAH Force invasion with APC's, Armored Personnel Carriers, small military tanks equipped with heavy machine guns and space for 8 soldiers. After studying the aerial photos, the Commander of the Peruvian Special Forces was convinced he could lead an assault team to the house. Even though Brazilian UN APC's and troops stood by on the outer perimeter of Cité Soleil in case something went wrong, it was unlikely they could reach the Commandos quickly. The commandos came from the sea through the swamp. It was a quick assault. The hand grenades woke up Cité Soleil and accomplished their lethal purpose. The Peruvian commandos confirmed Dread Wilme's death before withdrawal and disappeared back into the swamp. This type of commando operation was, unfortunately, a unique event since the battles in Cité Soleil were usually fought around, above or within the population and caused many injuries and deaths amongst them. Civilian casualties were the sad reality in the daily fighting with such a dense population living in mud or wooden shacks with metal roofs. MINUSTAH Military fired up to 10000 rounds a day with an estimate of 4 to 5000 bullets on the gang side. To put it in perspective, in the years between 2005 and 2007, stray bullets coming from the battleground of Cité Soleil injured 17 workers on the premises of Acierie d'Haiti on Rue National # 1. But the end of Dread Wilme spared the rest of Cité Soleil.

The operation against Dread Wilme had very negative coverage within the media inside and outside Haiti. There was not much reaction after Ravix, and Gren Sonnen found their violent end, but Cité Soleil received immediate media attention. It was a very political terrain and it seemed MINUSTAH had become too active and productive. At the time I didn't understand the importance of the gangs of Cité Soleil, especially with respect to the upcoming presidential elections. Political pressure was even coming from the MINUSTAH troop-contributing countries like Brazil and Chile to soften their approach. All operations regarding Cité Soleil were put on hold. But the respect the Peruvian soldiers gained from the gangs lasted for the rest of their assignment. They were based in 'Sode Cosa,' an industrial complex close to Cité Soleil. Abuelo and I were driving in our armored vehicle on National # 1 a few hundred meters from the large water tower next to the main road leading into Cité Soleil. This portion of the Route National # 1 was completely deserted, nobody dared to get that close to Cité Soleil. Also, we kept at least 300 meters distance, since we had already been fired upon further down the road a few weeks ago. We couldn't believe it when the old open willy's jeep from the Peruvian troops suddenly passed us, passed the water tower and went all the way to the entrance of Sode Cosa. This was usually a death sentence, but the Peruvians seemed completely relaxed about it, they didn't even drive fast. There was a driver, a passenger and one soldier in the back and all were utterly relaxed. Abuelo just said:" Maaan, you see, the gangs respect them, nobody fucks with the Peruvians." The operation against Dread Wilme didn't have a follow-up, the gangs in Cité Soleil remained in power and Dread Wilme was quickly replaced by a new name, 'Belony.' MINUSTAH was preparing for the main event of its mandate, Haitian democratic elections. The gangs in Cité Soleil did precisely the same.

CHAPTER 5

The Death of a General

Haiti, Port au Prince, January 2006

The constitutional obligation of the Interim government to organize elections shortly after the departure of Aristide was delayed and set back several times. Finally, 7th February 2006 looked realistic. The UN had set high standards for this election, all Haitians eligible to vote should get a chance. What was a fundamental right for the people in most countries was in Haiti limited to the documented part of the population which was mostly the Haitians living in the big cities. The United Nations created an electoral photo ID card which was for many Haitians the first photo ID in their lifetime. Some remote areas couldn't even be accessed with helicopters, UN electoral staff and their Haitian counterparts had to reach these locations on donkeys to register voters and assess locations for voting centers. On Saturday morning, 7th January, Sierra Base had an unusual broadcast. All Security Call signs had to report to the Christopher Hotel immediately. I got already heads up from Gus on the way. The MINUSTAH Force Commander, General Urano Teixeira Da Matta Bacellar was found dead with a gunshot wound to the head. The initial investigation soon declared suicide. A respected General leading the joint military forces of a large UN contingent killed himself four weeks before the main objective of his mandate and maybe the most significant event in his career, in his sport-dress. He was sitting on his balcony in his tennis outfit ready to play tennis, then suddenly something made him take his gun and end his life. So, General Urano got up this morning to go to play tennis, not to face his final judgment, right? He didn't write a note either. Of course, when it came to such a drastic step, nothing made sense around him, but anybody dealing with the Force Commander, especially a few weeks before the elections, knew him as an absolute professional, his suicide didn't make sense at all.

We knew he was agitated the day before; he was even the main subject of our last night beer conversation in Boucan Gregoire. At the end of yesterday's Core Group meeting, a meeting with MINUSTAH leadership and Ambassadors of United States, France, Canada, Brazil, the European Union, and Spain, the Force Commander had a severe fall out with the Brazilian Ambassador that ended with the Ambassador screaming at him. One of our colleagues in close protection spoke Portuguese and caught some parts of the argument. The Force Commander was supposed to do something and refused. They were screaming at each other in the main conference room of the Christopher Hotel next to the Reception area. At some point, the Ambassador handed him his cell phone with a high-ranking government official of Brazil on the other end. Our colleague assumed it was the Foreign Minister of Brazil. Again, the Force Commander refused something, and the cell phone conversation did not end better. We only knew their conversation was related to the upcoming elections. The Core Group had meetings almost daily about progress for the forthcoming elections. Hearing the following morning that he was found dead in his tennis shorts was just sad and wrong. Much more wrong and sadder was the stories the Haitian media started to spin immediately after his death about his involvement in all kinds of illegal activities. I knew that Gus, JT, and Bertrand had the highest respect for him, and the media rumors were disgusting, especially since many internationals repeated them without any critical thought. The investigation was in the hands of the Brazilian Military Police together with the Haitian National Police. The forensic capacity of the HNP was light years away from a modern 'CSI - Port au Prince' and didn't give anybody hope for answers. The elections were still scheduled for 7. February 2006.

It was the first election for me in a country that couldn't organize it by itself. On my level, I had little insight in the complexity of such a project but was lucky to meet people involved who were very experienced and could give me a glimpse of the big picture. Elections in Port au Prince were decided by the masses in the poor areas. In the regions, to become an elected representative for the lower chamber or the Senate, elections were won by the strongest man with the most significant arsenal. It was worth the fight since the official mandate provided access to official vehicles, significant influence or control of justice and law enforcement and made drug trafficking maybe not legal but definitely safe from Haitian or US prosecution. Even our colleagues in the usually quiet regions prepared for difficult times. UN Military and Police were distributed to voting centers in the capital and the provinces to ensure as much safety as possible. I patrolled together with Johnny, a retired Royal Canadian Police Officer, voting centers for high-risk areas of Port au Prince including the tabulation center in SONAPI. SONAPI was an industrial complex with large warehouses and sweatshops hosting thousands of cheap labor workers, many from Cité Soleil. For the elections, one of its warehouses became the brain of the upcoming elections. One of the main reasons for the delay in the election was that experience demanded that tabulation, official recording, and counting of the votes had to be under international control. These voices were heard and UNDP together with OAS, the Organization of American States financed the creation of a tabulation center in a warehouse in SONAPI.

Johnny and I watched it growing for the last couple of weeks on our patrols to SONAPI. It became a modern computerized tabulation center and 'Bea,' was the nickname of the man in charge. He had organized elections in such environments before and developed the plan to minimize fraud as much as possible. It didn't make his life easier or safer since the Haitian authorities, and some foreign influences made several attempts to gain control over the counting process. The tabulation center was part of a well-designed plan which was agreed on, other parts of the plan were dismissed with comments like: "We do not need your plan; we know how to separate ballots and bags." 'BEA' recruited and trained Haitian National Staff to do the final count and feed the computer programs. The initial count would be done at the voting centers, the ballots were planned to be brought to the different military bases who were in charge of securing and escorting these ballots together with the vote counts. The vote counts were supposed to go from the military base to the tabulation center where it was entered into the electronic system. Everything was ready for 7. February.

Election day, John Harrison picked me up at 0500 in the morning at Route Frères. It was still dark, but we could already see the masses in the street. For security reasons no private or public transport was allowed to circulate, everybody had to walk. We realized soon most people had voting centers as destinations. We made our way to SONAPI and found everything up running, BEA and the National staff were ready. There were 4 large voting centers around the gang strongholds of Cité Soleil and Cité Militaire for us to patrol. We couldn't believe how many people were already gathered at 0600 in front of the voting centers, and people were still coming. We couldn't feel any negative tension towards us. I had no idea what to expect from a Haitian election day, but it was amazing to witness how excited the Haitian people were about their democratic right to vote.

The Haitian authorities didn't share this excitement since none of them showed up at the voting centers for hours. The doors remained closed. The sun started to heat up the soil, and thousands of Haitians were sitting and waiting. It was close to 9 o'clock and still no sign, I couldn't believe how patient the Haitians were. Most of the voters remained silent, but some smaller crowds started to get excited and pushed at the gates to open or approached us complaining about the delay. These crowds were the younger voters, and I learned over the years that they had particular tasks in the election process. They were gang members and the controllers of the crowds and their votes. The masses sitting and waiting didn't get excited since their choice was made for them. To me, it looked perfectly reasonable at the time, except that everybody should have been upset about waiting so long.

Niko called me and asked me if we have any voting center open because the SRSG, the Special Representative of the Secretary-General and head of MINUSTAH wanted to see a voting center where people were actually voting. I told him, there were around 3000 people here who wanted precisely the same, he could join them, maybe it would speed up the process. Just at the voting centers, we patrolled there were maybe around 50 000 people waiting. At 10 o'clock Haitian election officials started to arrive and shortly after the voting started. Around the official closing time at 18:00 when the sunset began to take the light away in the voting centers, there were still huge crowds waiting for their turn to vote. The UN Police Officers at the voting centers told us that the authorities wanted to close because of the darkness. There had to be a solution, besides I expected a violent end of the evening when we had to tell the rest of the people, they wasted all these hours for nothing. Our Engineer from the Christopher Hotel had a solution. MINUSTAH Engineering Section had generator light towers in a storage area of SONAPI. Each of these light towers had four floodlights in each direction. We brought the light towers with the tow hitch at the back of our armored vehicle to the voting centers. In the meantime, UNPOL Officers used their flashlights and candles to provide light to the individual voters. It was so funny to watch how the UN Police Officers tried to provide light without actually looking at the voter's choice. Not that it would have made a difference for the voter, but the Haitian media would have accused MINUSTAH of denying a secret vote to the Haitians. It was a beautiful moment when each beam on the light towers started to glow and soon was shining bright. The voting finished around 23:00 and the voting centers finalized the process under the supervision of UN Police officers and closed between 03:00 and 04:00 in the morning. It was a great day because we felt our personal effort made a difference, and we could watch the result of it.

John and I witnessed the counting process in the tabulation center in the days to come, literally days. Separating bags and ballots turned out to be much more difficult as expected. The first escorted deliveries with ballots and vote counts took much longer as it was supposed to. Then, the intake and processing of these ballots and bags was a mess, even the votes from the big voting centers around SONAPI took days to count. Once these votes were received, Rene Preval had a significant early lead. It was no surprise; he was believed to be allied with Aristide and facilitate his return, and therefore the gangs mobilized their territories to vote for him. Rene Preval was not charismatic as Aristide; he was a technocrat, a professional politician and was handling the international community very well in his first term when he was President under the shadow of Aristide. Aristide was blamed in general for his shortcomings, and many people told me they were even not on good terms anymore. I started questioning this theory over the years and thought it was just a smart game to play, divide and rule. At least for this election, Aristide's zombies facilitated the unity of the gangs behind Preval's campaign. Preval needed it since the voters in the rest of the country were not expected to be in his favor. Once the votes from the regions came to Port au Prince with several days delay, Preval's lead started shrinking, and the trend seemed to continue.

But it took a long time for these votes to arrive and get registered in the tabulation center and the Haitian media started spinning the rumors about MINUSTAH influencing the choice of the Haitian people. In the Lavalas strongholds crowds started to celebrate Préval's victory as President even though the votes from the regions continued to reduce his lead. On Sunday 12. February crowds began to gather in Cité Soleil, Martissant and Bel Air and marched towards the CEP office, the Provisional Electoral Council. The CEP was the Haitian authority responsible for the election process supported by UNDP. It was in the Montana Hotel a little bit further up from the Christopher Hotel on Pan American in Bourdon. On the night of 13 February, reports of ballots with blank votes fueled the suspicion of the Préval supporters that the Interim government and MINUSTAH wanted to steal the elections from them. The first barricades were already set up at 05:00 in the morning, anything found in the area was used, vehicle wrecks, metal doors, rocks, old fridges, trees or burning tires. We were early enough to get to the tabulation center to check with Bea as usual. The blank votes made no sense to our colleagues or us who observed the same excitement for their right to vote like here in Port au Prince. Some people in remote places had to walk for several hours to reach their voting center. Who did that for just giving a blank vote? Such luxury was reserved for voters in western countries who believed they made a significant statement by casting a blank vote. Not in Haiti, voting in a reasonably safe environment was luxury. The media interpreted these blank votes as proof of fraud against Preval and declared him the victim.

By 09:00, the entire metropolitan area of Port au Prince was paralyzed with barricades. An angry crowd of estimated 2000 Préval supporters marched towards the CEP headquarters in the Montana Hotel. The group came from Cité Soleil. The UN Riot Police Unit at the main entrance to the hotel was challenged by rocks, and the crowd pushed to break through. The acting Force Commander did not want to interfere in the democratic process and ordered all UN Military Forces to remain in their bases. We didn't want to interfere in the democratic process either but had to get to the Montana Hotel. We had several staff members in support of the election headquarters of the government there. From the internet service to drinking water, everything was provided by the United Nations to ensure successful elections. Our way to the Montana Hotel was a violent obstacle course. Johnny and I in one vehicle together with SP1 and SP4 in the other armored vehicle left the UN Log base. We got accompanied by Sierra Zulu 3, our colleague from close protection who was stranded with his soft skin vehicle in Log Base. He was very welcome to join us on our trip. 5 Security Officers were the patrolling force of MINUSTAH while the UN military remained in their bases. 'Echo-6', from the Engineer Section, a former Military Officer kept us informed about the situation at the Montana Hotel on Security channel 2. In his last message, he reported increasing violence and pressure from the demonstrators and was not sure if the UN Riot Police Unit could remain in control.

Violence met us on the way as well. It was a long way through the roadblocks, and before we could remove the trunks, stones, and tires, we had to deal with the violent protesters. Young zombies were enforcing the roadblocks by throwing stones at anybody trying to get close. There was no way around or time to think about it. We had to show force and rushed at full speed through the rain of stones, jumped out, fired some bursts in the air and cleared a path for our vehicle to pass. We had to convince them that anybody who didn't run would have been shot. Once the crowd was disbursed, we had to deal with the barricades which were a serious threat to our vehicles, to our tires. Besides all the sharp edges of car wrecks or other old metal constructions used in the barricades, we had to watch out for the burning tires. Not so much the heat, but the bundles of wires inside a tire which remained on the streets. These wires were made of high tensile strength steel and gave the tire the needed stability on the road but were a dangerous vehicle trap when left lying on the way. It brought any vehicle to a halt within a few hundred meters if the axle or wheel caught it. To cut this tight wire salad free on an axle or rim was a challenging work of at least one hour. The closer we got to the Montana Hotel the less violent barricades we faced since we moved away from the hardcore Preval strongholds.

'Echo-6' reported to Sierra Base via radio that the UN Riot Police Unit was under severe pressure and a few minutes later we all heard Echo-6:" They breached the gate, they breached the gate, they storm inside." We could hear in his voice that he was running for shelter. None of us said a word, we just pushed harder and more aggressively. Several Security call signs tried to get to Montana. Some tried on foot or on motorbikes like Sierra Tango, our firearms instructor, and Franz. It seemed forever until we heard Echo-6 back on the air:" People are everywhere but not violent, most of them are in the swimming pool, it is a big pool party." It seemed none of us was breathing for the last minutes and took a deep breath now. After 99 barricades and one changed tire, we finally made it to Montana. The demonstrators had already left; they achieved their goal. They scared the hell out of the members of the CEP and MINUSTAH. They had a short refreshing dip in the swimming pool after a long day of demonstrating. The hotel didn't look like the worst-case scenario of looting our minds created after the emergency broadcast of Echo-6. As violent the crowd was to get into the premises, they were peaceful inside. It was one of the first amazing examples for me how organized and disciplined Haitian demonstrators were. Their task was done for this day because counting was still ongoing. The situation didn't improve much on 14 February, we removed barricades, scared stone-throwing demonstrators and checked at SONAPI for the latest election news. It became a daily routine. When news hit the media that burned ballots in favor of Rene Preval were found in the outskirts of Cite Soleil on 15 of February, we knew the shit was about to hit the fan.

I was curious how bad it was going to be. It didn't matter if these reports were anywhere close to the truth since the media was a daily tool to influence perception versus reality, the news itself was enough. It worked, it made Preval President. Out of fear of more violence Rene Preval was declared President shortly after midnight in a decision of the CEP and under significant pressure from the international community. It was assumed that Preval reached more than 50 per cent. That the counting process was not finished, and nobody knew at the time if Preval could reach above 50 percent was not important, he was elected President the second time. The violent protesters turned into cheerful crowds. The next day at our visit at SONAPI, we were surprised to hear that the story of the burned ballots was true. The Haitian media did not lie, we saw the burned ballots, they were in Bea's office in SONAPI. But even more surprising was that all these ballots were in the system, they were counted in favor of Preval. Because of the violent protests, the Haitian election officer in charge of a large voting center close to Cité Soleil did not wait for the ballots to be escorted by the UN military to the UN military base, he went with the vote count directly to the tabulation center. The UN military was supposed to bring the ballots to their UN base. Why the UN military decided to dump the ballots in a pile of burning garbage was a mystery, but it made Preval President. It was an unfortunate event that stole real elections from the Haitians. A few weeks later the tabulation center in SONAPI finished the counting process, Préval had less than 48 percent.

Preval wouldn't have made it, at least not in the first round. Once Preval was declared President and the democratic process was completed, the MINUSTAH military forces emerged from their military bases. The MINUSTAH Military leadership called it a 'show of force.' It was a joke since in the past days with all the stone throwing and barricades our thousands of MINUSTAH soldiers were invisible. Military leadership did not act because they did not want to interfere in the democratic process, but this is exactly what they did. Their passive role allowed violence to dictate the outcome of the Haitian elections. We would never know if anybody else would have had a chance to become President. It was possible that Préval would have been the favorite and likely to win in the second round anyway, but for some reason, it looked like MINUSTAH military preferred not to take a risk. There was still a second round for the 99 seats in the Chamber of Deputies and the 30 seats in the Senate scheduled for 21 April 2006 and created a functional Parliament, at least on paper. We soon had to realize that the Haitian interpretation of being an elected official representing the Haitian people was very different than what we had in mind. Sir Paul Collier called it Demo-crazy instead of Democracy in his book 'Wars, Guns and Votes'. He outlines that exporting successful democratic elections in a troubled country does not result in a functional democracy, it just creates Demo-crazy. However, the Haitian elections were declared a great success by the IC, the International Community. More than 7000 UN blue helmets and 1600 UNPOL Officers provided the necessary logistics and umbrella of security to facilitate President Preval.

CHAPTER 6
UN-involved in Haiti

Haiti, Port au Prince February 2007

MINUSTAH efforts were refocusing on their stabilization mandate. There was not much to stabilize in the regions since after the short-term electoral violence it became the sleeping beauty again. Violence was reserved for the metropolitan area of Port au Prince where the gangs controlled the slums of Port au Prince. MINUSTAH blue helmets were engaged in gun battles in Cité Soleil daily without effectively ending the domination of the criminal gangs. The UN troops were not allowed to attack these slums, they were just allowed to maintain checkpoints and military positions around the slums. The gangs just kept our military forces busy enough to maintain their evil image. It was a political issue I was told over and over again. The government of Préval did not forget that they were elected by the power of these gangs and didn't want any further attacks. Instead, a peaceful solution was preferred, and a disarmament program for the 'chimères' was implemented by UNDP and MINUSTAH. The DDR Section was created within MINUSTAH for this disarmament and UNDP and the IC, International Community, funded the government counterpart, CNDDR. It was one of the most significant budgets at the time and in the future of MINUSTAH. There was nothing to argue about the necessity of such a program for these young criminals in the slums, but there might have been an issue with the success criteria at the time. The success criteria for such a program defined by the Haitian government might have differed significantly from the original idea of the United Nations program. The gang members were offered training, some form of salary and reintegration into new neighborhoods in return for their guns.

My informants from Cité Soleil and Martissant wanted me to get them inside the program to have education and labor training for free as well. I told them I couldn't risk them getting involved with these gang members. They didn't understand why MINUSTAH was doing this for the gang members and not for the other young people in Cité Soleil. At the time, I didn't know anything about life in Cité Soleil. I considered my informants as an exception, and every other young man in Cité Soleil was a monster of darkness, a zombie. When I realized years later that the majority of people actually didn't want to be criminals, I had to understand these UN programs ignored the majority of young people and just helped the few violent ones. To MINUSTAH, gang members were VIPs compared to the rest of the population. The members of the DDR program received a photo ID card from the program, and the government declared them more less immune against any arrest attempt by the HNP. At the same time, the truthful intent of disarming the gangs and their power had to be questioned. The principal appointees from the government should have raised enough red flags to reconsider the blind support from MINUSTAH and UNDP for the government program. The man on top, Alix Bien-Amie didn't have experience with such programs or delinquent youth but was a political prisoner of the 'Baby Doc' regime. Political prisoner of a dictator was always great in a CV for a humanitarian project and didn't need any closer look into his skillset or experience. The real reason for his arrest was maintaining a Marihuana plantation and not the fight against the oppression of a dictatorship. But still, he didn't raise too many red flags, but the second in command did.

Jean-Baptiste Jean-Phillippe Delmas, nobody knew him by his real name but by his alias 'Samba Boukman.' Boukman was a historical revolutionary figure in the struggle for independence in 1804 and Samba in Creole means a singer. 'Samba Boukman' was not just a revolutionary singer with Voodoo credentials, he was one of the main political links between Aristide and the 'chimères.' He became after the death of 'Dread Wilme' the voice of Aristide for the gangs. He brought exceptional skills to the job which were not listed in his CV. He initiated and coordinated the slaughter and decapitating of HNP officers in the gang uprising during 'Operation Baghdad.' He was also a key mobilizer within the slums for demonstrations in support of Préval in the 2006 elections including the CEP raid at the Montana Hotel. The wolf became the shepherd. He was the least likely person in the country to have an interest in dismantling the force of the 'chimères' and most likely this was never his task. 'Samba Boukman' used the program to strengthen the organization within criminal gangs and united them under the CNDDR umbrella more than ever before. The money he had available got him access even to the few gangs with different political alliances. Nobody had oversight over him, not even his official boss. I saw him for the first time long before his government position in the Christopher Hotel. It was at the beginning of the mission during the peak of 'Operation Baghdad.' 'Samba Boukman' was invited and granted immunity from arrest for a secret meeting with the SRSG of MINUSTAH to negotiate a peace between the gangs and MINUSTAH.

Just before this meeting, somebody in the Close Protection Unit approached me about electronic surveillance devices, the SRSG had reasons to believe that information was leaking. The officer knew I had experience with such things. Most communication was still on an analog system which made a hack pretty straightforward, but the logistics behind and the hours to listen or recall required quite some effort. My quick assessment at the time was that electronic surveillance was too complicated and not necessary, people around the SRSG were more likely the leak. When 'Samba Boukman' entered the VIP parking lot the driver of the SRSG greeted him like a brother, a Haitian surveillance device, the chauffeur. It would have been interesting to know who in MINUSTAH pushed his application and how many more employees were hired with the same recommendation. It was most likely an international who served in a previous UN mission during the tenures of Aristide and Préval and went 'native.' 'Going native' was a term of the British Colonial times when Governors of the British Empire joined the native cause against the Queen. There was always a potential for biases and political preferences for international civil servants and were usually based on good intentions but could create in extreme cases a sabotaging effect. In MINUSTAH and other organizations, we expected some of these 'natives' in high and influential positions. The CNDDR program was never implemented to collect a significant number of weapons nor to turn gang members into peaceful citizens. The ruling system in Haiti couldn't allow it to happen because the gangs played an essential role in this system. For this role, they needed their tools, their guns.

Weapons, even old handguns were expensive in Haiti. An aged, rusty, .38 caliber revolver inside Cité Soleil was 600 US dollars. What would have been less than 30 US dollars in a gun shop in Florida, was still an expensive tool in Haiti. A new Glock pistol was 2000 US dollars in comparison to 600 in Miami. Anybody who bought and 'lost' one in Florida and shipped it to Haiti could make a good profit. Even more with ammunition, the price of one 9mm bullet in Cité Soleil was on average 3 US dollars when a good offer of 500 rounds of 9mm in Florida was available for 73 USD. 500 bullets could get you a lot of loyalty from any gang in Haiti.

HNP officers were always short on ammunition, especially since it was so expensive, anybody with access to HNP logistics preferred selling it to politicians or the business community instead of handing it out to police officers in the field. The politicians or the business community bought the gangs' loyalty with ammunition. This circle made the gangs so powerful and the HNP so weak. But the 'chimères' in control of highly populated areas could facilitate successful elections for the politicians and guarantee security for businesses around their strongholds much more than any HNP unit could. The politicians needed powerful gangs and even the business community preferred dealing with gangs than with effective law enforcement. HNP officers usually ended up as targets and were killed for their service weapons. Each additional weapon for the gang was one more shooter. One more armed bandit increased their power and control. The gangs had no access to ports in Haiti or gun shops in Miami, they received their weapons from their friendly business contacts or elected representatives in the parliament, Senator or a Deputy. A Deputy was what Haitians called a member of the lower chamber in the parliament. The parliamentarians used the gangs for elections and demonstrations, for cocaine trafficking they had the HNP on their payroll.

Cocaine was either dropped over the sea and picked up by fishermen or landed on improvised landing sites or roads inside the country. Marihuana arrived by boat from Jamaica. There were countless shipping vessels arriving at uncontrolled ports in Haiti from international waters. What was once used to send weapons to US allies in South America was today known as 'the Caribbean highway' for cocaine trafficking from South America to the United States, Canada or Europe. Haiti is one of the main transit points of this highway; the estimates of the US Drug Enforcement Administration, DEA, were most likely far below the real amount of cocaine shipped through Haiti. Haitians talk very openly about who was involved in drug trafficking, there was not much secrecy about it even though it involved so many names. The complete lack of any government control of Haitian airspace or seacoast made Haiti a paradise for any kind of smuggled goods. The open transit opportunity in Haiti affected many nearby countries, Haitian weapons were used by criminal gangs on several Caribbean islands. The Jamaican called it 'Guns for Ganja,' the exchange of Marihuana from Jamaica for weapons and ammunition from Haiti. The Senators and Deputies from the lower chamber in the parliament together with Haitian entrepreneurs facilitated the contraband. The weapons they bought for the gangs were not donations, it was an investment for future elections and the tool for the gangs. CNDDR was not going to change this.

MINUSTAH's mandate was to support the Haitian government. Since the Haitian government was elected based on the power of the gangs, MINUSTAH's efforts remained restricted to gun battles at the outskirts of the gang strongholds. The politicians continued running drugs, and the gangs kept their tools. The reintegration process of 'chimères' was as well an exceptional version and aimed to increase the power and influence of the government. Most gang members stayed in their territories, but some were actually moved into the Carrefour area. Carrefour, a commune in the South of Port au Prince was a highly populated area and was not yet gang controlled. CNDDR was going to change this and integrated gang members from Boston in Cité Soleil to Carrefour. The government killed two flies with one stroke. The gang in the Boston area had historical ties to businesses around National # 1 and the airport road and not to the Preval government. The integration into Carrefour removed these gang members from their business alliance and made them the new community controllers in Carrefour for the Preval government. That the DDR program had absolutely no positive impact on crime statistics was no surprise, but the fact that thousands of blue helmet soldiers couldn't change this either was unacceptable. The effective UN military operations from May and July 2005 were history and what was for the gangs and their political allies an illegal foreign occupation force became MINUSTAH 'Tourista' to the general population of Port au Prince. There was nothing to respond, they were correct to call us 'MINUSTAH – Tourista.'

The insecurity remained on the same level as it was before the elections. In December 2005 63 Kidnappings were reported to the Security Operation Center of MINUSTAH and this was just a portion of an unknown dark figure. Kidnappings were the most feared criminal incidents due to the related sexual violence. Ordinary Haitians were kidnapped by gangs in Cité Soleil or other slums, and the more valuable targets were kidnapped by criminal gangs in wealthier neighborhoods. If the kidnappers believed the highest possible ransom was met, they agreed to release the victim. In some extreme cases, the victims died in captivity. It was a form of terror, and it got so bad that the general population was afraid to go to church on Sunday morning. This terror started when Aristide left the country in 2004, the zombies left behind claimed he was kidnapped. Kidnappings in the years before never targeted the general population. The victims were either high profile targets for large sums of ransom, politically motivated or related to drug-trafficking. These kidnapping gangs were still operating in safer residential areas but targeted their victims based on inside information and did not just pick up random citizens from the street. But the zombies did. It was a shame for MINUSTAH. All UN Military and UN Police Officers deployed in the metropolitan area of Port au Prince did not find any strategy to counterattack this form of crime. Also, the creation of the Anti-Kidnapping-Unit consisting of HNP and UNPOL Officers did not change anything. Gus, JT and the men in the shadow had in several cases credible information regarding kidnapping gangs and passed it on to the newly established entity without any result. They even got suspicious that their data could compromise their CI's, Confidential Informants. In several cases, kidnapped victims reported after their release that the kidnapping gangs had very detailed information from inside the HNP including from the United Nations. Several kidnapping gangs consisted of 'Ex-HNP' or still serving police officers. An older lady was kidnapped in February 2007 and wanted to report the crime to the police after her release. She recognized the first officer she saw at the police station as one of her kidnappers. He was not even upset or disturbed, he just told her to go home to her family.

The population had no trust in the HNP and lost it as well in MINUSTAH. The general public started to express their disappointment towards us and questioned what all these militaries, police and civilians were doing in their country. International MINUSTAH staff members were not targeted in this kidnapping wave and could enjoy Haitian recreation. The population saw the white vehicles with the big black UN letters on the side parked outside the more delightful restaurants, driving to the expensive supermarkets or on the weekends to the beautiful beaches outside Port au Prince. Internally we even started to call our mission 'Beach-Keeping-Operations.' Most people forgot already that in the early days of MINUSTAH, two Russian MINUSTAH helicopter pilots were kidnapped by a gang in Cité Militaire. It didn't go as expected, and this incident might have been the reason that MINUSTAH internationals were excluded from the future kidnapper's shopping list. They didn't consider negotiating with Bertrand Bourgain. The kidnappers held the victims in Cité Militaire. The exact location was not known, so a rescue operation was not an option. But John Taylor identified the gang and started to receive inside information. Bertrand insisted on not paying a cent for the pilots and started calling the chief of the gang by his name and made it evident that they were known to us. They got either annoyed or afraid and released the contractors unharmed at a gas station close to Cité Soleil after a few days without a ransom payment. They even gave them 250 Haitian Gourdes for a moto-taxi to get home. Our national staff members driving in private vehicles were not as lucky, many became victims of this terror.

Franz and I shared their risk of being kidnapped. We got ourselves a private vehicle since we didn't like to be associated all the time with MINUSTAH. It allowed us to blend in. There was actually a rumor about a similar type of vehicle in the same color driving around attracting kidnapping attempts which caused an active intervention of armed individuals in a UN vehicle. It was said that the white Toyota 4runner was used as a bait, a very effective strategy that didn't last very long. Still, white Toyota 4runners became the safest vehicle against kidnapping threats in the capital.

The democratic elections and the new government did not bring any improvement for the general population or the security situation. Préval was elected on the masses of Aristide supporters, and the gangs felt encouraged and empowered. The foremost gang leaders had close contacts with the government and sometimes vehicles from the National Palace picked them up in their territories for dinner with the President. Actual figures for criminal incidents were incomplete at best. The murder rate was limited to the dead bodies found in the morning in the streets, anybody else killed was taken to private morgues by their family. Nobody had an idea of how many people were killed each day in Port au Prince. The improvement people realized was that HNP picked the dead bodies up and brought them to the morgue in the general hospital. In the past years, these bodies could lay for days, some even got eaten by pigs. This was the main reason I didn't eat any pork in the country. These were bodies mostly of criminals or people who were killed in an area where nobody knew the victims. The only fairly recorded number was related to kidnappings. The US embassy recorded 60 US citizens kidnapped in 2006, and Haiti replaced Colombia in the top position for kidnappings. The political back up for gangs from the National Palace made things more complicated, and it felt like operating behind enemy lines, since we were working against the gangs and against the government.

I started to get a feel of the gangs and managed to develop my own sources and informants for Cité Soleil and the gangs operating in Martissant. The absence of Haitian law enforcement in vast territories of Port au Prince and the complicated and hindering rules for any engagement of UN Military troops left a vacuum that we were trying to fill. We got involved in whatever we believed was essential to get involved in. Nobody stopped us. We were four in the Patrol Unit, JC, was in charge. He was Canadian and former Infantry Officer, Abuelo, Manu and me. Manu was a real rebel for many years before he joined the regular army after the civil war in his country. I never saw anybody as relaxed when being shot at as he was. Gus had Daniel joining him in the RSO office, and John Taylor received Jack, an IT-specialist with a gun. He developed the security database. There was Franz and Sierra Tango, the firearms instructor Ray. He was not just a sniper in the Special Forces of his country but also a bad-ass Thai boxing machine. None of us had to do it, we figured it was the right thing to do. Together with Tommy Dutch and the men in the shadow, we operated behind enemy lines.

CHAPTER 7
Safari at the Red Planet

Haiti, Port au Prince, July 2007

It was a routine morning on the way to the office, patrolling the areas around Cité Soleil, counting the dead bodies we found around the gang strongholds or dumped in Titayen on Soleil 9. We had our coffee in the office, knowing that at some point, we would be rushing with siren blaring through the intense traffic from Log Base to the scene of an incident. If there was no way through, we had to make one. We had to jump out with our rifles, banging on the other vehicles and make them move. Nobody questioned our authority. It was all about selling it, and they had to believe they, or at least their tires, would be shot if they didn't move. We were never stuck. It could have been a traffic accident involving one of our staff members getting harassed by an angry crowd or trapped in an office because of a gun battle outside. We were about to have lunch when Gus called us to say that John Taylor's contact just witnessed a woman taken hostage in her red Suzuki tracker, and the kidnappers took her in her car into Cite Militaire. The airport road was a long stretch with many large businesses along with the Lavalas gang stronghold of Cite Militaire. Cite Militaire was still home to criminal gangs but the UN Brabat, Brazilian Battalion presence limited their activities, and they no longer had full control over their territory. Rue Simon was one of the main roads into Cite Militaire and what took any other vehicle 30 minutes took us just 6 from our Log Base.

At the corner of Rue Simon and Airport Road was an old empty building named Red Planet. Businesses in the area paid for a police truck with 6 CIMO officers, CIMO is a specialized police unit. They were parked at the Red Planet during business hours to keep the gang members inside Cite Militaire. Salaries for HNP officers were never paid on time and often delayed for several months, so money from the businesses was needed, even though the share received by regular officers from the HNP officer in charge might have been minimal. It was not the first time we linked up with them for a zombie hunting "safari'. We informed them about the kidnapping; they were immediately on their feet and ready for action. They knew we were going with them. We had to move fast but left our vehicles behind to avoid another bulletproof glass looking like a slice of swiss cheese. Gunshot impacts on bulletproof glass were impossible to hide, it looked impressive and cried out, "this bullet would have fucked you up." For anybody else in the security section, it cried out." What did you do, where have you been?". For insurance, our transport section had to report and replace any damaged armored window. This automatically involved our Security Investigation Unit, SIU, which concluded findings and recommendations for the UN insurers. The previous time, insurance refused to pay based on the SIU report and Bertrand had to write a justification stating that we acted on his direct orders for operational reasons for the insurer to accept and pay.

The population knew very well what was happening and before a shot was fired, they took their children and ran into their homes. A deserted street during the day was the first sign of serious danger in Haiti. It was not always what you could see, sometimes it was the absence of the norm.

Even though the bandits no longer had full control of this neighborhood, they still maintained a strategic look-out position at the main road to cover their retreat. They would have opened fire to slow us down and alert their fellow gang members. We knew these positions already and advanced fast to close in. The CIMO's were used to operating with us, and we moved on each side of the street, maintaining eye contact with each other. After a few hundred meters we saw the victim's Suzuki at the end of the large portion of the road. Maybe the kidnappers were still walking with the victim and hadn't reached their hideout yet. We had to hurry; to know where to go, you just had to pay attention to the people in their homes. Many were looking out of the half-open doors of their little shacks and pointed in the right direction. All of them knew that kidnappers came through. The population didn't support the criminal activities of these bandits but also couldn't do much against them. They were themselves hostages to these gangs.

Each time I was in combat with HNP officers, whether part of a specialized unit or ordinary street cops, I was always impressed by their bravery and skills. Once we gained their trust, they would have faced any threat with us, including death. Their monthly salary was maybe 150 US dollars if they got paid at all. They still risked their lives, even though none of the widows or families of HNP officers injured or killed on duty would get any compensation. The sad part was that most of the low-ranking policemen were not much corrupted and wanted to do their job. Even at the red planet, the businesses didn't pay the CIMO officers to fight the gangs, they just wanted them to make sure the gangs didn't disturb normal traffic and businesses during office hours. But sometimes when we joined them, they had an excuse to do their job. It was ironic because we also were not supposed to be there fighting the gangs. We all knew the kidnap victim was not a UN staff member. According to the general UN Security mindset or rules, we were not supposed to chase kidnappers in gang territory. We shouldn't have been in gang territory at all, but nobody was there to stop us. And in case we had to justify our actions one day in front of our friends from the Investigation Unit, we still had a way out. There was a small little clause in our use of force policy, if a Haitian law enforcement officer requested our assistance in pursuit of a crime, we could get involved. We just had to make sure there was always an HNP officer who needed us, even though we had to call them after the fact.

Boom, I froze, a 7.62 mm round going off next to me made my ears ring. The end of the barrel was next to my face, and the pressure of the bullet leaving the barrel of an M1 carbine was like a slap in the face. The CIMO officer with the old US army rifle from the Korean war fired another shot. He was shooting at a small hole in a wall around 50 meters from us, a bandit look-out position. The bullet impacts around the small hole gave it away. It didn't matter if he saw somebody there, it was preventive and the signal to move. He stayed covering the hole and JC and I went to have a quick look behind the wall at a gate next to the hole. When the shooting started, the kidnappers must have known something was wrong. Gus had alerted already the Brazilian Battalion about our presence and the situation and they sent foot patrols to the area. If the kidnappers had made it to their hideout, it would have been impossible to find them, not even the population would have been able to help. They would have entered one of their houses, gone through a hole in their back wall, crossed a yard or deserted warehouse area and climbed through another wall and another hole. I always thought it would have been great to have dogs to track them. It was not our intent to get in a firefight with the kidnappers, but if they hadn't made it to the hideout yet, the risk for them of running into a Brazilian patrol would be too high for them. They knew we were behind them, we just had to keep up the pressure.

It worked, the kidnappers left the lady standing and took off. The population brought her to the nearest Brazilian patrol. Later in the day during the debriefing with John Taylor, the victim told him that the kidnappers became very nervous once they heard shots fired and received a phone call about some mercenaries moving with HNP after them. A significant portion of our impact and success was that nobody knew exactly who we were. Even though we were driving white vehicles with big black UN letters on the side, our armored Land Cruiser looked different from any other vehicle used by UN Military, UN Police or other UN civilians. The myth around us was that we might have been US mercenaries and US Marines were standing by to back us up. John Taylor's informants reported that the bandits were not afraid of the UN troops, they were just scared of one white vehicle with some mercenaries inside, one of whom was always wearing a green hat. Our tendency to appear wherever something big went down was mostly coincidental. Today, it was a successful hostage liberation. As much as we derived personal satisfaction that our action spared a woman from days of gang rape and her family countless hours of crying and negotiating for ransom, it did nothing for MINUSTAH's image. We couldn't tell anybody about it, except Tommy Dutch and the others at evening debriefing at Boucan Gregoire. Even the HNP officers couldn't claim any official award because the kidnappers certainly had a better political connection. To free the lady from the kidnappers, we were each other's justification. The HNP officers claimed they had to protect crazy MINUSTAH people and we assisted HNP while doing that. As long as we didn't get injured or our vehicles shot to pieces, nobody knew our activities in the red zone. The red zone was Las Vegas and Abuelo always stated:' What happens in Vegas stays in Vegas.'

It was actually sad how easy it was to make a difference in this lawless environment; sometimes, it was so smooth we didn't even realize it. Later that evening, I was sitting in the Boucan with Tommy Dutch when a friend passed by for advice because he just received a phone call from somebody claiming they had kidnapped his son. He hadn't spoken to the son yet and had only received the call from the son's cell phone. That was usually the way the kidnappers made the first contact and suggested that his son was actually a hostage. To chase kidnappers on the street was one thing, but to see the fear in a father's eyes was something completely different; it became terrifying. His son had been at a friend's house and the friend confirmed that he had already left.

The father had nobody to turn to, but he knew Tommy Dutch. Most families never involved HNP for a good reason, and just tried to deal with it on their own. It was already late in the evening, and I was about to finalize the night with a cowboy coffee. Dutch created the drink; it was a mix of flammable liquids with coffee and cream. The father told us what he knew. The area where the son was taken pointed at a kidnapping gang targeting victims on Delmas 75, 83 or Route Frères. We didn't know an exact location yet but knew that some of their kidnapped victims were held in the area "Jaquet Toto'. I didn't need to hear more to take action.

I ran outside to my armored Toyota to make my way to the area. I had all my gear including the MP5 inside the armored car. It was perfectly safe since nobody could smash the window and lock picking was not frequent. Also, most locals around believed we were crazy or possessed by Voodoo spirits and wouldn't have wanted to mess with our equipment. I still remembered the hope in the father's eyes when I gave him a quick assessment of the kidnapping incident. His faith grew when I immediately got ready for action. It was good he had no idea how many bottles of Prestige I already had, it might have lowered his expectations. It was not the moment for a great plan, I just couldn't sit there and watch this father in pain and fear. I intended to look for the car so all Zombie Hunters could start working on it; to underline my readiness, will, and effort I switched on the blue lights and the siren when I left. The siren was loud and very unusual at night in Port au Prince, sirens were reserved for politicians and public officials to move faster through the heavy traffic during the day. People must have wondered what was going on, especially in the area of "Jaquet Toto'. Unfortunately, I gave up my mission a few hours later without result. The next morning Gus called me into his office; his cell phone was going crazy. He received several phone calls from people he knew and some who got his number from Tommy Dutch. They congratulated him for his great team and work and that we were unbelievable. Gus had no freaking idea but pretended otherwise, of course. He couldn't reach Tommy Dutch yet, and I had no clue what was going on. It turned out that just my patrolling with sirens and blue lights made kidnappers believe something big was going down. Several "white guys' looking like a swat unit patrolled the area. MINUSTAH in action, they hadn't seen this before. So, they let the son go.

As unbelievable as it was that just the perception of a MINUSTAH response could have such an impact, we weren't even surprised. The previous week, JC and I witnessed heavily armed MINUSTAH soldiers watching gangsters shooting into opposing territory not more than 20 meters away from their position. The UN soldiers watched like it was a movie. We wanted to check out the new location of the Sri Lankan UN contingent in Martissant a little bit further up the hill from the main road National # 2. The only concrete building with four floors in the area. The "Lycee de Martissant' was supposed to become a high school, but the security situation kept the building empty for years. Finally, the building found a purpose and was rented by MINUSTAH as a temporary base for a platoon of the Sri Lankan MINUSTAH contingent. The Sri Lankan UN Contingent was in charge of all Martissant and Carrefour in the south of Port au Prince. Martissant was on Route National # 2, the road leading to southern Haiti. Route National # 2 divided Martissant in two parts, one part was a slum a few hundred meters wide with tiny shacks towards the sea and the other side was an endless compilation of shacks and simple brick houses growing up the hills like Favelas in Brazil.

It was the only road south from the capital and traffic through Martissant was a nightmare. The way was in terrible condition and partially used as a market. The sewage system was like in the rest of the capital, nonexistent, collapsed many years ago and the functional remains blocked with trash. This created a permanent layer of some form of slimy black film covering all deep holes in the road. The road was initially built with two lanes in each direction, but space was tight because of delivery trucks and piles of trash between the market stands. A broken-down tap tap, the local form of public transportation could cause a standstill for an indefinite period. You had to carefully follow the vehicle in front to avoid your tire getting stuck in a big hole under the black slimy lake, especially with a heavy armored vehicle. We had been patrolling the area for some time, developed informants and identified the gang leaders in charge. The gang clashes on the hillside started to hit the local news because many women and children were killed with machetes or shot during these clashes. The main rival gangs of Ti-Bwa and Ti-Machete moved during the night into the territory of Grande Ravine with guns and machetes and killed anybody who could not escape. Grande Ravine retaliated the night after causing the same terror, and the vicious cycle continued. It also didn't help MINUSTAH's reputation since these killings took place under a significant UN Military presence from Sri Lanka, but we were about to understand why.

We were driving on Rue De Dalles, the only road leading through the "Favelas' and came to the point where a market borders the 3 gang strongholds of Ti-Machete, Ti-Bwa, and Grande Ravine. The market was one of the reasons the gangs were fighting since it was a financial source from extortion. But violence going on at the time was beyond the usual gang clash, it was related to the upcoming local and municipal elections in December 2006. Martissant was supposed to participate in these elections. It was the last chance to gain public funds, titles and official license plates for vehicles to run drugs. Each gang was fighting and killing for their political connection. The population had no voice or vote in it. It was decided on the battlefield between the gangs. If no winner was declared, the violence continued to cancel the elections in the area. The same happened if a voting center was controlled by one gang and impossible for the other gang to influence. The other group would inflict enough violence to cancel the elections in that district. The entrance to the UN base in the high school was 30 meters above Rue De Dalles between Ti-Bwa and Grande Ravine. It was 10:30 in the morning and the market was deserted, not a soul was on the street. That was never a good sign, we opened the doors of our armored to listen. Nearby, we heard single shots and some automatic gunfire, 7,62mm caliber rounds.

When we arrived at the high school, there were a minimum of 40 or 50 soldiers present. Most of them were in rooms on upper floors looking through small concrete windows; they were all watching the fight, we couldn't believe it. This was their interpretation of peacekeeping and stabilization. The commander explained to us that there was no problem because Haitians were fighting Haitians and not fighting the UN. We had informants telling us that the UN soldiers had some form of agreement with the gangs and even provided gang leaders with bulletproof vests and medical attention when one of their soldiers was injured. We didn't believe our informants; we couldn't imagine it was so bad. First, we thought it was a rumor to discredit the MINUSTAH troops, as usual. Also, they reported to us that the UN troops didn't intercept any armed gang members passing their patrols, even though they openly carried guns. On a positive note, our informants' credibility was much enhanced. The shooting continued during all our discussions with the officer in charge and his weird interpretation of his mandate. There was bloodshed not more than 20 meters away, and a platoon of professional soldiers didn't feel it was their concern. There was not much to do, except writing to Gus about it and Bertrand would bring it up in the meetings. I also shared it with our colleagues of Civil Affairs and Human Rights since we worked very closely with them on a regular basis related to the gangs of Martissant and Cité Soleil.

If we believed we had witnessed something scandalous, we had no idea. We started to patrol the area by foot, we thought we needed to fill the vacuum of non-presence of UN troops, the so-called UN-presence. We encountered a house with only one Sri Lankan soldier in front of it. Just one soldier alone was not right and not supposed to be. Any patrol or static position would have had a few soldiers. Before he saw us, we saw two or three young girls or boys in front as well. It was challenging to say what gender because all of them seemed below thirteen and had weird make up. When the soldier saw us, he said something to the three young people, and they went into the house. It didn't look right, there was obviously something fishy going on. We mentioned it to our Austrian and Italian colleagues from Civil Affairs. It didn't take long for them, together with Andrea from Human Rights, to get to the bottom of it. The Sri Lanka Battalion in the early days of the mission did not interfere in the gang clashes or criminal activities because it was part of an arrangement with all the gangs in the area. The gang part of the agreement was that they provided the soldiers with a house in each territory with young boys and girls as prostitutes. More than 100 soldiers were repatriated, and a few months later an official Board of Inquiry tried to settle an agreement with the victims and their families. The Battalion was replaced by a Special Forces Battalion from the same country.

The damage done to the young boys and girls was valued, estimated with a price to compensate for the pain and abuse. No healing was offered, but for the families of the victims, it was still a form of compensation they would have never expected. Sexual abuse must have been so typical in these slums of Haiti that I sometimes believed the population first needed to learn what actually constituted sexual abuse. In the early days of MINUSTAH, an interpreter gave me an idea about how regular sexual abuse was. He worked with the Jordanian UN contingent in their base close to Cité Soleil, the biggest slum of Port au Prince. One day a small boy was banging on the gates of the Jordanian UN base all day long and finally started banging on the commander's car. The commander asked the interpreter to translate what was the issue. The boy complained that the soldier on night watch asked him for a blow job but refused to pay. The boy was less than eight years old. The commander settled the case with an amount of money the boy agreed on, the issue was resolved and didn't leave the contingent. The same interpreter also explained why many times demonstrators from Cité Soleil made goat noises towards us and imitated goat horns with their index fingers. It had to do with the sexual intercourse of the soldiers with female goats before the goat was slaughtered grilled and eaten. I was stunned, and it seemed the abuse of goats was also new for the inhabitants of Cité Soleil, but not the abuse of children. MINUSTAH and the sections involved with the leadership tried to make an effort to set things right and took responsibility as a result of our reports. Unfortunately, in the years to come, we had to learn that such statements were not well received by different UN leadership in other missions that preferred to cover up wrongdoings and punish the whistleblowers.

CHAPTER 8
Cité Soleil, The Root of all Evil

Haiti, Port au Prince, September 2006

Our reports were the basis for Gus, the RSO, to advise our Chief of Security. Much of our data from the field described a very different situation than was expected according to strategic UN military deployment and operational planning. Even though we couldn't enter Cité Soleil, our armored vehicles allowed us to get close enough to encounter many unoccupied UN checkpoints and static UN military positions around Cité Soleil. This gave the gang members significant freedom of movement and opportunity to bring kidnap victims into Cité Soleil. Our reports usually resulted in Bertrand Bourgain openly accusing the military of being lazy bastards and responsible for the insecurity in the capital. Needless to say, the Force Commander, a Brazilian General had a severe head to head argument with our Chief of Security in every leadership meeting. It was an insult to the General and his troops, and it was not our business. Most Heads of UN Agencies and other witnesses agreed with the Force Commander. Most likely the newly appointed SRSG who arrived in June 2006, Edmond Mulet thought precisely the same, until we showed him pictures. Bertrand Bourgain kept quiet for one week, and we took photos, every morning and every afternoon of empty UN military checkpoints. We passed several popular gang ambush sites 4 times a day and didn't get shot once in the entire week. We must have been some 'blancs,' foreigners again possessed by a Voodoo spirit. I didn't know what surprised the SRSG and Force Commander more, that Bertrand Bourgain could shut up for one week, or our photos. The Force Commander must have been furious. He was in full control of the Brazilian contingent but had to rely on the word of the other contingent commanders. The SRSG and the Force Commander wanted to see it for themselves.

On a Saturday morning, the SRSG and Force Commander with heavy Brabat, Brazilian Battalion convoy protection were scheduled to visit some of the UN checkpoints in our photos that were not within shooting range of the gangs in Cité Soleil. We were checking the area in advance of the visit. We headed down with both of our Patrol Vehicles and were impressed by the UN military presence in the area. Suddenly, every position was occupied, even the two locations we specifically wanted to point out had been reinforced with more sandbags and Jorbat, Jordanian Battalion had two APCs, armored personnel carriers, parked next to each of them. We messaged on the radio to Sierra-Papa, Gus, all clear and fully secured. We were told the convoy with the VIPs were 20 minutes out. There was no point for us sticking around watching this theater. Everything was set up and looked perfect. However, when I met Gus for a beer in Petion Ville he told me we still proved our point; 20 minutes after we watched and waved at the two fully occupied checkpoints, they were empty, completely deserted, no soldiers, no APCs around. The only possible explanation was that the Jorbat troops thought that we, our two UN Patrol vehicles, were the VIP delegation. Of course, they were never there, so they didn't know we were always there. Within seconds of our leaving the area, they must have been out of the checkpoint, into their APC and back to their base, because 20 minutes was an impressive time to evacuate the checkpoints. I was told the words the Force Commander used were much worse than lazy bastards. Edmond Mulet set things in motion, wheels always turned slowly in the United Nations, almost like Haitian evolution, but the change was about to come.

The speech of the new Principal-DSRSG in November 2006 was short, but I remembered this part:' I don't want to hear the rules which prevent us from doing something, I want everybody to focus on our objectives and how to achieve them...'. Everybody working longer than six months in the Department of Peace Keeping Operations had heard about Luiz Carlos Da Costa, the man who started as a mailman in UN headquarters in New York and became, not just the highest-ranking civilian staff member from Brazil, but a legend within Peace Keeping Operations. I was suspicious, we all heard such speeches before, and somebody with his career must have been a very nice guy who didn't piss off anybody. Even so, Edmond Mulet needed such a person. The SRSG was trying hard to move things in a different direction and needed all the help he could get. Reported criminal incidents and kidnappings reached their highest recorded levels since MINUSTAH was established, and there was still a sizeable dark figure of violent crimes that never got reported. Haitians called us MINUSTAH -Tourista, but nobody questioned Bertrand's and our credibility anymore. We became the eyes and ears for any security-related incident, not just to Gus and Bertrand, but to mission leadership. We needed to provide an almost real-time update or background information on any development. It was great but intense, and Ray gave us a hand every day. We were rushing with a siren from one incident to the other. Most events we looked into were linked to the gangs of Cité Soleil, the place which was off limits for MINUSTAH operations. But they kidnapped busloads of passengers on Route National # 1 and brought them into Cité Soleil. Cité Soleil was the root of all evil and had to be changed.

The UN Military conducted its first operation on 21 December against Bois Neuf, the former home of 'Dread Wilme' in the northern part of Cité Soleil, next to the sea. The new gang leader was 'Belony.' The operation was a failure, and the following actions were not much more successful either. The lack of equipment and skills of the Uruguayan infantry contingent based in Port au Prince was a significant factor in the shameful performance. A friend of mine, the World Food Program Chief of Security and former Uruguayan special forces member, explained that these Uruguayan soldiers were not professional soldiers. They were recruited for UN missions and sent to peacekeeping operations with almost no training. It was to make money for the soldiers and the country. Their salary was still better than at home in their civilian job, and less than the country received from the United Nations. The country could make money by contributing troops to UN missions. Most countries today provide troops for this reason. The Force Commander's tour was up, and before he left, he moved Cité Soleil into the AOR, Area of Operation of the Brazilian Battalion.

Lieutenant General Carlos Alberto dos Santos Cruz was the missing link, the third Musketeer and together with Da Costa and Mulet, MINUSTAH was reloaded. He brought with him Brazilian Special Forces who took a break from jungle warfare and criminal gangs in their Favelas and joined the Caribbean 'Beach Keeping Operation'. The demands from the population and private sector were finally heard. In February, MINUSTAH Brabat Special Forces took over control of the main 'bases' in Cité Soleil in a very short overnight battle, but the foremost gang leaders Amaral, Evens, and Belony were not there anymore. They were brought to safety long before in vehicles from the National Palace. They found refuge in the countryside where their families came from. Most gang members escaped the assault as well and joined the gangs in the hills of Martissant. There was a large amount of ammunition and some weapons seized by the Brazilian Special Forces, but JT and Gus knew most weapons were buried in cemeteries or were moved on fishing boats to other locations for different times to come. However, Brabat was now in control.

This was Cité Soleil, we could finally see it for ourselves. The gang leaders were the rule of law, the police, the judges and the jury. The few international NGO's operating in Cité Soleil could only go as far as it was permitted by the gang leaders, because, they decided over the portions and the form of distribution of any aid in the area. They were the lifeline to food, fresh water, medical attention, and education. For us these NGO's were in the past years the allies of the gangs, they were part of the problem. But when I was faced with the reality of Cité Soleil, I started to see a different world. Actually, our ineffectiveness in Cité Soleil left the NGO's no choice other than dealing with the gang leaders if they wanted to bring help to the people most in need. Even though some NGO's might not have changed a lot, just the fact they were there counted for the people. But others, especially one NGO had a tremendous impact. Hands Together, operated schools and clinics in Cité Soleil for more than 13 years, they had schools in every 'base' of Cité Soleil and for older children two big centers including one high school. They provided food, uniforms, and tuition for more than 6000 children in their schools. They registered 2000 'barefoot' children who had no parents, families or homes and offered them the same service. I always heard about Father Tom or his operational director Douglas Campbell and their support for the gangs. But when I got to know Cité Soleil, I started to understand that they were actually the only ones fighting for the people regardless of who was in charge. When I visited the schools of Hands Together, I realized the masses of young people did not rape and kill. All these young people were potential victims of such crimes themselves, and these schools were the only hope they had. It was maybe the only grace and gratitude shown to them in their entire lives. Being labeled as a child from Cité Soleil closed most opportunities automatically outside Cité Soleil. The population of Port au Prince wouldn't trust anybody coming from Cité Soleil, they were all criminals. The best jobs they could hope for were as cheap labor in the sweatshops around the slum.

Also, the education system was designed to create sweatshop workers and nothing beyond. Father Tom had to learn that dealing with the gangs was much less complicated than dealing with the ministry of education since Cité Soleil was controlled by the Brazilian UN troops. The department of education started to dictate the method of learning in Hands Together's schools, even though the government provided nothing except official state school certificates for the students, for which Hands Together had to pay. Hands Together students were not even allowed to sit in circles and engage in discussions according to the department of education. They had to focus on repetitive learning, discipline, and authority, just what was needed in a sweatshop. Or as King Leopold II of Belgium wrote in a letter to his Colonial Missionaries before they left for Africa: "Teach them to read, not to reason." I could never confirm if the message was authentic, but the mindset was the same.

Most of the families were single households with one mother and several children. Not many people had a job. Just to clarify the definition of a job, begging was considered a job. Any person who could leave Cité Soleil and be accepted in some wealthier area to beg on the street safely had a job. The people of Cité Soleil lived with the threat of being harmed by criminals every day. If it was not the gang in their own territory, it was the neighboring gang, and they relied on their own gang to protect them. If it was not the gangs, any simple sickness could be a life-threatening situation. It was a no-win situation for anybody. Even gang members and gang leaders did not live long. It seemed the name of the gang leader was just famous and influential until he was killed and replaced, the same importance was granted to the next leader. When a leader was killed, he was either killed by an ambitious 'soldier' within the gang or during a clash with HNP or a rival gang. If it was not physical violence, it was a Voodoo curse. Haitians were very skeptical in general about any loss of life that didn't result from a physical impact. Then they suspected poison or Voodoo spirits were involved.

In one of the meetings with my informant, I learned that Ti-Claude, a small kidnapper at the time from 'Ti-Haiti' in Cité Soleil was about to die. Somebody cursed him with a powerful and deadly spirit, and he was already so weak that he couldn't stand up. His 'Ougan,' his Voodoo priest, needed to perform a ritual to move the spirit into something else, a cow or donkey, some animal because this spirit needed to kill something. The problem was that the 'Ougan' was asking for 3000 US dollars and his gang members were waiting for the money from a 'friendly' businessman in the area. There must have been time pressure; otherwise, they would have just kidnapped somebody for ransom. It worked out since Ti-Claude lived on for quite some time. When a gang leader died, the most violent and ruthless member of the gang was going to claim the title. The next leader was usually worse than the previous because he had to prove to all the inhabitants he was in charge. He was the new contact for the politicians and businessmen, he received the money, weapons, and ammunition. He was the person in charge of humanitarian aid, he was king. But he was just a name, a name we were hunting. The name of the gang leaders was not significant, what was important was their position and function as a tool to control thousands of people. Having a gun provided all that a young man could wish for, money, beer, parties, and girls. I had no doubt in my mind that I would have been a Cité Soleil gang banger if I had been born here.

And yet, so many of these young men didn't become criminals and didn't choose violence. They were at risk every day to become the next gang recruit. I wondered what made them resist. I was even more amazed when I realized it was actually a daily struggle for them not to become a gang member and it started at an early age. Whenever I had a chance, I asked students from Father Tom's high-school or other youth how they could avoid becoming a bandit. I received answers like:" You have to be strong, you have to say no." They explained further if anybody offered a coca cola, a sugar cane or anything else, the answer had to be no. If you said yes once, you were in and could never say no anymore, even if the recruit was just five years old. They were used as delivery boys, messengers or as lookouts for enemies, police or possible targets. The child might have had a chance if the mother at home realized he had a coca cola or anything the child, or his family could not afford. If she made a strong statement, punishing the child and returning the temptation to the gangsters, it might work. Most of the children had a maximum of one parent at home, and if this parent had a job or tried to look for a job, the child had a better social status in the neighborhood but was also at higher risk to join a gang. Parental supervision seemed to be one of the most important factors in whether a child was a potential recruit or not. Another factor for not joining a gang was:" You had to be busy." They explained to me that you couldn't hang around, the gangs would never accept anybody just hanging around without being part of them. The youth had to make themselves invisible; therefore, the schools of Father Tom were a central place for them to hide and be busy somewhere else. His schools prevented thousands of children from joining a gang. On weekends Churches replaced the schools and the youth gathered there for much longer than just the Sunday mass. It offered the teenagers a selection of non-criminal soccer teammates.

Hanging out with the bandits implied being part of them and this included playing soccer. "Never play soccer with them, especially when you are good," was one of the comments of a high-school student. But places to play soccer were rare, and around the church, the youngsters could enjoy their favorite national sport. My informant simply said he was free. He was poor but could leave Cité Soleil without being afraid to get arrested or killed, the bandits could not.

After the Brazilian troops took Cité Soleil, most bandits left the area, especially the well-known ones. The rest stayed behind to maintain their territories but kept a low profile. Many returned only during the night. There was a new gang in town that aimed to take over everything, the Haitian National Police. The HNP under the command of Inspector Rosmond Aristide. His family name was not always Aristide, but he was on the protective detail of President Aristide and admired him so much that he became Aristide. I did not recall the story of his name change, it might have been marriage or another legal form, but he adopted his idol's name. He also had the trust of President Préval to keep Cité Soleil in check. Inspector Rosmond was a proud patriot with political patronage. This patronage made his actions legal and him the enforcer of the law. I started to understand the dynamics of human rights violations under the laws of Duvalier, the military junta or Aristide. Implementation of the law did not consider human rights; violence was the standard method of the lawman. It didn't matter much if it was a dictatorship or democratically elected government, it didn't change the technique. He made firm arrangements with most of the gangs since he came from the same place as Rene Monplaisir and Samba Boukman, communicators between the 'bases' and the President, but not with Boston. Reginald Boulos was one of the business elite who had a long history with the leaders of Boston, one of the largest territories in Cité Soleil with a strategic position along the main route to the North, Route National # 1. He started to reestablish his influence in the area again. Since he was part of the popular movement called the group # 184 that was organizing and financing the demonstrations against Aristide in 2003, Rosmond tried to undermine his efforts. Inspector Rosmond used the neighboring gangs to kill anybody joining an alliance with Boulos. He even dressed gang members in HNP uniforms and launched 'joint operations' in Boston. The results of these operations were never found since the bodies of the victims were chopped up and disposed of in plastic bags. His method worked, Inspector Aristide kept Cité Soleil safe and gang violence at a bare minimum.

Since Cité Soleil became accessible in February 2007, it was the place to go for any VIP and any international organization. We in the UN Patrol Unit provided the escort and coordinated military support if needed for all these visits. Even the Diplomatic Security Service, the RSO office of the US embassy coordinated with us their visits. Their trust in our experience on the ground was the best evaluation we could get. The goal was to bring immediate relief to the people of Cité Soleil funding quick impact projects and identify and find donors for long term projects. Where there was money, Haitian authority was not far away. The mayor of Cité Soleil didn't have his office in Cité Soleil and didn't seem to be from the area, but he was the elected official authority and therefore the point of contact. He made contact with the gang around the future mayor's office and hired them as his security guards. He provided them with weapons to gain power and influence in other territories as well. As fast as the international community wanted to bring humanitarian aid to the people of Cité Soleil, Haitian businessmen, politicians and the HNP tried to get hands on their own gang and strengthen their influence. The first projects were cash for work kind of programs which was supposed to inject money quickly into society and improve their living conditions and offer them jobs. They were also quick cash programs since it involved paying workers. We almost had an hourly schedule of escort runs between Cité Soleil and the meeting point at Tebo-Base, an empty building on Route National # 1. We escorted USAID, European Union, WFP, UNDP, FAO and any other international organization who wanted to see Cité Soleil and bring aid and quick relief to the people. There was just one problem, we escorted them all to the same project. The mayor of Cité Soleil took cash from each organization money for 'their' project but sold them all the same project. The project was located in the territory of his loyal gang, and he employed the families of the gang members. His security detail grew daily, and it didn't take long until they performed their duties with automatic assault rifles. Everybody wanted to become the next chief of Cité Soleil, and everybody tried to get there by reestablishing the power of the gangs. The mayor even did it with international aid money.

Our reports about this lack of coordination and photos of his security details with 'long guns' slowed the mayor down. My Austrian colleague from Civil Affairs put a stop to this development, and formed a joint committee with UN Military, Police, Security, Human Rights, HNP and the Mayor's office to coordinate all relief efforts. The situation remained complicated because of too many entities trying to control the 'chimères' that were left behind again like zombies. In one of my first conversations with Father Tom, I asked him from his viewpoint, what was the best time for him, his organization and the people in Cité Soleil; He said:" when the US Marines were here." I was surprised, it was not what I expected, and he continued:" They were very friendly and respected." I was even more surprised, and with a smile he imitated somebody holding a rifle in his hand and explained," Because when they said a friendly good morning, they did it with their gun in their hand, Haitians respected them." Even Hands Together which many of us accused of being friends of the gangs just wanted the overall security to deliver their programs peacefully. In general, people just wanted security overall. In Hands Together schools children were asked to talk about or draw what they feared most in life. Usually, the answer was: "the shooting at night." They did not choose to live without police or law and order. Slums like Cité Soleil were always controlled by some form of civilian gang or militia. The 'Tonton Macoute' of 'Papa Doc' and 'Baby Doc,' were the 'chimères' of Aristide.

They were never supposed to be community leaders; they were always community controllers. From the first time we drove into Cité Soleil, we never experienced hostile actions towards us from the population. Haiti was the poorest country in the western hemisphere and poverty was everywhere, but Cité Soleil was, even by Haitian standards, the absolute worst. Their faces were marked with hardship and suffering, but none of them seemed to blame us or our military for it. The first faces were mostly curious, but soon we received some smiles. People were barely dressed; many children had no clothes at all. It was usually the arrogance and misconception of internationals who never lived without the basic need and right for security who had comments like:" We don't want military escorts; we don't need armed escorts." Maybe not the international and humanitarian aid workers, but the people of Cité Soleil, and Haitians in general, wanted to live without fear. They wanted to see MINUSTAH military do their job.

The Brazilians had the advantage that the majority of the country loved Brazilian soccer and had a great connection with the people. After a few weeks, women started to change their appearance with simple improvements in hair-style and makeup. They looked like they found some form of pride or joy again in their lives. The portion of the Route National # 1 which divided Cité Soleil and Cité Militaire had not been used for years by any vehicle, and slowly traffic started picking up again. A large water tower marked the entrance to Cité Soleil. Many buildings along this main road and inside Cité Soleil showed the signs of massive gun battles. We watched Cité Soleil changing for the better.

The HNP officers were happy about the construction of a new police station at the main square in Cité Soleil, but not so much about the one at the small 'wharf,' the small port of Cité Soleil. The Inspector told me a long time before it was finished, no HNP officer will step foot in it. When I asked why he just replied because of the spirits. Of course, I thought, because of the spirits. But he was serious. There was a police station there in the past, and HNP officers were killed and burnt inside. The fear that evil spirits were still there would keep the HNP officers out of it. Cité Soleil also became a courthouse, the judge was Judge Leveque. I knew his name already, to release a bandit from prison was usually 3000 to 4000 US dollars depending on who was paying; for a gang leader he charged much more. It was justice on demand because he only showed up at the court if he was paid by one of the parties involved. He could facilitate any arrest; it was just a matter of price. I was never told how much he charged Reginald Boulos to arrest Inspector Rosmond over the influence of the gangs in Cité Soleil, but Inspector Rosmond was arrested. He was released after a few days and most likely the judge gained from it as well. I was not sure if they were appointed for life because Judge Leveque was always around. Within all the gangs, the politicians, the HNP and businessmen trying to get control of the gangs, the judge was the biggest bandit of all. Everybody focused or always blamed the corruption within the HNP without realizing that the real damage and impact of corruption was coming from the Haitian Justice System.

Cité Soleil became our main patrol area, sometimes we just stopped by Amaral's house. Amaral was the gang leader of Belekou, in the South of Cité Soleil and was after 'Dread Wilme' the new root of all evil for MINUSTAH troops. I stood in his yard and looked around. I saw a one-story building, painted, which made it unique in Cité Soleil. He had a wall protecting it with a metal door and a peep hole, I thought the peep hole was hilarious. Him looking outside and the street full of Brazilian Soldiers, who is there? Certainly, the best house in the neighborhood of 'Belekou.' When Aristide departed in 2004, his residence in Tabarre was completely looted. Not completely, the rotten bundles of US dollar bills and human baby skulls in the cellar were left untouched because of the evil Voodoo spirits related to them. Amaral's house didn't show any signs of vandalism. The furniture was still there and in good order. It looked like he had time to pack, most of the clothes or other items were gone. This was where Amaral was eating and drinking, the person we had heard so much about for the past two years. After the death of 'Dread Wilme,' he was the new chief of the Zombies, enemy number one for thousands of UN soldiers and UN Police Officers. I looked at the Enduro-motorbike in his yard, it was untouched, nobody dared take it away. Amaral was still in control, even though he was hiding somewhere in the region. I was told the motorbike was a present from the singer Wyclef Jean, one of the Haitian success stories which made it to the top in the United States. It was even registered and had a license plate on it. For what I wondered, he couldn't go anywhere with it. He was such a big name he couldn't leave the worst slum in the Americas. MINUSTAH spent millions of US dollars on troops and equipment just for him. The Secretary-General in New York had every morning the latest update about Osama Bin Laden and was asking after it, what's new about Amaral? The notorious gang leader of Cite Soleil challenging MINUSTAH Security forces. His 'soldiers' had gun battles with thousands of rounds of ammunition for hours with Brazilian and Jordanian soldiers. He was the chief of a few hundred square meters of human waste, that was all it was. The humidity and mosquitos killed me in the afternoon, it must have been a nightmare later on at night. This was his home, his life. He couldn't even get the weapons or ammunition on his own. Some politician or business person with access to the Dominican Republic or shipments from other countries had to deliver it to him. His house was less than 30 meters away from the sea which smelled terrible because of the canal full of garbage and human waste. Such a famous gangster living so close to the sea should have lived in a large villa with a 30-foot powerboat in front of it. Something was not right, somebody wanted him here and made us focus on him. I looked up to the clouds covering Kenscoff, the hill above Petion Ville, where the wealthy and beautiful had their big villas and parked their Mercedes G-Class and Porsche Cayenne.

CHAPTER 9
The Ibo Lele Hotel and the Haitian Cocaine Family

Haiti, Port au Prince, March 2008

Haitian coffee is excellent, simple pure and natural and the best time for it was in the morning before the Caribbean heat would sneak through the mosquito nets on the windows. On Sundays, I could enjoy this freshness of the night until the heat slowly filled up my small apartment. The US TV shows and movies provided by Tele Haiti kept me in an 'after-sleep' bubble ignoring space, time and the world around me. The TV set and the lights in my apartment were powered by a battery inverter system that provided electricity for almost 2 days and could be charged by the generator of the building since city power was rare. The fridge was old and didn't close well and would have drained the batteries within 12 hours. The occasional package of chips for dinner didn't need to be stored cold, and I was used to drinking my water warm. It was also more convenient to drink red wine at home instead of carrying up heavy cases of beer. The hot water for coffee could be done on the gas stove. It was a precious morning in March, and I enjoyed my coffee and my TV shows and was still in my bubble. Until the ringing of my cell phone made my bubble pop like a needle in a balloon. It almost felt like I was the balloon. A call on Sunday morning was either an emergency or an informant, definitely annoying. My informants didn't have credit on their cell phone and would have just rung me once to make me call back, and on Sunday, this could take a while. But the caller seemed to expect me to take the call on his expenses because it kept on ringing. Damn, I had to get up now. To my surprise, I saw Abuelo's name on display. We had no task scheduled for today. A call from him on Sunday morning was very unusual. 'Grandfather bull' knocked himself out with sleeping pills for most of the weekend to recover from the busy week.

I heard a rough morning cigarette voice with a touch of Al Pacino in the movie Scarface:" The man in Ibo Lele, Commandant just woke me up, I had like 10 missed calls from him. He wants us to meet him. Come up to Ibo Lele, but not on the terrace we meet in his room". My mind got immediately sucked back into my Haitian reality of informants, demonstrations, gangs, and politics. Meet Commandant? Why in his room? The Ibo Lele Hotel was usually empty, who could see us? Automatically while my mind was spinning, I lit a cigarette and told Abuelo with at least the same rough voice I would be there in 20 minutes. "Nobody is shooting at me, be there at 1030hrs," he replied and hung up. I should have known better. Abuelo lived just a few minutes from the hotel, but he needed more time to get ready, he was metrosexual like Brad Pit, he explained to me when we first met in 2005. I was surprised to hear that Brad Pitt was homosexual. He must have read my mind and clarified: "I am not gay"; and explained further that metrosexual meant taking care of yourself using cosmetic products beyond the reasonable standards and did not identify any sexual preference. Abuelo needed these 90 minutes to take a shower, then moisten his skin with body lotion, dry his colored hair under the air conditioning while combing it into the correct position. Then put menthol anti-sweat powder on his feet and baby powder on his balls and his ass. I know these details because one morning he came cursing into our office after he mistakenly used menthol anti-sweat powder on his balls and ass and it was burning like hell. For our operations in Port au Prince ganglands, he was dressed in perfectly up to date 511 khaki or black combat clothes and body armor and the latest Calvin Klein scent. Abuelo didn't talk much about his past but was a stone cold professional in times of danger. He was one of the first United Nations Security Officers arriving in Haiti in 2004 and was hired directly from Iraq where he ended his 25 years of service as a contractor to the US State Department and Department of Defense. He was recruited during the war against drugs in Latin America and received his US passport before he ever set foot on US soil. English lessons were not part of this program, he learned it from Sunny Crockett and Ricardo Tubbs on the TV series Miami Vice. I first met him in April 2005, shortly after my arrival. We both stayed, like many other staff members in the Ibo Lele hotel since it offered 24 hours of electricity and a restaurant.

The view from the Ibo Lele Hotel was amazing, it was overlooking the airport, the lakes towards the Dominican Republic and the Bay of Port au Prince. The shiny reflection in the metal of the roofs of the shacks in Cité Soleil looked beautiful and peaceful from up here. I hadn't been to Ibo Lele for a long time or talked to Commandant and was curious about what was going on. I took my MP5 from under the bed and my Glock 19 that was covered by a t-shirt on the small table next to my bed. I didn't intend to hide my guns since I never left without them, I didn't want my main tools of defense visible to any attacker just in case anybody managed to get inside my apartment undetected. On weekends I didn't dress tactically, a simple t-shirt and jeans did it because the MP5 remained in my moving gun safe, my car anyway. I just stuck my Glock 19 in my pants with a simple holster inside the waistband.

The traffic was not bad; it was already later in the morning; still, any old, broken water truck or tap-tap could transfer your trip in a never-ending story. A tap-tap was the typical public transportation. A vehicle in which the part behind the driver's cockpit was cut off and replaced with a platform. On this platform were two benches and a roof. Many tap-taps were colorfully painted with faces of their saints, Jesus, Maria or Brazilian football stars. When somebody wanted to get off, he had to tap-tap on the metal, and the driver would stop instantly, regardless of the consequences. Any passenger was a customer, no tab-tab was full, there was always space for one more. Einstein stated, time and distance were relative and should be measured together, Haiti had its own particular way to test his theory. A length of 200 meters could take 2 hours and the detour of 6 kilometers if there were one available could be much faster. Therefore, the detour would be called a short cut, space and time measured together; it was correct. The 'short-cuts' were usually dirt roads in terrible conditions through narrow streets and small houses. These dirt roads were the sidewalk, the laundry place, the soccer field and for some the extended living room. Caution was required while driving. Petion Ville, named after the founding father Petion, was once a small village above the communes of Delmas, Port au Prince, and several other municipalities. Today all these communes were glued together by tiny brick houses of poor neighborhoods. The infrastructure and roads connecting these communities were built under Papa Doc in 1960 for a few hundred thousand people. Today more than 3 million people used the same infrastructure. There was no flexibility on the streets of Port au Prince.

The Ibo Lele Hotel was on Monte Noire just above Petion Ville. It was said that the Ibo Lele was one of the hotels Bill and Hillary Clinton stayed during their honeymoon in December 1975 when they witnessed the first Voodoo ceremonies in the outskirts of Port au Prince. Ibo Lele is a Haitian Voodoo 'Loa,' spirit related to the Ibo people, but also means in Creole the 'Ibo' people singing or screaming. The 'Ibo' or 'Igbo' people originated from Igboland in Nigeria and Equatorial Guinea, and it was believed that their love and will for freedom was one of the driving forces behind the slave revolution that resulted in victory over the French in 1804. The rebellion in 2004, two hundred years later, was led by two men, one of them lived in the Ibo Lele Hotel. He was a gentle older man, a grandfatherly type and, according to Wikipedia, a notorious war criminal and human rights violator under Duvalier and the military junta of Cedras.

Everything was relative in Haiti. Louis Jodel Chamblain was a patriot with political patronage. Niko always called him a lonely patriot. When Aristide was about to return in 1993, Aristide supporters brutally killed his pregnant wife while searching for him. Chamblain escaped to the Dominican Republic until 2003 when he returned to Haiti with a rebel force. He was sentenced to life in absentia and took advantage of the Haitian Justice system with the same political patronage after his return in 2004. His appeal resulted in a retrial and he was sentenced to one year in jail, which he served until 2005. It was a perfect example of Haitian justice. It took me some time to understand that he had no money, he lived in the hotel for free and was like the chief of security. This seemed strange since everybody else involved in the rebel movement appeared to be very wealthy, but but in retrospect was simple to understand. He went into exile in 1993 before drug trafficking in the country boomed and made people rich and greedy.

I parked my armored Toyota in the almost empty parking lot. Abuelo's car was already there. I walked through the corridor with the Voodoo paintings to reception, it had been a while, but nothing changed. The man behind the desk did not notice me as he was focused on the small black and white tv, watching a football game. Behind the next corner was a huge terrace with tables and chairs and some couches. The waiters of the restaurant one floor below next to the swimming pool, relax on the sofas, some sleeping. I silently passed them without disturbing their siesta. Usually, I would have asked them for a Prestige, Haitian beer, but things were different this Sunday. The pool and restaurant area were empty. So at least in the Ibo Lele Hotel, everything seemed perfectly normal. I wondered even more, why we didn't meet together on the terrace as usual. The empty hotel made a profitable business unlikely and was obviously either a costly hobby or a front for other financial activities, but it made it a very confidential meeting place. The concept of money laundering as a crime was not much considered or understood in Haiti. All these 'flourishing' businesses in a country with a UN peacekeeping force, no functional state institutions, no customers, no tourism and 60 percent of the population living on less than one US dollar a day had only one purpose: to justify to US authorities their bank accounts and beautiful villas in Miami Beach that they paid for in US dollars.

I remembered his room was just after the open area with the couches. When I reached Commandant's room, I noticed his door was slightly opened and just entered. Abuelo and Chamblaine were sitting around the small table. We brotherly hugged and sat down. Chamblaine started:" I got a phone call from Guy, he asked me to talk to you guys from MINUSTAH.," he paused and looked at us. "To negotiate with the US embassy how he can turn himself in. He wants you to be his proof and evidence that he came voluntarily. But he doesn't want the DEA to be involved." Oh Boy, Guy Phillippe wanted to turn himself in and wanted us to help him do it. My first question was:" Is he serious?" Chamblaine was positive and seemed very excited and happy about it. This needed more than a quick thought. Guy was not just a drug dealer wanted by the DEA, he was one of the key players in the Haitian cocaine family since 1993 and his cooperation with US authorities could be a life sentence for dozens of people in Haiti. The face of Guy Phillippe had been on Interpol arrest warrants for months and on the top 10 most wanted list of the US Drug Enforcement Administration, the DEA.

Less than two years ago in 2006, his face was on many walls throughout Haiti as a presidential candidate. Before that Guy Phillippe was the face of the rebellion against Aristide in 2004 and he expected to ride the wave of liberation all the way to the presidency in the 2006 elections. He did not even garner 4 percent of the votes. Guy was a frequent guest in the Ibo Lele, and we all talked to him and Chamblaine. In those days Guy was a hero, the rebel against Aristide and the chimères. I saw Haiti in black and white. Over the last three years, I started to learn there was nothing black and white in Haiti, it was all green, like the US dollar.

Before Guy fought Aristide, he was like a son to him. He was Aristide's favorite police officer. He was young, and part of a Haitian group selected for training at the police academy in Ecuador in 1992. The program was financed by the Haitian army. After graduation in 1995, the Haitian Armed Forces was replaced by a new police force, the HNP. The 'Ecuador Boys,' as Guy Phillippe and the others were called were integrated as high ranking police officers in different departments in Port au Prince. Guy was a real sunny boy and played ping pong with Aristide every Friday after he handed over the money from the drug dealers in his jurisdiction to Bob Manuel, the Secretary of State for Public Security at the time. The newly established HNP was the authority, representing the country, representing Aristide. The HNP protected and controlled the transit of the Colombian cocaine shipments and the money transfers and made sure the fair share went to the country. The elements of the HNP which didn't actively secure and monitor transit operation were investigating and arresting anybody who tried to establish their own cocaine business and bypass the country. The logistical part of the trafficking operation was in private hands; the brothers Jaques and Hector Ketant. They transited the Colombian cocaine through Haiti, shipped it to the United States and facilitated even the distribution at the destination. Anybody bypassing the Ketant brothers was avoiding the share for the country, called Aristide.

The 'share for the country' was like an expensive membership in an automobile club, just that it was usually planes instead of vehicles that needed the country's service. When a two-propeller aircraft from Venezuela had an engine failure at 0100 in the morning the 'share to the country' paid off. The plane from Venezuela was not part of the official flight schedule and landed in Titayen on the Route Soleil # 9, North of Port au Prince close to Route National # 1. Most of the Colombian cocaine came by plane via Venezuela. On the ground waited several vehicles marking the improvised landing strip with the headlights. The vehicles also transported the cocaine to storage in Port au Prince. The plane normally left once the 1,5 tons of cocaine were loaded into the vehicles, except that this plane had technical problems. The man on the ground in charge, a young 'Lieutenant' in the Ketant cartel, alias 'Kiko,' knew what to do. He burned the plane and called the commissaire of Delmas 33, Guy Phillippe, who responded. The driver of the recovery truck must have been surprised to see police presence on all roads in the middle of the night on his way to the accident scene. He must have been even more surprised when he saw what he was supposed to recover, the remains of a burnt aircraft. Water trucks were already in place to clean up the scene, by sunrise, all traces of the night's events removed. 'Kiko' informed Jaques Ketant when everything was arranged. All communication was via police radios on a separate frequency.

It was all a big happy family between 1993 and 1999 until greed started working its evil magic and created plots and intrigues. The different entities involved began to complain about the high 'share for the country.' The HNP complained it didn't receive enough salary from the 'share for the country' and the logistical part complained that the 'share for the country' was too high. Guy and his friends wanted more. A split started to grow within the HNP over loyalty to Aristide. Aristide must have smelled the betrayal and started to gather his grown-up orphans, his monsters of darkness, around him. A clash between the 'Chimères' and the HNP was inevitable. In October 2000, just before Aristide's scheduled reelection to the presidency, he visited the office of the Provisional Electoral Council in Delmas 48. The commanding officer of the HNP on site was an Ecuador Boy and did not want to grant access to the armed 'Chimères' who were escorting Aristide with credentials from the National Palace. The HNP officers were outnumbered and were disarmed. Tires were found, and the police officers were prepared for necklacing. But the deadly match did not strike this day. Jacky Nau, the Ecuadorian comrade of Guy, did not die this day, but the support from the Ecuador Boys for Aristide did. Shortly thereafter, the Ecuador Boys and other high-ranking officers were accused of treason and arrest warrants were issued for them. They joined Chamblaine in exile in the Dominican Republic. In 2001, Guy Phillippe was blamed for a failed coup d'état attempt, and Youri Latorture, who was still with Aristide in the National Palace was a suspected supporter. Both continued to plot against the country.

Aristide faced the threat of his Ex-HNP enforcers plotting with other members of the Haitian cocaine family to overthrow him and take over the business. He couldn't trust anybody anymore. The terror of his 'chimères' between 2000 and 2003 and the ties to Colombian drug cartels increased international criticism and political pressure from the Bush Administration. Aristide remembered what happened to Manuel Noriega and ordered to clean house. The chief of HNP, Rudy Therassan with a team of assassins killed Hector Ketant at his residence on 13. February 2003. When Therassan was arrested, and 1.9 million US dollars in his bank accounts were seized he claimed he killed Hector in self-defense. This didn't fit with the crime scene, which was a blood bath looking like Zombies had ripped him apart.

Nobody wanted to transport the corpse of Hector Ketant to the morgue because it was believed there was an evil spirit in him that could kill. Voodoo was not just big in Cité Soleil, it was also a leading spiritual force for the drug dealing elite in Haiti. I was told Hector was very violent, but Jaques, his brother, was described to me as a gentleman. Maybe this was the reason why Therassan granted him a fast bullet through the head when he had his foot on Jaques Ketant's neck three months later. Therassan and his enforcers brought Jaques to Titayen on Route Soleil # 9, a popular execution site in a garbage dump. Just before he pulled the trigger, he was stopped by a radio message. He was ordered to bring Ketant to the residence of Aristide where he was arrested and deported on a DEA plane to the United States. He named many of his partners in crime and also the millions of US dollars he paid to Aristide. People always wondered why Aristide was never arrested. They didn't know that Aristide had him almost killed and handed him over to the US authorities since the official version of Ketant's arrest was a bit different. Aristide must have made a deal with the DEA. Actually, Ketant was one of many who was arrested and extradited to the US while Aristide was still in office in 2003. This might have been the reason why Aristide was never arrested or indicted, he sold out many others.

Even after the successful coup d'état against Aristide, he was flown out by the US and French authorities to exile, not to US custody. The failed attempt of Guy Phillippe and Youri Latorture in 2001 finally succeeded in 2004. Guy Phillippe struggled to gather a enough Haitian fighters in the Dominican Republic, he needed the Ex-Fadh. Since Guy Phillippe and his entourage were never army officers and for too many years very close to Aristide, they were not trusted by the Ex-Fadh, but Chamblaine was. He could gather them and provide the needed rebel force. Youri coordinated these efforts with the popular uprising against Aristide in Haiti organized by the Haitian business elite. Coup d'états were the standard form of ending the term of a Haitian government and creating new governments, sometimes with democratic elections in between. Aristide was the only president who was reinstated once since he remained the constitutionally elected president. The second time, in 2004 the Chief Justice of the Supreme Court became the legal replacement for Aristide as President and appointed a new Prime Minister. Knowing the dynamics of Haiti, I was convinced that this choice was agreed upon within the Haitian business elite and suggested to the IC, the International Community before the appointment of the Interim President. The new Prime Minister, Gérard Latorture was the Foreign Minister of Haiti in 1988 and had served for many years as United Nations official in several countries. He might have had an excellent record with the UN, but in Haiti, he had one major issue. Actually, the issue was a reoccurring pattern of leading Haitian politicians, their family members, Gérard Latorture was Youri's uncle.

Youri Latorture was a former Haitian military intelligence officer who learned his tactics and trade directly from Lieutenant-Colonel Michel Francois in the military junta of Raoul Cédras. The tactics were suppressing political opponents through torture, and the trade was Colombian cocaine transiting through Haiti. These special skills and experience made Youri Latorture a unique player within the Haitian cocaine family, and he played a significant role during the presidential terms of Aristide and Preval. He sensed the winds of change in 2001 and joined the Anti-Aristide movement as a student in Canada until his uncle became Prime Minister. His uncle knew who his nephew was and what he did and still granted him full authority. Youri Latorture was the real decision maker in the Prime Minister's office and made sure all port authorities were in trusted hands. He was called Mr. 30 percent, his 'share for the country.' The new licenses for international cell phone providers were very lucrative contracts at the time, and Youri profited through it until he was arrested. The DEA arrested him based on 4 sealed indictments at the Miami International Airport. He was lucky, his uncle's intervention via Washington got him a one-way ticket back to Haiti, but he was warned. Back in Haiti, the Latorture's applied a successful strategy to keep Youri safe from future prosecution, democratic elections. Youri became a member of the legislative power in Haiti, he became a Senator of Haiti in 2006. Youri was smart and concentrated on his career as an elected representative of the Haitian people.

Guy Phillippe had a similar plan, he just wanted more, he wanted the presidency. He wanted to become the new leader of the Haitian cocaine family since the one on top, Aristide was finally gone. All of them must have felt safe to do so since the general belief was that Guy and the rebels acted as the extended arm of the CIA to enforce US foreign policy by ousting Aristide. Actually, this argument was not unfounded, Guy and Chamblaine were rewarded with a high US department of defense medal for their leadership in the armed uprising against President Aristide. It must have been an unpleasant surprise when the Blackhawk helicopters made the banana trees in Guy's garden bend to the ground and dozens of raiders from the DEA office in Florida fast-roped into his garden in 2007. I met the one who had him by his shirt but couldn't secure him, he ran off into the banana trees. I heard 'Abuelo's' voice:" What do you think about it?"

Abuelo interrupted my mind's wandering and brought me back to the Ibo Lele. I looked at him and his hair and was wondering if his hair gel would resist a burning tire. Maybe he had some particular 'desert storm' version. Because this was the kind of death waiting for us when word got out. The images of the necklaced victims passed through my mind. These endless pain in their faces with the rest of the tires around their burnt bodies. I was always trying to guess how long they might have suffered and wondered, how do you get them to kill you fast with a bullet before they lit the match? Maybe a joke. "You want to do it?" 'Abuelo' didn't let my mind go. I looked at them both and concluded that we had to involve our leadership. We couldn't do this under the radar.

I asked Chamblaine what he thought we should do. He agreed, we needed to involve MINUSTAH leadership. He also understood that this was what Guy wanted. He could only trust Chamblaine with such a request. Chamblaine was not in the cocaine business and was not afraid of Guy talking to the US. But for so many people around us nothing would have been too cruel or violent to stop this from happening. Suddenly a chainsaw came to mind. Jaques Ketant, the gentleman, cut a man accused of stealing from him in half with a chain saw. When I heard this story, my first thought was, I never saw a chainsaw in Haiti, labor was so cheap everything got chopped up with machetes; Jaques Ketant must have imported the chainsaw for special events.

Who knew what was trendy in the cocaine family of Haiti, certainly not jail time. When Abuelo and I left Ibo Lele, I realized the list of people who could not afford to have Guy Phillippe cooperating with the US authorities started right here, in the Ibo Lele Hotel. The hotel was owned by three sisters of the Haitian elite. Two of these sisters were married to two comrades of Guy Phillippe, the Ecuador Boy 'Gogo Noel' and high ranking HNP officer Will Dimanche. Guy Phillippe and his friends were the extension of the National Palace, untouchable and irresistible. This power made them acceptable to the highest levels of the Haitian elite all the way up to the Ibo Lele. I understood now why we didn't meet on the terrace. But on the other hand, things out of the ordinary tend to attract attention, maybe we should have met in the garden.

It was time to check in with our new partner Niko. In January of 2008, the RSO office was thinning out. Bertrand Bourgain left the mission and promised Gus and John Taylor reassignments out of Port au Prince. Daniel became the RSO but already had an offer for another mission and was just waiting for the release and medical clearance. Abuelo hated to write reports, so I replaced JC as Officer in charge of the Patrol Unit after he was reassigned to coordinate Security Training Programs in the same office with Ray. Their office was next to ours in Log Base, and JC together with Ray remained available to be the backup patrol, 'the last resort' as we used to call it. Since Daniel was RSO, I was promoted to Deputy RSO. It sounded great but just meant that I did the same as before and additionally replaced Daniel when he was on leave. I had a tendency to forget this fact when my presence was required in some important meetings. Niko joined us in patrol after switching positions with Manu once Abuleo agreed to it. Abuelo hated change and argued that Niko was involved in humanitarian projects in Haiti. He concluded that Niko might have had an issue shooting at bandits. I remembered Gus looking at Abuelo with a big question mark in his face when Abuelo stated:' Ya, he builds schools and stuff for children. He is a tree hugger". "With a gun," I added. Niko was my choice and Gus wholeheartedly agreed. He convinced Abuelo with the argument, Niko was some form of Mother Theresa of the Waffen SS. As questionable the underlying moral of this comparison was, it worked. Niko waited at the poolside cafeteria which was new and not related to the 'typhoid kitchen.' The pool was painted in blue but never filled with water. The mission was afraid it could create the image of UN staff members having a great time in Haiti. I guessed this ship had already sailed since Haitians called us MINUSTAH – Tourista.

Weekends were quiet in the HQ since most staff enjoyed the beaches. Niko assumed Da Costa was already in the office since he saw the SUV limousine and the backup vehicle of the protective detail at the VIP parking lot. After I explained the situation to Niko, he went up to the fourth floor to speak with Da Costa directly. Since Bertrand Bourgain left, we maintained direct communication with Louis Carlos Da Costa. Bypassing our chain of command was a violation of all reporting procedures, but we couldn't care less. Our new Chief of Security was now called Chief Security Advisor. He was the 'new generation' of UN Security from the UN Department of Safety and Security, UNDSS was created after the deadly bombing of the UN HQ in Baghdad to lead all UN security operations worldwide, including DPKO Security. He was not a leader or decision maker like Bertrand, he didn't need to know about our meeting in Ibo Lele. 1400hrs, Da Costa's office; his personal assistant walked us into his office where he was sitting with another man in a business suit on the chairs in front of the balcony overlooking Port au Prince. Da Costa was very respectful, and his smile made everybody feel welcomed and important. Da Costa introduced us to the head of the DEA office of the US embassy. Both were listening to my brief summary. Da Costa's smile got bigger and bigger watching the DEA station chief, while I was talking. He always liked to hear our input about the reality of MINUSTAH operations on the ground, the bandits and their political affiliations. This time he enjoyed it more than usual.

I tried to make it as short and precise as possible and paused to receive questions, but it took some time for the head of the DEA to respond. "Why would Guy Phillippe contact you guys?". I explained to them that we knew Guy from the beginning of the mission, we sat with him sometimes at the Ibo Lele Hotel and with his trusted friend Chamblaine. I wanted to explain who Chamblaine was, but his gesture with his hands told me, there was no need to explain. I clarified that we did not know Guy Phillippe very well, but we had no reason to question that Chamblaine believed Guy Phillippe was serious. The DEA chief now smiled back to Da Costa and said:" you were right about them" and he continued to us," I am authorized to support all your efforts in bringing him in. However just to be clear, we cannot guarantee him any deal because these deals are up to the judicial process. He has to surrender himself to US Justice first. Usually, judges consider such action in a reduced sentence, but nobody can tell him before what the sentence will be. First, he has to come in". I also clarified that Guy mentioned no DEA and I would refer to Mr. Darrel as a representative of the US Ambassador. Before we left, Da Costa said that we could use any logistics from MINUSTAH available to facilitate the mission. I personally hoped we could do this as low profile as possible and avoid involving more people.

Abuelo went to Chamblaine to fill him in and let Guy know. Our initial plan was to get a VIP armored SUV Limousine with tinted windows from MINUSTAH and just pick him up. It was a long drive on bad roads, but it was the way we made the least noise with the least number of people involved, we thought. By tomorrow, Monday afternoon we expected to have an idea about possible timing. Niko, Abuelo and I stayed together for some time on the parking lot. Abuelo was worried about the number of people knowing about our mission and the time it took us to get to Pestelle and back. The road was long, and it was too easy to block it with a small violent protest. If anybody would have just believed we were about to bring Guy to the US authorities small protests were our least worries. Abuelo mentioned:" Man, you know, this narco-stuff is complicated, this is not like Cité Soleil, with the drugs, you never know from where the threat is coming from or how many people will try to kill us."

CHAPTER 10

Guns for the Gangs

Haiti, Port au Prince, March 2008

On Monday Niko was checking which armored vehicle was available to pick up Guy and I did my usual tour around the gang strongholds to collect the latest news from my CI's, Confidential Informants. I couldn't meet them at the office because they never trusted our security guards at the gate or other National staff working in MINUSTAH. It would have been their death sentence if they had been identified as informants. I knew in the meantime that many MINUSTAH national staff members were actually eyes and ears for Haitian politicians. Some were even serious criminal offenders. Most of our English-Creole interpreters for military contingents hired at the beginning of the mission were deported from the United States because of their criminal records. Nobody in the Recruitment Section wondered why they were speaking English with strong New York or Miami accent, although the gang tattoos should have given them a hint. My CI's were my eyes and ears living within the gang strongholds of Port au Prince. To work with Confidential Informants was unique and very stressful. To figure out the quality of a CI and establish a fruitful permanent contact took a minimum of 6 months and out of 15 contacts 3 or 4 remained. I never talked much politics, I focused on the gangs, and my informants were mostly ordinary people living close by them. If I talked to individuals from the upper class, HNP or politicians, I never knew what agenda was behind their comments or information. My CI's or personal contacts never knew which information I actually filtered from them. Like Mackency, he was our eyes inside the demonstrations, but also a self-declared journalist and always had a 35 minute political analyses prepared for me. I pretended to listen out of respect but couldn't bother. But he was crucial to our task of monitoring demonstrations. He was inside the crowd and could give us updates about the routes and plans. We were always in front or in the back of the demonstration and needed his information to stay safe; otherwise, I would have never dealt with him. He was the reason why I was going slowly mad and always heard my cell phone ringing, even in the middle of the night. Whenever I checked, nothing, I just imagined it. Whenever he felt something was necessary, he didn't stop 'ringing' me until I called back. Usually, it was related to money. Also, now, I needed to give him money for the week.

I met him in the parking lot of a supermarket in Clercine, close to the Aristide Foundation. He mentioned that Lavalas had received money to give to popular movements for demonstrations in the coming weeks. No specifics about timing but we heard from different corners about mobilizations for more significant demonstrations shortly. Interesting was the part that money was supposed to be passed on to a popular movement. This usually indicated violence. If Lavalas organized protests in its own or Aristide's name, the demonstrations were very well organized and disciplined. But if the demonstrations were held by their affiliated popular movements, Lavalas and Aristide were not responsible for violent actions during these events. The organizations were unions of former port and telecommunication employees who protested about their frozen salaries. Many of them 'chimères,' who never worked at these institutions but received a check for their loyalty to Aristide. It was called a 'Zombie check,' and was government money channeled to 'friends' or affiliated gangs, and thousands of such checks still exist today.

My next contact was Moses. For him, I needed a lucky hit, because he never had a phone. I had to find him around the old post office in downtown Port au Prince. Moses was a former gang member from Martissant who quit killing for the gang but was still smoking weed with them. I had to catch him between 10:00 and 11:00, so he was awake but not yet stoned. He was still a hardcore Aristide supporter and would have never told me anything which he believed would have harmed his hero's interest or image. But Moses gave me insights on the gangs of downtown and Martissant, his neighborhood. I usually drove around in the area until I saw that he saw me and waited close to the Venezuelan embassy on Harry Truman Boulevard. His gang friends believed I bought weed from him. I almost gave up today when I suddenly saw him in the mirror running towards my car. That was the only good thing on Monday, he needed money, but also a shower, our conversations in the enclosed armored vehicle could be painful. He partied with his friends all weekend because Danny Toussaint and Evens Paul delivered money from Youri Latorture to the gangs in Martissant and downtown. Danny Toussaint was a pro-Lavalas operative from the early days. Danny Toussaint and Youri had a shared history from their time in the Haitian Army and at the National Palace. Danny Toussaint was well respected within all Lavalas gangs but seemed to have a particular relation with gang leaders in the Martissant area. Evens Paul was the Mayor of Port au Prince under Aristide and maintained close ties with the gangs in the downtown area. The only reason anybody handed out money to the gangs was because they needed them. It was said the money was for 'désordre,' violent demonstrations. When, was not mentioned, but "soon." When I started working informants, I learned the names of politicians and members of the business community because of their associations with the gangs. I had to ask then Gus or John Taylor who these people were. It seemed that Youri Latorture together with Danny Toussaint and Evens Paul was a controversial group since it was believed that Aristide was a dividing factor between them. For now, I had no reason to question Moses, at some point all these political players had been united under Aristide, why not again.

The longer the contact with a Confidential Informant was, the more personal it became. The longer we knew each other, the more I became their 'patron' their 'credit-union' and responsible for the well-being of their family. MINUSTAH had a Section with a budget to pay informants, the Joint Mission Analysis Cell, JMAC for short. They offered to register our informants, but JT and Gus advised otherwise. JMAC was a big Section whose primary function was to analyze security developments. It was established in 2005 and big news at the time in the UN and DPKO. New York HQ didn't consider that this was not just big news for the United Nations but also for politicians and business owners in Haiti. They had a perfect read on any development within MINUSTAH and even the UN Security Council in New York. They sent people to MINUSTAH HQ to bring information and get registered as informants with JMAC. It was a win-win because JMAC even paid them money. The data was not always wrong but directed and controlled from somebody outside with a political agenda. JMAC never considered the possibility of counterintelligence or misleading information, and it was difficult to realize since the JMAC informant handlers were usually UN police or military officers who rotated every 12 months. I maintained in early 2008 a close relation only with JMAC under Ray Basden and the targeting cell with Herve and Jose, two UNPOL officers. But I still kept my informants apart and paid with my own money; thus it was also my information and my decision what I did with it.

Informants were serious business because any mistake could have killed them. It was a particular form of exploitation and a very personal issue. I was asking them to risk their lives for information for very little money. It was not the money that made my work with them successful, it was the respect and honesty I had for them. I didn't have to do it, but there was no other way if I wanted to know what was going on in the ganglands. In extreme situations, when one of them got in trouble or injured, I got in my car and met them at a time and place I was never supposed to be and brought them to the Doctors Without Borders hospital. The most difficult situation was when one of them was arrested, because I couldn't just go to the police station and expose them as informants. And even if they didn't care about our work relationship, they would have expected me to pay an amount of money I couldn't. To be a prisoner without political connections and money could be a sentence for life, a short life since the living conditions in Haitian jails were terrifying. The focus on human rights violations by international organizations was always the Haitian National Police, but in fact, the Haitian Justice System was a far greater human rights violator in the country than the HNP could ever be. Naive as I was at the beginning of MINUSTAH I asked via our Justice Section. The only answer I got was that there were many innocent people in Haitian prisons. They were correct, on average 88 percent of the inmates never saw a judge and spent years in jail. The worst example was a young HNP officer who worked with me on some kidnapping cases years later; he was arrested for murder, no victim, no witnesses. A judge was paid to open a case for a crime that never existed. I knew the background story and political reason for it, and there was nothing I could do. MINUSTAH Justice Section blew me off as usual. He got sick and died a few weeks later.

But the threat for Confidential Informants was not just coming from the Haitian side, I even had within MINUSTAH some very suspicious encounters. I once received a phone call from somebody far above my paygrade asking me who my informant was. I didn't understand and thought they wanted to evaluate how credible his information was because it was related to the killing of a Nigerian UN Police officer. He was shot and killed in a market in Bel Air. It was not an armed robbery; it was an assassination. Even though, he was in civilian clothes the bandits knew that he was a UN police officer. After his death, his colleagues dressed him on the scene in his uniform for insurance purposes so his family could get some financial support. In a gang territory, nobody gets killed without authorization from the gang leader, and for the killing of a UN officer, permission beyond the gang leader was required. It was the time when the Disarmament Program of the government successfully united most of the gangs under their leadership and control. The Nigerian police officer was killed when 'Samba Boukman' and Pascal Clerge, alias 'Di-Lou,' the gang leader of Bel Air had a meeting. According to my source, 'Samba Boukman' authorized the assassination. I stated it in a report and shortly afterward received this strange phone call. The person demanded the identity of my source and I wondered why. I understood that my statement was very controversial since MINUSTAH and UNDP financed the DDR program of the government, but I didn't expect my report to be distributed that openly. Of course, our new Chief had no idea what kind of information he was reading and shared it with all Section heads. I never knew the intent of that phone call but wondered what would have happened to my informant if I had revealed his identity. I was actually tempted to throw Mackency under the bus. Maybe I would have stopped hearing the phantom phone calls.

My third meeting on this day was with Rudolph, a young Haitian who lived in Cite Soleil with his mother and younger brother and sister. He approached me 2 years earlier asking if he could wash my car. He wanted to finish his school but couldn't pay. I agreed, and he started telling me about his life in Cité Soleil. He became my best eyes and ears and a friend. He was the youngest but the only one of my three primary informants who understood the concept of a salary. His salary at the time was not more than 100 US dollars, sometimes with telephone cards or other extras, but he knew that he didn't have to give me any information to receive his salary. I didn't need rumors or for him to create data, I just needed to know what was happening. No news was good news. His school was close to Log Base, so I met him in the parking lot of the airport. Cité Soleil entertained exciting visitors over the weekend; Youri Latorture came with Rene Monplaisir to Cité Soleil and met with gang leaders and Lavalas activists.

I was not an expert in Haitian politics, but I knew that this didn't make sense. On the other hand, Moses also reported Lavalas and Youri connections. I clarified whether Youri went himself or sent a representative. This was significant since many times, even though the 'big boss' was mentioned, just a messenger or representative was actually handing over the money, ammunition or message. He clarified that Youri himself came. He didn't know yet what they were talking about, but they must have received weapons and ammunition. He heard the gunfire when they tested the weapons close to the sea at night. He believed it must have been two or three automatic rifles.

Guns for gangs were a common form of showing respect to the gang leader when a business person or public official needed them for a special mission. They would give a new 'big gun' to the leader and some older weapons to his high ranking 'soldiers' to provide them with the superior fire-power they needed. Even more important was the ammunition for guns the gang already possessed. Youri's name came up a lot lately, but him in Cité Soleil with Rene Monplaisir was surprising. Rene Monplaisir was a known Lavalas activist and one of the community organizers for President Preval in Cite Soleil. He was unlikely to betray his political alliance with the President. Préval must have known about this meeting. The real surprise was that gang leaders and other Lavalas radicals sat down with one of the key players of the coup d'état against their idol in 2004. For them, Aristide was still the highest power in the universe, he was their 'Ougan,' their Voodoo priest and they all would have died for him. Even if it might not have made sense to me at the time, I knew Rudolph didn't create things, the meeting happened. Youri was a strategist and his ability to plan and look ahead made him essential to many other politicians. It was not a surprise; he was a law student and was a trained military intelligence officer. I would like to have known what Youri had to offer to Lavalas for their participation, it must have been something big. But for the moment the weapons information caught my attention since I was chasing a container of weapons which reportedly recently arrived at the port in Port au Prince.

A friend in South Africa informed me about a container with weapons leaving South Africa on a ship to Venezuela with final destination of Port au Prince, Haiti,. We tried our contact at the port who bragged a few days ago about the great container x-ray machine they received from some willing donor country in the fight against contraband and drug-trafficking. It was Pepe, chief security at the port and a good friend of Tommy Dutch. He was in exile for many years in the United States since he participated as a Haitian Navy Officer in a failed coup d'état against 'Papa-Doc.' He liked to portray himself as a freedom fighter against oppression and dictatorship. Tommy Dutch's version was a bit different. He was actually partying and fell asleep drunk on the Haitian Navy ship which participated in the failed coup attempt. He was pardoned by 'Baby Doc,' the son of 'Papa Doc' ten years later and returned to Haiti.

The main port of Port au Prince was assumed, like any other port in Haiti, to be a significant hub for weapons, drugs, and money trafficking. The last effort of K9 dog units didn't work out well after the dogs were poisoned. The solution was technology. Donated by some country, the latest technology container x-ray was installed, security personnel were trained, and the generator ran out of fuel. This was the end of the fight against contraband with the x-ray machine. The lack of electricity and the lack of interest to invest in generator fuel by the port authorities kept the port as the import-export companies liked it, free trade. But Haiti was a small universe, I got my confirmation of the weapon delivery two weeks later. I personally saw the weapons in the hands of international security contractors. They received the guns from Youri Latorture. He was not just a Senator since 2006 but also the owner of a security company, National Security. This company provided security guards for all the stores and offices of Digicel, the new mobile service provider. Digicel contracted a small army of more than 60 international close protection officers from an international security company, for the protection of their upper management. Youri's company, National Security provided the legal status to this international security company.

Youri also provided them with the newly arrived South African 9mm pistols and some South African produced Galil's as a backup. I had never heard much about Youri Latorture until his name surfaced in the gang territories a few months previously. Niko knew him very well. He met him many times when he was protecting the SRSG and visited the Interim Prime Minister, his uncle. They all saw Youri as a lovely guy. However, the lovely guy needed a backup plan for the DEA efforts in the country. It seemed to me Youri was reaching out to old Lavalas connections of the Haitian cocaine family and trying to improve these relations again, while Guy Phillippe was waiting for our pickup.

CHAPTER 11
Zombies on Crack Cocaine

Haiti, Port au Prince, April 2008

Guy was looking for a way out and was waiting in Pestelle, a village closed to Jeremie, for our pickup. Niko identified the armored SUV limousine we could use; it was in the workshop for maintenance. Armored SUV limousines in Haiti had no easy life and spent half the time in the workshop. Our vehicles were heavy duty, uncomfortable but perfect for Haitian roads. We had no tinted windows and didn't want to take the risk of bringing Guy with it. The transport workshop told Niko that we could have the car on Wednesday at the latest. Our colleagues from the transport area were experienced Field Service Officers and when they said Wednesday, it couldn't be done sooner. Transport was going to drop the vehicle in Log Base and leave the key with the Security Officer in charge, the mission was on for Thursday morning. Rudolph gave me a 'ring' on Wednesday afternoon when I called him back, he told me that several guys from Cité Soleil left for Les Cayes. He said there were two or three buses full leaving Cité Soleil. I never heard of anything like this, it sounded like a gang retreat. I didn't pay much attention to it, everything was ready for Guy. We thought it was better to have Chamblaine with us in the car since there was still a possibility that Guy was not serious and wanted to set us up. Niko ran into some issues in Log base. Transport dropped two armored vehicles, the new SUV limousine with tinted windows and an old one. The old one should have been given to the Police Commissioner until we were back from the mission, but of course, this didn't make sense to the Security Officer in Log Base. Niko just sent a short message to Da Costa, and the Chief of Administration called the Security Officer with the message; whatever Niko was asking for had to be granted. I realized one thing, all MINUSTAH personnel did not waste a second when an order came from Da Costa. But it triggered the suspicion of the Security Officer who immediately reported strange Patrol Unit activities to the CSA. The CSA must have been worried when he realized that his Patrol Unit, the 'loose canons' were on a special mission. It didn't take long until the Chief called Niko, then Abuelo and finally me. I gave him the same answer as my partners, he had to clarify it with Da Costa. I was sure it didn't satisfy him, but we couldn't care less. We just wanted to get this over with since more and more people knew something special was going on.

We left Port au Prince early morning. Chamblaine tried to reach Guy but couldn't get him. We were just before Leogane on National # 2 when we received reports of violent protesters and burning tires in front of the UN Regional HQ in Les Cayes and on main roads throughout the city. Les Cayes had no history of civil unrest or violent demonstrations, but this morning it was burning. Our trip was shorter than expected, and I remembered the retreat of the gangs in Cité Soleil to Les Cayes. We had to cancel our mission since there was no way around Les Cayes on the way to Pestelle. Guy Phillippe was later in the day in contact with Chamblaine and told him that Les Cayes was not going to stop for some days, and he couldn't leave his family behind. Friday was more violent than Thursday, and UN residences including the UN Regional HQ and UN Military base in Les Cayes were overrun and looted. His wife, two children, and his brother's family were with Guy in Pestelle, his condition to surrender was that they had to come with him. The DEA didn't hesitate to offer transportation to all of them, his brother and family had no US visa and would have gone first to the Dominican Republic to receive permits from the US embassy there. His wife and children had a US passport and could fly with him on the DEA plane directly to Fort Lauderdale. We just had to get them to Port au Prince. We needed our MINUSTAH helicopters.

Da Costa received us in his residence close to the Montana Hotel. It was Saturday and was watching his favorite team Real Madrid. At half time he sat down at his computer on a small table and filled out a special request for a helicopter flight on Sunday and the waivers for transportation of non-UN staff members on UN helicopters. He called the Chief Aviation Officer, gave him our names and told him that we were going to provide the coordinates and we had the waivers, special permits, for the passengers we were going to pick up to board. Nobody needed to see the waivers. He clarified that it was understood, since he didn't like the scenario and complications we had with the armored vehicle. The official documents he filled and approved at the same time for a particular helicopter flight with non-UN passengers would normally have taken several days. He did it in the 15 minute half time of Real Madrid. Before we left, he told us:" Tell your friend to let Guy Phillippe know, if anything happens to you, I will send the Brazilian Battalion to hunt him down and bring him to justice." I could see, he was worried and concerned. Maybe we should have been as well.

Sometimes I didn't want to see the obvious. I met with John Taylor for a beer on Friday while the riots were going on in Les Cayes. He was back from leave and waited to fly on Saturday with the UN helicopter to his region if it was possible. I could see he was convinced Guy would not show but didn't want to destroy my enthusiasm. Sunday morning, Chamblaine, Abuelo, Niko and I waited in our office in Log Base to get a message or call from Guy. The helicopter was ready for take-off. It didn't happen. Chamblaine already knew it when we picked him up this morning because he was 10 minutes late and didn't look very motivated. After a few hours, we had to cancel the mission. Whatever went wrong, we had to accept it. We knew we had troubles coming to Port au Prince and had better prepare for that. I knew from Rudolph that the troublemakers who messed up Les Cayes were back in Port au Prince, their retreat was over. Since I was acting RSO, on Friday I requested from Military Operations reinforcement for all MINUSTAH facilities of Port au Prince, especially Log Base. I was lectured Friday afternoon by our Chief of Operations, that in his humble opinion, I didn't see the big picture. If I had been present as RSO on Friday in the Senior Management Team Meeting, I would have known that the military was aware of possible demonstrations and was going to prepare accordingly. Besides, he advised me to focus on the great opportunity the CSA had organized for us the coming week. The new training course of UNDSS about the future approach of UN Security in the field.

When the CSA introduced his colleagues from New York and thanked them for coming first to Haiti, he advised us there would be many changes, and we would have to adapt to the new policies. We would not monitor demonstrations anymore; our UNPOL officers together with the HNP were supposed to that. In my mind, I thought:" Good luck with that." This wishful statement of the Chief Security Advisor and the trainers showed us how little experience they had in the field. Even though the UNPOL leadership had a great story to tell on paper about their achievements and the positive development of HNP to justify their program, it was unfortunately only on paper. Niko asked if we were going to pay for the HNP's fuel. The trainers looked confused, and Niko explained that most of the time the HNP couldn't respond with us to incidents because their vehicles were either not operational or had no fuel in the tank. The trainers were convinced that somebody high up in New York was going to find a solution for it. The trainers assured us that New York was here to support us in the field, like when a hurricane hits Haiti. The 'guys' from New York with their laptops were trained and prepared to come and help. Ten people in a flooded area who need transportation, food and a place to stay, obviously with electricity and the internet for their laptops didn't sound much like support to us. But the main new rule, we would not risk our lives anymore. The CSA must have asked them to be very detailed and specific about this new approach.

The training started but didn't prevent us from monitoring the security radio channel, Channel 2. It didn't take long to have an excuse to get out of the classroom. Sierra Base was calling for any Sierra Papa, Patrol call sign for emergency response. Niko responded, and Sierra Base informed him about a civilian UN call sign attacked by violent demonstrators in downtown. Ray and JC were even faster into their body armor than we were, they assumed that it was so dangerous, 'the last resort' had to leave the classroom as well and accompanied us. I guess none of us was ready for change yet. There were violent demonstrations in downtown, and one UN vehicle was attacked with stones not far away from it. The driver left the car in the street and found shelter in a gas station. We went to pick up the driver and the car. The violent demonstration remained in the downtown area, the official reason for the demonstration was the high cost of living, like in Les Cayes. We knew this was just the slogan for the international press. This was the mobilization, the 'disorder' we heard about for the last few weeks and paid for by Youri. Our trainers from UNDSS were impressed when we brought the UN vehicle back to Log Base with smashed windows and sprayed with graffiti. They didn't know that this was just the beginning. Mackency and Rudolph reached out to me about the gangs smoking 'crack' cocaine and preparing for a rough day. It seemed 'crack' cocaine was given to the gangs specifically to increase the violence because I didn't hear much about crack cocaine on average days. We prepared for a difficult day. Jose, our friend from the JMAC targeting cell joined Niko to be with him in the area of Petion Ville, JC and Ray stayed in the area of Log Base, and Abuelo and I took care of downtown, at least that was the plan.

We went the next morning towards lower Delmas close to the seaside. Main Delmas was a road going through all of metropolitan Port au Prince from the sea at La Saline, the first slave market of the island, all the way up the hill to Petion Ville. There was a report of a crowd gathering close to the church St. John Bosco which was a few hundred meters away from the sea. Since 2005 we must have monitored hundreds of demonstrations already and had a great idea about the dynamics of it. Mackency reported from different gatherings in the Martissant area, this sounded different than the usual demonstrations. On a typical day, the initial meeting was in Bel Air close to the church Perpétuel Secours. The Voodoo Priestess 'So Ann' or another Voodoo priest close to Aristide and their Lavalas movement initiated the gatherings with a Voodoo ceremony. I was always surprised by the mix of church religion and Voodoo, but it was somehow very flexible. Many of the voodoo spirits were actually related or similar to Catholic saints and churches were usually built on spiritual energy places. Aristide was a Catholic priest and believed to be into Voodoo and its black magic as well. The black magic priests were the guys who zombified people; at least Franz loved to scare newcomers to Haiti with this unique threat. The gathering in Bel Air usually started marching to St. John Bosco church, where Aristide preached many years, where they met with 3000 to 4000 supporters from Cité Soleil. Even though we knew this demonstration was not the normal officially announced Lavalas demonstrations, it usually didn't change the opening ceremonies and locations. The report came from UNPOL, which indicated to us that this was not real-time information and around 90 minutes delayed. Until the HNP officers in Bel Air informed their commissariat in Port au Prince which relayed it to the communication center and finally was picked up by a UNPOL working there who sent an email to the UNPOL communication center in the HQ, it usually took 90 minutes to two hours. Rudolph had reported to me much earlier that gang members were leaving Cité Soleil for gatherings at St. John Bosco. Mackency was in Martissant and said that gangs were warming up and already burning tires. We calculated a two-hour delay from UNPOL and our driving time to meet this crowd on the way up around the main Delmas and airport road; we were so good we had them right in front of us.

As we turned from the airport road into main Delmas going up the hill direction to Petion Ville, we saw a crowd of at least 500 people in front. As arrogant as I could be, I just said:" Boy, are we good. Let's follow them." I assumed we were right behind them. I saw Abuelo looking in the back mirror and heard: "Fuck." Abuelo was a cold fish, and this meant nothing good. I turned around, the group in front of us was not the only group, there were groups on the left, on the right and behind us and the rocks came flying in. I was sure when we turned there was just the crowd in front of us, where the hell did these guys come from? The noise of one rock was annoyingly loud, our vehicle got hammered with hundreds. These demonstrators were not the regular crowd. They were all hardcore' gang bangers', I never saw so many in one place. And even they looked more zombified than usual, they were zombies on crack cocaine. We hit the Zombie Apocalypse. On our normal patrols, we never paid attention to the number of rocks and potential barricades laying around in the city. It made violent demonstrations so much easier. Delmas was a big road with a dividing concrete wall to keep us on the two lanes going up with no street in sight the coming few hundred meters to make a turn into safety. It was like fresh bloody meat thrown into shark infested waters; we were the meat. The stones were flying, some ran up to our car with sticks, they tried to roll big rocks metal frames and other items into the road, but Abuelo hit the gas. Wow, they were really focused on us. These guys were dedicated, and sooner or later they would find something that could stop us. Suddenly we heard a high pitch noise of a siren, we knew this beautiful noise came from a Brazilian APC. The APC was coming in full speed from behind us and made everybody move. It was sent to evacuate the Force Commander from a meeting in the Prime Minister's office in Delmas 60, they must have already known this was about to get ugly.

We didn't know if the APC was just so much more impressive or these demonstrators had a particular beef with us. They tried to separate us from the APC. Abuelo almost touched the APC with the front bumper of the car and stayed on it to keep the cover. I jumped in the back of the vehicle. We had no side doors behind the driver and passenger side, just an opening on the backside like in an ambulance. The car had seats along the sides in the back for eight people facing each other with their backs against the windows. The seats could be folded and fixed on the sides and left a reasonably large storage area and the possibility to move. In the back, we could open a small door on the right, and the bigger part could remain closed. It was a great vehicle, whose armor saved us many times. But it became problematic when we were ambushed and risked getting stuck. Ambushes in gang areas were usually from the front and both sides from higher ground and they could shoot at both of our side doors. It was most of the time impossible to open any of these doors to shoot back or exit the vehicle safely. The back doors in the direction we were coming from were the best option to open and usually also the way out. With these crowds around us, we would have never been able to open our side doors in time before they could either block us in and burn us or try to grab us. The back was the only option to exit the vehicle and engage. I held the handle of the small door as tight as I could with my left, MP 5 submachine gun was in my right. I was ready for an impact and even the vehicle flipping. I just had to be fast enough to open the small door and let my submachine gun talk. 30 rounds had to get me enough time for the first magazine change to continue shooting and keep the crowd away and not get hit by a stone. Now I just had to focus on what happened next.

My sign to open and shoot was when we stopped moving, I didn't look forward, I didn't even look at the 'crack heads' attacking us. I just glanced through the bulletproof glass of the back door on the passing asphalt. We were still moving. I knew Abuelo wouldn't stop for anything. They could have thrown themselves in front of the vehicle, Abuelo would have just put the car in 4-wheel drive to increase the traction. I saw the rocks rolling down which must have bounced from our vehicle. A solid rock on an armored window made a nasty noise and the first time it happened, I thought we were shot at with a rifle. But a bullet impact was much more ear friendly. Until you turn your head to the glass and see the result right there at eye level a few centimeters away and you thank the quality of the bulletproof glass. I saw the stones rolling down but didn't hear their impact. I just focused on the street and our movement. At some point, no rocks were rolling anymore, and I realized Abuelo turned into a side street. We were driving until we believed it was safe enough to open the doors and have a cigarette. None of us said a word for a while, we knew the APC saved us from our last fight. If we had got stuck, we would have had to exit the vehicle and go berserk to have a chance to survive. We gave the others heads up about the violence towards us and that this was not the usual crowd.

All staff members had to remain indoors, regardless if it was a supermarket, bank or their residence. Whereever we were moving it didn't take long until a violent crowd chased us through the streets. Scouts on motorbikes were driving around, and whenever one of them spotted us, it didn't take long for the crowds to come and hunt us. We started to feel very uncomfortable and weren't used to not being in control outside the gang strongholds. Many of our staff members had violent crowds in front of their residences. The scouts on the motorbikes knew precisely where we lived. It seemed our UN HQ was not on the target list, but the Log Base definitely was. Rudolph told me that Cité Soleil had the task to storm the UN Log base as they did in Les Cayes. Ray and JC kept hundreds of Zombies at a distance for hours. In between, they even took the trainers from New York to the airport to take the flight out of Port au Prince which arrived in the morning from Miami.

All other flights were already canceled. The trainers were lucky Ray and JC knew them because of their work relationships in the training office, I would have let them wait until the host government, an HNP patrol could bring them to the airport. We had several staff members requesting evacuation from their residences, but only Niko and Jose managed to extract some to the Ibo Lele Hotel. Our military never reinforced our UN bases. JC and Ray kept the violent crowds away from UN Log Base in the days to come. We all tried to get to people in need and many times almost became the people in need ourselves. Our tools to reach the end of the day were tear gas and rubber bullets which we collected from friends over the years. These were not standard Security equipment, and our stocks were limited. As a last resort, we could fire shots in the air, just above the heads to scare the hell out of them. We were lucky that Cege had just joined us as our Logistics Officer, and he had enough ammunition available. He also didn't make it complicated or ask for permission. He was a Field Service old timer and former Special Forces; he knew what had to be done.

The riots paralyzed Port au Prince and were a serious challenge to many UN Military bases. It seemed their strategy to limit our response capacity by attacking UN Military directly at their base, worked very well. The Sri Lanka Battalion in Martissant was assaulted by the crowds and had to be rescued and evacuated by the Jordanian Battalion. The Jordanian Swat unit supported friends from the US embassy Diplomatic Security Service who were challenged by some zombies close to their consulate in downtown. Our military tried to avoid clashing with the violent demonstrators since it was officially about socio-economic issues until the masses wanted to break down the fence of the National Palace. Then MINUSTAH was forced to protect and support the host government. It did not look to me like they really wanted to storm the palace. Preval, the President, was at his house in Canape Verte and didn't seem to be targeted. It was just the trigger to get MINUSTAH military involved in the violent clashes and turn the violence against MINUSTAH in general. It worked perfectly. We couldn't make it to the National Palace ourselves, but when Mackency described the situation there, I called our photojournalist about it. I was sure he didn't want to miss it. It must have been just a few minutes later when I heard Abuelo:" Maaan, he is crazy." We saw him flying down Canape Verte on his motorbike. On Friday the violence continued, and there was no point in being exposed anymore. Also, Mackency called me earlier that the zombies had our vehicle numbers and the order to burn them, he didn't specify with or without us. I ordered all patrols to look for shelter. Ray and JC in Log Base, Abuelo and I joined Niko and Jose at Ibo Lele.

The President announced a speech on the radio after lunch. When I was told what exactly he said, I thought things would get worse. To me the statement didn't have much of a calming message, it was almost provocative. But something else was announced, and this was really strange. The Senate lost their confidence in the Prime Minister and voted him out of office. I could not believe that in all this mess and violence in downtown, the parliament was actually in session and made a decision without being bought and paid for. We were asked to check the reaction of the people after the President's speech. I should have referred our leadership to the new approach and suggested they check with HNP, but we had many scared staff members in their residences, trapped at the airport or other locations, so there was nobody else.

Getting back into the mess after a few peaceful hours of rest was painful. Like in the army during long marches in cold weather, as long as the body was warm and moving it was ok. Any stop even for not more than a minute, when the body lost temperature, and the wet underwear and socks started to cool down or freeze, the first steps were the worst. I stepped out of the car before each corner to take a 'quick peek.' I was tired and didn't want any stones flying after us anymore, I would have just opened fire above the crowd. A lot of debris in the street, containers, burnt vehicles, smashed and looted shops, but no violent crowds. Many young people walking down the road back into their neighborhoods, the zombification process also worked the other way around, they became normal 'gang-bangers' again. A few hours ago, they wanted to kill us, and now they didn't even look at us, it was just business. We couldn't figure out what made them stop. If they were paid just until Friday afternoon, or until the Prime Minister was removed, or if there was a command and control structure in place which ordered a stop. Whatever it was, the 'food riots' were over. When we drove down main Delmas carefully passing all obstacles a closer look confirmed who was the main strategist behind these riots and proved our contacts correct. The Digicel stores had the biggest and nicest window fronts, there was not even a scratch on them. Shops left, and right of them looted, burnt and smashed, only the mobile service provider Digicel store without a scratch. I later heard people talking about that the Haitians liked Digicel, that's why they didn't attack the stores. The rioting population was a few hundred gang members who didn't care about anybody or anything, and they would have loved new cell phones. They did what they were told to do, and the Youri connection was obvious. All Comcel shops were looted and destroyed.

Another excellent indicator, which told us who was behind the 'food riots,' was that the parliament was in session on Thursday and the demonstrators did not mind them working. At the same time, the US consulate and embassy next to the parliament faced violent crowds and had severe attacks on many of their sub-offices. On Thursday 10 April, while the streets were burning just outside, 18 Senators declared that the Prime Minister should resign within 2 days because of his failed economic policies. They returned to their seats in parliament even on the most violent day on Friday to decide; they didn't wait for his resignation, they just voted him out of office. The Prime Minister knew the reason. Two weeks ago, he had been in Washington and gave a speech in which he strongly expressed his support for the DEA arrest operation against Guy Phillippe. The Senate couldn't care less about the economic situation of the country since the cocaine business was running very well. They just needed to be safe from US prosecution and also needed to show Guy Phillippe there was no reason to worry or run.

The riots could have been much more severe, they stopped just in time. One or two more days and we would have had serious issues of supply and communication. The cell phone towers would have gone down without fuel in the generators. The same for our residential generators and food and water supplies would have been exhausted. The most fantastic experience I took from these days was the discipline of the violent crowds, to hit only the identified targets. The vehicles of the people living in my apartment building were all smashed. Jonas, the nice man who took care of the building, told me he heard the scouts saying:" This is MINUSTAH location." The official short-term goal was achieved, the Prime Minister resigned. From a military tactical viewpoint, it actually looked like a tactical reconnaissance operation. They were testing response capability and successful strategies to paralyze the city. The crowds were attacking UN residences and UN facilities to measure the response. They tested whether they could cut off the fuel supply from the terminals in Carrefour. The airport was closed, and several passengers who arrived before the airlines canceled all flights had to stay at the airport during the night without food or water. They tested very well the strength and tactics of the UN troops and the HNP capacity and could paralyze the city for a few days. It was challenging to explain my reconnaissance theory because not many people witnessed the organization within the riots. Ray and JC did not allow the zombies to take UN Log Base, not on their watch. But in the long run, if the zombies would have taken UN Log Base, maybe it would have been easier for us to explain our observations and conclusions. These riots looked like reconnaissance or a test run to me, a test for what, I couldn't say.

CHAPTER 12
TIH, This is Haiti

Haiti, Port au Prince, May 2008

A conversation with my contact in South Africa made me see the riots from a much larger perspective. His contacts in the Air Force Base in Pretoria told him that Aristide, who was in exile in South Africa at the time, was ready at the Air Force Base of Pretoria to board the Presidential plane. My contact did not know the planned destination of the flight, but the Presidential plane was fueled up for long distance and ready to take off during the riots in Haiti. My friend mentioned that the French and US Ambassadors to South Africa intervened and stopped him from leaving. My South African friend had already explained to me that Aristide had to make a move soon since his friend President Mbeki was about to finish his term at the end of the year. Publicly, his most likely replacement Jacob Zuma stated he didn't want Aristide to remain in South Africa. There was a good chance that Aristide wanted to make a surprise visit back to Haiti. This could have been the prize Youri was offering the Lavalas gangs and could explain the support from the Lavalas gang strongholds and Lavalas leadership. It also proved Youri being part of the extreme anti-Aristide wing wrong, or maybe this never existed anyway because it was all just business. I wondered if a possible return of Aristide could have been the motivation for Guy Phillippe to seek justice and safety with the US authorities. If he had the choice between payback from Aristide for his betrayal or US jail time, I guess the option of a US jail sounded much better. The riots in Les Cayes could have been a message for Guy to stay put. But it might have been as well just a training exercise for the big event in Port au Prince. One thing was for sure, Youri had no issues working with Lavalas even on a possible return of Aristide. Preval must have been in on this deal as well, which was less surprising. Bob Manuel, the close friend, and advisor of President Preval could have used his friendship with Guy to guarantee his safety as well. The real lesson for me was that all the anti-Aristide talk was not a non-negotiable principle and Haitian politics was much more dynamic than it was said to be.

The good old days of the MINUSTAH Security Section were over, we knew. But we didn't know yet how much. The weekly Senior Management Team meeting was held on Monday after the riots. I failed to attend again but was told later that a comment was made to investigate if the actions of some Security Officers during the riots followed the United Nations Use of Force Policy. Da Costa and SRSG Anabi made clear there was no need for further such discussions. The request was made by the Security Section itself, our Chief of Operation. It was definitely time to move on. Abuelo and Niko followed the example of John Taylor and Gus, they were moving as RSO's into quiet regions. I planned to follow Bertrand to Chad and was scheduled for a job interview at the beginning of May. But United Nations recruitment was like Haitian evolution, really slow and it could take up to 6 months for New York to facilitate such a move. I continued representing the RSO office and the Patrol unit. After the riots the fear of violent civil unrest was high, and when staff members encountered demonstrations, our UNPOL operations did not yet know an event was happening. The same chiefs who told me not to monitor protests anymore were the first to call me and ask me if I could check what was going on and if we needed travel restrictions. I ended up doing more or less the same as before, just alone. I always arranged fairly neutral meeting places with my informants, but since every gang member in Port au Prince was throwing stones at my vehicle, I had to consider my personal safety and that of my informants.

The gang territories were quiet after the riots, at least no more information came about unusual amounts of money or weapons handed out to them. The only data out of the ordinary were reports of production of uniforms. The news was still linked with Youri Latorture, but also with 'Ex-Fadh' elements in the Central Plateau. No further details. Niko was RSO in Hinche and had information about frequent meetings between Youri and these 'Ex-Fadh' members. It was in September when a group of twenty people in new green uniforms occupied a former Haitian Army building in Cap Haitian. The building was empty, and no violence was related to this incident. The HNP and MINUSTAH didn't know what to do with this group, and after a few days, they just disappeared. It didn't attract much attention but fit well into my reconnaissance theory. Youri Latortue was the known strategist in the riot scenario and was calling for the reinstallation of the Haitian military. He also needed a security force he could control and trust to be safe from joint HNP/DEA operations. My conclusion at the time was that if there was a riot scenario for a few days and overnight some form of security forces deployed and saved everybody; it would be the perfect way of introducing the Haitian army again. I distributed my information not to the Security leadership, but to friends and the Chief of JMAC at the time, Ray Baysden. Even though my theory must have looked like wild speculation, Ray did not question my mental state and liked my analysis. Considering his extensive experience in Haiti with the US State Department, I was happy and proud of the positive feedback on my last information report as RSO of Port au Prince.

September was Hurricane season, and while Youri was busy organizing riots, he neglected Gonaives, the capital of the department he represented as a Senator. The water canalization system planned and financed after the deadly hurricane Jeanne in 2004 to avoid thousands of victims in the future was half finished when it ran out of money. The money disappeared earlier than expected by international donors. Hurricane Ike would have been a minor event if the half-finished canalization hadn't given the rainwater a destructive force. The new canals successfully collected all rainwater but found no finished passage towards the sea and created a tsunami-like wave from inland through the country. The strength of the water was impressive. Walls, houses, trucks were moved or flattened. The helicopter pilots told me of many dead bodies caught in the mangrove trees in the bay of Gonaives. Survivors of the Land-Tsunami-Wave had to seek shelter on roofs and higher ground. The Argentinean Battalion of MINUSTAH in Gonaives had experience with other storms and hurricanes and did a great job. They knew the AOR, Area of Operation very well and the problems therein. One of their rules for food and supply distribution was that only women were allowed to stand in line and receive it. It kept troubles away and in Haiti, like in many other countries, it was mostly up to the women to maintain their families and organize the little they had. The UN base was well located free of any flooding and was the main helicopter terminal for relief supply. It was also the safe haven for many internationals rescued from their roofs. I saw a young lady sitting and smoking, she looked exhausted. She must have been one of these staff members rescued from the shelter, I thought. She looked even more confused when I approached her about it, it turned out she had just arrived that morning. She was a staff counselor. She came here to help anybody who needed her counseling. I was not sure if it was just the result of hiring inexperienced psychologists for a salary no experienced psychologist accepted, or the UN had a genius approach to healing anybody with post-traumatic stress in an instant. As long as the staff counselor seemed more stressed than the potential patient, any patient must have been reassured about their mental health. Gonaives was a short but nice break, even though the destruction of a Hurricane which cost many lives didn't sound like it, but it was a few days real fieldwork, and I thought I contributed something.

Back in Port au Prince, there was still no news from Chad, and I was reported for a hit and run accident by Haitian civilians the next morning. The damages of the parties involved were minor and had nothing to do with the UN rumors circulating that I rammed vehicles and pushed them into ditches. One vehicle had the light hanging out, the other the bumper light broke, and one car had a black line at the weak part of the driver door. It was no surprise that my armored vehicle had no scratch, the damages wouldn't have impacted my 'beast,' and actually, the damages were standard Haitian vehicle condition. The initial investigator, Sierra-India-5 and I did the report. I did not argue about the damages or the statements of the parties involved, except that I did not remember having had an accident in the heavy armored. A significant amount of gin and tonic might have influenced my perception as well. I remembered heavy traffic in heavy rain and some form of congestion which I thought I outmaneuvered perfectly. My friends tried to warn me for some time, they thought I was burning the candle at both ends. I was on the eve of destruction and didn't realize it, like tunnel vision in stressful situations. I knew the consequences of not reporting an accident. It was not the first time this happened to staff or security personnel and usually resulted in a withdrawal of the driving license for one month. SI5's investigation was not sufficient, and the Chief Investigator was asked or decided himself to redo it. The investigation report was extended for drinking and driving. Pending the outcome of the investigation, he collected not just my driving license but also my weapons permits. Investigating me for drinking and driving at the time was almost like investigating me for breathing, it didn't need a very skilled investigator. I didn't argue much because I was not the first and wouldn't be the last and had to expect to have the driving license revoked for another month. To take the weapons before completion of the investigation was unusual, especially with my history, I felt pretty naked.

I was re-assigned pending the outcome of the investigation to Sierra Base, the Communication Center. I couldn't drive any UN vehicle and had no weapons, at least no official UN-issued weapons, and Sierra Base was the perfect spot for me. Jim Kafouri was working there as well after he returned from a long but successful fight against cancer. The medication killed his cancer but not his humor. When I replaced him for my first night duty, he looked at me and said:" You fucked up and got assigned here, so if anybody who fucks up gets assigned to Sierra Base, where do they put me when I fuck up?" A few days later, I received phone calls from friends in other sections who saw the final investigation report. They advised making a short clarifying memo because, with the conclusion stated in the report, I would lose my job and be out of the UN. It was not just that an accurate blood alcohol content was noted in the report, even though I was never asked for a blood or breathalyzer test. I was also described as a person out of control who should not have access to weapons and ammunition. I met the Staff Counsellor in the Christopher Hotel who was very experienced, and it was good for me to talk to him. Da Costa sent me since he didn't see me as a gun swinging crazy person and wanted to counter the investigation report with a professional opinion. In our talk, he made me also realize that we all had our limits. Stress at work and in my personal life was a bad mixture. He also gave me a professional certificate for being still under control and not being a threat to myself and others. But nobody was aware that the alcohol content was completely made up.

The report did not mention that the blood alcohol content was calculated based on the Chief Investigator's estimation of my weight and the amount of alcohol I could have possibly drunk. Actually, his estimate was most likely on the lower end of the real blood alcohol content, but he could have never known. He did all this from the office and was even too lazy to go at least to the bar where I was drinking. Abuelo would have said:" He got greedy." I wrote a clarifying interoffice memorandum to the Board of Inquiry, Legal and some other sections and gave my friends the ammunition needed to backlash the investigation on our CSA and Chief Investigator for obvious bias against me. I knew that my investigation was dropped, but I was never informed about it officially. Da Costa told me that the offer from Chad was coming soon and I stayed in Sierra Base for the time being.

It was close to the end of 2008, and things actually seemed more secure. Kidnappings were still in an average of 30 reported incidents per month in the metropolitan area of Port au Prince but more related to organized crime outside gang strongholds. Gang violence reduced significantly. There were no upcoming elections, and the criminal gangs learned to maintain a low profile. They buried their 'long guns' in cemeteries or other locations and kept their handguns for their daily criminal offenses. In Log Base our old Patrol office became the office for the Fire Marshal. I enjoyed usually taking a lift down to Log Base to visit Ray, Cege our new Security Logistic Officer and the Fire Marshal, call Sign Sierra-Foxtrot, SF.

I took a ride back up to Christopher Hotel with Sierra-Foxtrot when we heard over the radio that a school building in Nerreth, Petion Ville collapsed. We changed routes and headed that way. The Fire Marshal was an old experienced professional and thought it was necessary to get involved. It didn't take long to find the location; a large crowd was in the small street on the way to the school. We left the car and ran down the hill. First time in all these years I froze because of dead bodies. There must have been 40 or 50 dead children already laying on the street in front of the collapsed building. They were already pulled out of the rubble, and many were dusty, bloody and deformed. They were all children. The building was at least three or 4 stories high and collapsed entirely to the back. People were mostly on the building or around the building digging out anything human. There were many legs arms heads or other parts visible in the rubble. It was a mess. I was terrified, and in shock, all these dead children were the ages of my daughters. I didn't know what to do and just followed SF and tried to translate for him any question he had to people at the site. It didn't take long for the Haitians to know that there was an international on the scene and a man ran after us to tell us that his daughter was trapped inside the building.

There was an opening, a door and it was possible to crawl into the ground floor. It was just a little bit lower than the street. The opening led to a room under the rubble which didn't collapse for the first four meters. The concrete pillars and columns formed small chambers in between the ruins. SF inspected the inside, there were at least three young girls, all three were conscious. SF went back outside. There we met other Security Officers, and the Fire Marshal wanted to ask them to prevent people from stepping above the areas where the girls were trapped. But the Security Officers had a message actually from the Acting Chief Security, that this was not a UN matter, it was a Haitian civilian matter, we should let the host government take care of it. Fire Marshal checked his phone and realized he had a few missed calls but didn't care anyway. He told them he was going to stay. He continued examining the house very carefully. The upper floors all had fallen towards the back of the school into a ravine, a dry river bed. No people were standing on the rubble above the three girls. He received a phone call and answered a little bit annoyed with:" Who the fuck is it?", It was somebody who asked for a situation report and then what we needed.

Sierra-Foxtrot replied we needed doctors here with IV's for three young girls who were trapped inside the building. Also, a no-fly zone for helicopters or heavy trucks to avoid vibration and further destruction. He handed over the cell phone to me and asked me if I had something else in mind. On the phone was Joel Boutroue the DSRSG for UN Humanitarian Agencies, like Da Costa a man of his word we trusted. He told me that US and French teams with rescue dogs and other professional equipment were expected to arrive this evening or night. I warned him about complications at customs. The customs officer didn't care much about their daily routine, but if international rescue teams were coming with equipment and dogs, it was an opportunity to make them pay to clear it, especially if there was time pressure.

Sierra-Foxtrot was already back under the school and coordinated the opening of the small holes to the chambers to prepare them for the doctors with the IV's. Two girls could be freed and brought out without visible severe injuries. The doctors had arrived in the meantime and managed to lay an IV for the girl who was still trapped. It seemed she was seriously stuck with her foot. Outside the building, UNPOL and HNP officers organized the transportations of injured or mostly dead bodies. Nobody knew how many so far, I saw a mother looking for her seven children. People around told me that the school grew another floor every year and the magistrate closed it for some time because the school built new levels without authorization. Once payment was made for the authorization, the school was reopened. It was already 22:00 and the girl was still trapped.

They still tried to get her free, but it was difficult. The doctor started to be worried about her strength and said that if he had to amputate, he had to do it soon because of her physical condition. That was not what I wanted to hear. The rescue teams arrived and were stuck in customs until further notice, but it seemed unrealistic that they could be on the scene before 2 or three 3 in the morning. It would have been too late, according to the doctor. The father of the girl was inside with us. They were discussing the amputation in English; the father didn't understand a word. The doctor decided at 22:30 to amputate. Fire Marshal saw that I didn't want to be part of this and asked me to bring out the father and keep him there until everything was finished. I just felt fear. I was not sure why I felt sorry for myself since the girl, the father and so many other family members had so much more reason than me to be scared or fearful, but I couldn't help it. The father seemed much calmer than me. It was almost 23:00 when they brought her out on a stretcher. I was afraid, but I had to look, and I saw both feet looking out of the white sheet which covered her. She still had both feet. They didn't cut off the foot. The Fire Marshal came out and told me that he wanted to try it one more time before the doctor gave the anesthesia, and the foot got free. Very easy he said, he didn't understand what made the difference. With this positive image in mind, we closed the site under the building until the rescue workers came in the early morning after customs was satisfied.

I had to get ready for Chad and had to hand over my contacts. I never heard from Moses again after the riots. Mackency was handed over to the new RSO, and Rudolph had a small job in a Prestige depot. He also got a passport so I could send him money via Western Union. In one of our last meetings Rudolph had just come from a police station and the courthouse where he denounced a school owner of the attempted murder of his cousin from Jeremie. At first, I thought he was trying to get some more money out of me until I heard the story. Rudolph couldn't make this up. His cousin came from the region because he had a job painting a newly constructed school building. At the end of the work he was pushed into an unfinished room in the basement, and people inside the dark room started hitting him. He was screaming, and somebody from upstairs came to check. When the person opened the door, he escaped. I figured there must have been some dispute among the workers, or maybe they didn't want to pay him, but Rudolph gave me an entirely different reason. He explained to me that they tried to kill him, so the school would be a good business. I couldn't follow, and he told me that the owner went to a Voodoo priest to demand help from a dark spirit to become rich. They wanted to bury his brother from the region inside the basement as a gift or sacrifice to the evil Voodoo spirit. Since nobody knew he had family in Port au Prince, he would have simply been missing without a trace. I was speechless, but for him, it was completely normal and also for the judge and the police. He said:" Most likely under the supermarket here is also a dead body."

I looked around, we were in the parking lot of a supermarket, and I looked at the entrance and the parking lot. It was a new supermarket, fairly significant with seven or eight cashiers permanently occupied inside the big hall. The parking lot was tiny compared to the size of the supermarket itself, maybe 12 vehicles could park. I also never saw more than two customers inside. This supermarket was just a front to launder money, not to do real business. I just hoped this supermarket didn't need a sacrifice to make money. But I had to admit, I actually didn't know anything about it.

Before leaving for Chad, I visited Gus with Tommy Dutch in Jacmel. Gus was about to retire and leave Haiti, so we wanted to make sure we had one more beer for the road. It was the first time I left the West Department of Port au Prince for a recreational trip. It was an unbelievably beautiful drive through the mountains, and Jacmel was a relaxed, quiet place compared to Port au Prince. I knew I always worked in the worst parts of Port au Prince and my Haiti was not the Haitian experience of most other UN staff members. But when I experienced Jacmel I told Gus that this didn't look like Haiti, it was so beautiful, and his answer was:" No, this is Haiti, Port au Prince is not Haiti." After all these years I considered myself an expert and realized I didn't know Haiti at all. The night before my departure, we all got together one more time. The men in the shadow, Tommy Dutch, Ray, John Taylor, Gus, Niko, and Abuelo. One of my mentors, a Zombie Hunter from the US embassy brought me a t-shirt. It showed a human skull with two guns in a circle and in the middle of the t-shirt was written, no diamonds, no oil, same problems, TIH, This is Haiti.

CHAPTER 13
Life was worth less than an old rotten football

Chad, Abeche, January 2009

I went from one beach to another, with a lot of sand, but no sea, the desert of Eastern Chad. The Peacekeeping mission MINURCAT was established by the Security Council despite the recommendation of the DPKO assessment team not to engage in a peacekeeping operation on the border to Darfur. The mission had no political mandate and was supposed to provide the security umbrella to the extensive humanitarian service for a large number of Sudanese refugees from Darfur and internally displaced Chadians in vast camps in the border region between Chad and Sudan. Coming from the Caribbean 'Beach-keeping' operation, the reality of standard field missions caught up with me again. The starving children of Haiti with mango, banana and coconut trees, access to the sea and frequent tropical rain became relative when I was flying for hours over the deserts of the Sahel zone bordering the Sahara and looked down to villages which were without rain for eight to nine months in a year. How they survived in this dry and hot climate was a miracle to me. Life was not much worth in Haiti, here, life was worth less than an old rotten soccer ball; children were playing soccer early morning on dusty ground with an old rotten football. They might not have looked like privileged children to western eyes, but they had families, homes and a school to go. If the ball had gotten into the dusty road and I had the choice to run over the child or the ball, there would have been no question, save the child and run over the ball. But if I had let the children take a vote on what they wanted to come back to them, the boy would have been dead. This was their reality, and we lived in it.

Life was a constant struggle for survival for most people in Chad, and it usually introduced itself quickly to any newcomer. For example, when a five-year-old child begging for money came across a newly arrived international helper, and he gave him some small amount of cash, drawing a beautiful smile from the kid until a nine-year-old hit the five-year-old in the face, took the money and ran. He was running because he was chased by a group of 15 other kids. The impression of shock in the aid worker's face, sadness and not knowing what happened was as I imagined, the expression of a young deer standing in darkness on the road looking with big eyes into the headlights of the car. Wrong help could cause even more pain, and it was essential to adapt to it. It didn't matter if it was the Middle East, Haiti or Africa, there were always poor children around. Even a water bottle inside the vehicle could cause complications. It would have looked bad drinking it in front of them and to give it to one was not an option, it would have never been enough for all of them and could trigger a fight. A great thing to give to children was a soccer ball so they could use it to play together, I just had to keep in mind that on the grounds they were playing, the soccer ball didn't last longer than a week, just in case I came back.

It took me some time to adapt, my spoiled background as a 'Beach-keeper' could even be insulting. My good friend Steven was based in Eastern Chad already before MINURCAT and was Security Advisor for an international organization. We both were based in Abeche, the regional capital of

Eastern Chad and my Area of Operation. When he showed me the Chinese restaurant, I was quite impressed; the restaurant was a concrete building and looked fairly authentic inside. I have never been to China, so authentic meant an ordinary Chinese restaurant in Europe or the United States. The Chinese government built a road for the country of Chad and had their workers stationed in the town. The restaurant was mainly built for these workers. It even had a bar and behind the bar a large freezer to store the beer. Sunset in the desert was early and fast and at 17:40 light was fading away inside the restaurant. At 18:00, the generator was switched on and ran until around 23:00. Those 5 hours of electricity gave the clients not just satellite tv entertainment but also cooled the beer in the freezer. Steven brought me into the restaurant the first time in the afternoon around 16:00. I was not aware at the time that the fridge was without electricity since the night before, and this was considered normal. When the Chinese lady placed our beer bottles on the bar, I checked the temperature. I was accustomed to do that in Haiti, and if it was not cold enough, I would send it back for an exchange. I happened to mention that the temperature of the beer bottle did not meet my expectations, it was too warm.

I triggered a dramatic response, Steven was outraged. I didn't know at the time that he served in the DPKO mission in Darfur for more than two years before his assignment here in Chad. Darfur, just across the border five hours driving time away was, like the rest of Sudan, under Muslim law and alcohol was strictly forbidden. Sometimes they could find on the black market 'Johnny Walther,' a cheap sort of whisky in small plastic bags. Steven and his colleagues in Darfur would have died for a beer regardless of the temperature. I was shocked and was just happy; I never considered an assignment in Darfur. I didn't care about rebels, gangs or wars, but I also had my limits, no beer was definitely too much hardship. I made an effort to be more sensitive towards my colleagues who had such traumatizing experiences, and I started to drink the beer in any condition and temperature.

Staff tended to complain about their own mission administration after some time, and I believed it was normal. If anybody ever complained about MINUSTAH; MINURCAT opened a new level to the negative. It was like DPKO established the first field mission in Africa, ever. The Chiefs deployed in Chad were promoted out of other missions. This was a new UN approach to get rid of useless staff members by promoting them to another mission. I always wondered why many of us had such difficult times to move on to other missions or even get promotions until I overheard a conversation of two Section Chiefs. One was telling how happy he was that he got rid of his most useless staff member. The Chief of Administration in the other mission informally called the supervisor who told the story. The Chief Administrative Officer wanted to make sure the person could handle the job. The Section Chief sold the useless staff member to the new mission as a superstar just to get rid of him. The more skilled and useful a staff member was, the more likely this person was going to remain in his level, position and mission. Of course, being labeled as a gun swinging nut-case was another strategy to move to another mission, at least in my case it worked. The mission in Chad gathered a significant amount of inexperienced Section Chiefs, and such Chiefs were the most difficult to deal with. The less competence and self-esteem they had, the more ego they developed. The final argument was, I am right because I am the Chief. I even came across a name for such a syndrome. The Dunning-Kruger effect, the 'verywellmind' website called it fools were blind to their own foolishness, or low ability people who do not possess the skills needed to recognize their own incompetence. This was either an epidemic for UN mid-level management or a part of the recruitment requirements. In Security we were lucky, Bertrand was in the capital, and in the East of Chad was his Deputy Edward Brakatu from Ghana, the most courteous and hardest working Security Officer I ever met. I was convinced that the living conditions and challenges in Eastern Chad were the main reason for his heart attack and early death shortly after the closure of MINURCAT.

Most of the other Sections were not so lucky and had to deal with incompetent, inexperienced Chiefs, which also had a severe impact on my tasks as the Regional Security Officer of Abeche. Since University degrees were recently required within the UN to be a decision maker, it ruled out most of the field-experienced Field Service Officers. Franz was working on his University master's degree studies in the time I left MINUSTAH for this reason. Most of the experienced FSO, Field Service Officers were close to retirement and had no interest in studying. They were regarded as trouble makers because they dared to raise their opinions about the errors of the leadership. The good thing was that all these experienced trouble makers were deployed in the East away from the decision made in the capital of Chad, in N'Djamena. The mission was actually supposed to be only in the East of Chad and never deployed in the capital of the country, but the leadership of MINURCAT ignored this. They stayed with their essential staff and assistants in the capital. When I arrived in Chad, the mission was actually already deployed for a year, and they had just started to move the mission to the East. The recruitment for our National staff members was done in the capital which had a sizeable Christian population. The East was an entirely Muslim community, and when the Christian National staff members were sent to work in the East, we faced the anger of the population because it looked to them like the UN didn't want to employ people of the Muslim faith. It took the DSRSG, who was deployed in the East, some time to explain this to N'Djamena. The mission was implemented slowly, and it looked like we made things more complicated for the UN Agencies in place. Some didn't care, like the World Food Program (WFP) and the Mine Action Unit of UNPOS since they did not rely on the concept of MINURCAT.

Half of the MINURCAT staff never left the capital during the entire period of MINURCAT. It was like two missions in one country, one in the capital acting like an extended New York HQ and one field mission in the East. I preferred the East, 4 hours flying distance from the big-shots, but it was regrettable to see experienced Field Service Officers be outcasts for the last years of their career. As if all those years in dusty, dangerous places like Somalia, Iraq, Afghanistan or Angola away from their families didn't count. Unfortunately, this was the path the UN, or at least DPKO seemed to be going. When these officers retired, all their experience was lost forever. But until then we made the best out of Abeche.

The security situation was stable for most of our stay, and if changes were about to come, we had a few weeks or even months' notice before a rebel attack. The first indicator for rebel mobilization on the other side of the border were car hi-jackings; when rebel groups prepared for an attack, they paid each recruit around 500 US dollars to join their movement. When the recruit came with a Toyota pick-up or Land Cruiser, they paid 5000 US dollars or even more. Depending on which side prepared rebels for their attack would be the direction in which the vehicles went. If many vehicles were stolen in Eastern Chad, we knew the rebels hosted in Darfur prepared to attack Chad. Many of the Chadian soldiers or government supported rebels came from similar tribes as in the Darfur region and were recruited in the same refugee camps. There was not much loyalty, the war was their business since they were 11 years old. The country paying was the country they were fighting for. Some soldiers changed sides several times. The stolen Toyotas became a 'tactical,' a vehicle with ten soldiers in the back and a heavy machine gun mounted on it. These types of vehicles were used the first time in 1987, at the end of the conflict between Chad and Libya which resulted in the defeat of the Libyan troops. To this day the war was called 'Toyota War' because of the advantage the light infantry vehicles offered the Chadian troops against the Libyan tanks. The stolen cars moving to Darfur could go on for weeks, but we knew that we came closer to the possible attack when the MIG 21s, the Russian fighter jets of the Chadian Air Force were moved back to N'Djamena. The aircraft were usually based in Abeche for Reconnaissance flights along the border but moved back to the capital before possible attacks.

The reason was the calculation that the rebels when crossing the border could reach Abeche within 4 hours. The two MIG 21 needed around this time from being alerted to get ready to deploy and engage. The chance that the rebels could reach the MIG 21 before and destroy them on the ground was too high. This was usually the time to start evacuating most civilian personnel into the UN Military camp. Steven and I were still relaxed in our outpost, the Chinese restaurant. We knew, as long as the General of the area who owned most of the houses the UN rented, was in his white Chadian traditional clothes, the attack was not imminent. If we saw him leaving in the morning dressed in military camouflage, we moved to the UN Military camp as well.

Not all car-hijacking incidents were related to rebel mobilization, sometimes it was just a violent form of getting a ride. In one case a UN helicopter was hi-jacked when it happened to land close to two high ranking Chadian officers who needed a ride. The usual incident was that one or two Chadian fighters with Kalashnikovs forced a vehicle to stop, even if they had to shoot at the car. Depending on the driving skills of the hijackers, the drivers of the vehicles were either left behind or had to be the chauffeur for the hijackers. The Chadian soldiers or government supported rebels knew that they were untouchable, above the law. Any form of interaction with them could cause serious harm to International staff members of the United Nations or other organizations. My friend Chris, a MINURCAT staff officer, organized me two bottles of red wine for a birthday party, but I ended up celebrating the good health of two of our colleagues who were just ambushed by hijackers. Our Irish and Greek friends left the military camp to drive to our civilian offices, a few hundred meters away. They were stopped by two military men with AK47's. Both Ladies reacted fast and very well. They left the engine running, got out of the vehicle, didn't look at the assailants and laid down on the floor beside the car, never looked up. Even though they heard the car leaving, they waited some time before they got up. Another UN vehicle passing by brought them to our offices. It was a dangerous situation which both of them managed very well.

We had a good team spirit among all of us working in the East, and I believed we supported each other through times like this. A few days went by when I received a phone call from the Staff Counsellor. She needed to talk urgently with my Irish colleague, she seemed very nervous. It sounded like somebody was in danger. I went over to the Humanitarian Coordination office where my Irish colleague worked to check if she was ok. When I asked her if she received a phone call from the staff counselor, she rolled her eyes and told me that the Staff Counsellor was stalking her via email, cell phone, and desk phone for few days, but she didn't want to talk to her. I thought fair enough, not knowing that I was about to be stalked next. The counselor did not stop calling and writing me emails until I went over to my colleague's office with the staff counselor on the phone and begged her to take the counseling. When she took the phone, she was listening for a while, just interrupted the other end in a very calming tone and I heard comments like, "I understand", "yes, please calm down", "all will be ok", "yes you can contact me next week again", I understand", "there is no reason to get upset". Wow, I just saw my colleague counseling the counselor, and I remembered the young Staff Counselor in Gonaives after the hurricane.

In isolated areas, we all somehow became staff counselors since life in our camps sometimes felt like in prison. I witnessed certain stress factors I never paid much attention to, like the challenges my female colleagues faced in environments like Eastern Chad and surely in many other field missions. Abeche was a reasonably big town with a UN Military presence, but some of our female colleagues worked in much more remote places and had interactions with the official representatives, the religious leader or the Chadian Generals in charge of their regions. I had to admit, they managed these situations better than many of us male colleagues, but they were exposed on their own and faced an underlying threat I never thought about. The situation was even worse for females working with NGO's, Non Governmental Organizations in remote places. We knew of incidents with female international staff members of NGO's related to sexual violence in Eastern Chad and in Darfur. But we always heard it as confidential information from our contacts, the organizations kept such incidents very secret. The victims were just brought out and sent home. Many young volunteers for such NGO's were not aware of the possible dangers they could face and were placed in situations that were irresponsible and negligent from these organizations. Even life within UN premises could be intimidating for female colleagues, especially when older men in field missions tended to overestimate their looks and considered themselves irresistibly attractive. I witnessed my female colleagues managing such situations with a routine which suggested that they were frequently exposed and used to an amount of ignorance which must have been very disturbing and needed more awareness from us men.

In Haiti for most staff members, life was a reasonably healthy working life. They came to the office between 08:00 and 09:00 and left at 17:00. When the 7.0 earthquake hit at 16:53 for 30 seconds Leogane, a small town 25 kilometers south of Port au Prince, and the destructive power spread out in a circle, most UN staff members were still in their offices in the Christopher Hotel. These 30 seconds on shaking ground and in trembling buildings must have felt never-ending but there was no time for people inside the Christopher Hotel to get out to safety. The building collapsed on itself together with many other buildings in the capital. I received the first messages early in the morning about an earthquake in Haiti and I went from my sleeping container to my office container to check the news. The first headline was Christopher Hotel and Montana Hotel collapsed in the earthquake. I was shocked and couldn't imagine the amount of destruction the quake must have brought to Port au Prince. The memories of the dead children at the collapsed school in Nerreth came back into my mind. And now our own colleagues were under the rubble. I remembered our Engineer told me that he never knew the structural condition of the main building of the Christopher because the owner never provided them any construction plans for the building. The owner just told them it was built according to the Haitian standards, like the Montana Hotel with too little steel. An annex building attached to the central tower of the Christopher was constructed years after the main Hotel tower, and the steel was still visible on the roof, and our Engineer was satisfied with that. This building did not collapse. The Log Base close to the airport were all container buildings, and the staff members were safe. Everybody wondered at the beginning of the mission why Log Base did not become a container city with 2 or 3 floors like in other missions and could have provided enough space for the whole purpose. The choice and will of one man, Hocine Medili who wanted the Christopher Hotel as HQ became the graveyard of many colleagues and friends.

I was trying several cell phone numbers of my friends and colleagues in Haiti, but all cell phone communication was down. I could reach Cege via our UN satellite system on his extension. Nothing happened in Log Base, and the connection worked very well. He was one of the few points of contact for so many family members and colleagues who were seeking information about their loved ones. He gave me a quick update on the situation, and it sounded terrible. The central tower of the Christopher Hotel, a 6-story building that had two more floors beneath the entrance level towards the back to the swimming pool was reduced to a pile of rubble two meters above the parking lot. Ray, Franz, and the Fire Marshal were ok and working at the rescue operation at the Christopher Hotel, but it didn't look promising. Tarmo, our colleague from close protection, could send a radio signal from somewhere under the rubble that he was still alive but trapped in a small chamber. He was at the SRSG office on the fourth floor and collapsed with the building and was now somewhere in the rubble on -1 or -2.

While our colleagues in Haiti were working with minimal breaks, the United Nations and its organizations prepared their response teams. The World Food Program (WFP), United Nations Office of Project Services (UNOPS) were first responding agencies beside UN Security Officers in general with the lead of UNDSS. The WFP and UNOPS, like the US State Department, selected teams of officers who had already years of experience in Haiti so that they could replace colleagues and support the ongoing rescue operation with the necessary local knowledge. UNDSS had a different approach, to be selected for such missions was a privilege since most of the time it involved extra money. Most of these Security Officers were never in Haiti before. The MINUSTAH Security continued to do their job and had to take care of the newcomers as well. MINURCAT sent two Security Officers based in N'Djamena since none of the personnel in the East could be spared. One of the two Security Officers had served in Haiti.

The following afternoon Cege told me that they did not have any radio contact with Tarmo for a few hours. They expected the worst. But the Fire Marshal was still hopeful and believed it was not Tarmo who was dead, it was just his battery. He had a good idea of his location and was working on it. It was time for Steven and me to go to the Chinese restaurant. At 18:00 the generator provided us with live news from Haiti. It was an unforgettable moment when Steven pointed at the TV. We saw pictures of what was left of the 6 floor building and the ongoing rescue operation. I usually saw former colleagues on top of the pile. This time in the spotlight on top of the collection of rubble was standing Tarmo, he looked like always, maybe a bit tired. He had to save battery and switched off the radio. It was a miracle, he had just a few bruises after he went from the fourth floor down to -2 with tons of concrete where the Fire Marshal found him after more than 48 hours. Every aftershock in this small chamber must have been a nightmare. He was one of the very few who were so lucky, he knew his friend and colleague Karimou from Niger, who was on duty with him that day was killed instantly a few meters away from him. The rescue of a Danish UN staff Member after 5 days from the rubble of the Christopher Hotel was another miracle, the last one. The wreckage turned into a graveyard. More than a hundred staff members, friends, and colleagues died in the building including Mr. Anabi and Mr. Da Costa, maybe the best leadership DPKO ever had. The landlord of the Christopher Hotel came to Log Base at the end of January to claim the rent for the Hotel for February since the contract was still valid. Edmond Mulet was back from New York as SRSG and thought Franz was crazy when he delivered him the message. MINUSTAH did not continue to pay for the graveyard.

A few months after the earthquake the country of Chad and the United Nations agreed to end the MINURCAT mandate by 31 December 2010. This message was very well received within the

MINURCAT staff, and everybody hoped to get to the mission in Haiti which almost doubled in size because of the reconstruction efforts after the earthquake. It was around this time when Abuelo wrote to me from his leave in Chicago that he was diagnosed with cancer in a very advanced state. He was about to begin chemo and radiation therapy at the same time because of the severity. He didn't feel ready to die and was going to fight. It was a long and hard fight. I could almost feel the pain when he described his medical treatment and the impact it had on his body. It got so bad that I was afraid of reading his emails. But he did not give up, and the messages became better and better. He was diagnosed cured before we met again.

In Haiti, many high-level officers and Section Chiefs returned to MINUSTAH and remembered the work of the 'old' Security Section under Bertrand Bourgain and Gus. They requested to bring back the old 'patrol' unit. Many colleagues and section chiefs were asking for my return. The person who brought the CSA in Haiti the list of Security Officers from the closing mission in Chad told me that there were two names which the CSA crossed out, me and JC. My Austrian colleague from Civil Affairs in Haiti was working in Ivory Coast and got me in contact with the Security Section in her mission about a possible assignment when I received an email from the CSA in Haiti. He stated that they were working on my offer, I should stand by for a few days. I couldn't believe it. The chief administrative officer based in Abeche had moved to MINUSTAH and recommended me because of my performance in Chad. There were not many arguments left for the CSA, except his personal reasons. But personal reasons were not enough when the CSA was faced with a real Samurai. She was with MINUSTAH in the early days as a high-ranking Political Affairs Officer and returned to Haiti on a temporary assignment. Whenever I needed a piece of advice from a brilliant person at a high level in the United Nations system, she was the one I asked, if she was available. She didn't take no for an answer, and her comments were sharper than a samurai's sword. She was not just a great adviser but also an idealist and just the fact that she was still working with the United Nations made me believe that the UN was supposed to be a great organization. Only on my level, it didn't look that great anymore. The worst case I came across was when a newly selected security officer arrived and couldn't speak a word of English. But he succeeded in an interview with a recruitment panel in New York via telephone in perfect English a few months ago. He forgot it in the meantime. Of course, and nobody in the mission said a word, because he was either somebody's friend, family or paid somebody in the mission to get hired.

Once qualified or not, they were staff members and inside the system they were protected by the political correctness and cultural diversity. Anybody who criticized their performance didn't understand their cultures and needed cultural awareness training. The culture was incompetence and was created by corruption. To point out errors was defined as racism or intolerance towards the persons' cultural background. This was actually the real racism within the organization and an insult to all the brave and professional colleagues I worked with from all corners of the world. If they were Europeans, South Americans, former Para Troopers from Nigeria, soldiers from Sierra Leon or former Gurkhas from Nepal. I would have gone into any battle, any day with these brave men. The 'culture issue' of the UN was just a front to protect corruption and incompetence. I didn't expect much difference anymore when I moved back to Haiti, but at least I was in a friendlier environment and maybe with my contacts I could still make a difference. I did my second check-in for MINUSTAH on 24 December 2010. I usually went from mission to mission with a small backpack as hand luggage and a significant military rucksack as check-in luggage. This time I had one additional large bag with me since I got divorced during my time in Chad. It contained all my belongings. Like many others in the field, we tend to pay for our freedom. I heard many sad stories about divorces and failed long-distance relationships but usually, the trigger for most divorces was the email or text message from the girlfriend in the mission area which the wife happened to read. The real victims were always the children. But, if my daughters were unhappy in a relationship, I wanted them to do the same when they were older. They should end it and move on.

CHAPTER 14
The return of a President and a Dictator

Haiti, Port au Prince, January 2010

The earthquake brought Haiti into the world spotlight and I thought that this was the chance for the country to finally get on its feet. The MINUSTAH budget and Personnel increased to almost double the original 2004 size. The security situation was reasonably good, even in Cité Soleil and in Martissant since there were more than 10 000 UN Military troops deployed in the country. Only kidnappings had a short break and continued soon after the earthquake on similar levels as before. I was surprised to see that Haiti didn't look much different. It was almost one year after the quake, and it didn't seem worse, but also not better. It took me a while to realize how many hundreds of thousands of people lived in very simple tent cities. There were some significant changes which were very difficult to get used to. The Boucan Gregoire, our favorite bar and restaurant, was still there, but with a different name. It was called 'Mosaique' now. The owner and its staff were the same as when I left two years ago; this was a positive indicator that the owner treated his team fairly and with respect. He also kept the price of the local beer on two dollars and didn't increase it like most other humanitarian friendly restaurants to 4 or 5 dollars, even though the local brewery didn't change the price after the earthquake. It was the form of support the Haitian restaurant owners showed to the large international community that came to help Haiti. The amount of money donated to organizations involved in the reconstruction of Haiti also attracted many vultures.

Timothy Schwartz, a Ph.D. Anthropologist, wrote in his two books' Travesty of Haiti' and 'The Great Haiti Humanitarian Aid Swindle' about it. Timothy Schwartz definitely didn't write these books to make friends. His focus was on the numbers and statistics and showed the extent of the corruption related to the earthquake money. Timothy didn't judge the intent of the people; only judged them by their results. Some of the outright scams he discovered were disgusting and a disgrace, but unfortunately very unlikely to be the worst. The UN would be screwed if he were ever be tasked to survey its organizations. He wouldn't care about color, race, culture or if the people involved were nice, he would just state the facts, and it would be a bombshell. Sometimes, even if the intent might have been good, the survey showed a bad result or at least an unexpected one. Absolutely unexpected was the result of his survey requested by a US organization about the death toll of the earthquake, in which he estimated 40 000 to 60 000 casualties. This number was much lower than the figures stated in general by the Haitian government, which was above 200 000. When the survey was submitted to Washington, the Haitian government and large organizations like the Clinton Foundation invested significant efforts to discredit the survey, the work and the person of Timothy Schwartz in general. The lower number of deaths could have impacted the continuing donations. The frustration resulting from these personal attacks and the greed that was preventing Haiti from rising out of the ashes could be read in his second book about the Humanitarian Aid Swindle. The only two persons who received a positive review in his book were

Jean Penn with his organization and William Evens II, the President of the Petion Ville Club, the country club that provided the land for Jean Penn's organization to host thousands of people.

I remembered the club from the happy hour every Wednesday. The club was not far from the MINUSTAH HQ, and many staff members used the opportunity to go to the public event of the historical country club from 16:00 to 22:00. We could only be in the restaurant area, but I could always see the beautiful long swimming pool and part of the golf course with real beautiful grass. It looked like a peaceful oasis in a violent desert to me. Now, the golf course was a tent city with the population of a mid-sized city.

The focus of MINUSTAH at the time of my return was the security issues related to the Presidential elections including electing 10 Senators and 99 Deputies. The first round was held on 28 November 2010 before my arrival. No Presidential candidate reached over 50 percent and the first and second place candidates were supposed to go to the second and final round. But claims of irregularities delayed the run-off for a second round. Mirlande Manigat, an older woman, supported by Youri Latorture was number one. I didn't know much about her, and it seemed she didn't have a terrible reputation. But a candidate supported by Youri Latorture and his entourage from the parliament didn't sound like a promising future to me.

On the other hand, the candidate who claimed the second was not a great option either. The candidate and close friend of President Preval, was Jude Celestin. I knew about Jude Celestin and his close relations with the gangs of Cité Soleil, especially Amaral. His appointment for the director position of the CNE, the state institution in charge of all heavy machinery for road construction gave an excellent example of his policy. The former CNE director Robert Marcello was kidnapped by the Amaral's gang in Cité Soleil. Amaral, who was in hiding at the time, ordered his gang to kill the victim and bury the body. From other sources, we were told that Robert Marcello refused to give Jude Celestin a state contract to purchase CNE equipment of almost 100 million US dollars without a bidding process. There was no bidding process necessary anymore after Jude Celestin replaced Marcello as the director. Rudolph, my informant, lived still in Cité Soleil and reported to me that Cité Soleil was still well controlled by the Preval government. The government mediator for Cité Soleil, Rene Monplaisir established a training camp in Bon Repons, at National # 1 close to Cité Soleil to train future Presidential Guards for Jude Celestin. It seemed the people around President Preval were very convinced about the victory of Jude Celestin.

The candidate who came in third was Michel Martelly, everybody knew him as 'Sweet Mickey', a singer, and entertainer. The excitement for this candidate was overwhelming when I arrived in Haiti, and I was not surprised that Martelly claimed voter fraud and irregularities. Countrywide demonstrations were held in support of Michel Martelly. Even Rudolph told me that if Cité Soleil could have voted freely, it would have been Michel Martelly. There was a lot at stake, and the Haitian government controlled most of the foreign money donated for the earthquake, even though the international community should have known better considering the history of corruption. The upcoming elections were all about controlling the money; some wanted to gain control over the funds, Preval and his entourage did not want to lose it. Haitian emergency laws, when applied after natural disasters, suspended all legal requirements for public bidding processes, and the government could distribute money and contracts without limitation or control to their partners and friends in the private sector. Any destruction in Haiti, whether due to a natural disaster or just deterioration of infrastructure due to lack of maintenance, was either a long-term or short-term investment for the Haitian business elite. It had to be built up again at some point by Haitian companies with foreign aid money. A few Haitian families owned most of the wealth in the country, and every family had their political preference. Some families were big enough to have all political choices covered, so regardless of the current political leader, the family always came out ahead.

The family Vorbe was such a big ruling family. In the last few years, the family benefited from the close relations of Joel Eduard 'Pasha' Vorbe and Dimitri Vorbe with President Aristide and President Preval. Just after the earthquake, President Preval purchased 200 000 units of food rations from Dimitri Vorbe for 20 US dollars per unit. That Dimitri Vorbe bought expired rations for less than 2 dollars per unit in the Dominican Republic, and just changed the expiration date did not worry the US embassy too much since this was considered a normal business in Haiti, or free trade. That none of said profit would be taxed was also no surprise. The US embassy was more worried about recent violent incidents which concurred with violence documented on a photo series from January 2004, when anti-Aristide protesters were shot and killed by 'Chimères' in the streets of Port au Prince. One of the 'Chimères on the photos was Dimitri Vorbe. I never saw these photos, but John Taylor had one which showed a similar scene with a dead Haitian civilian and Dimitri Vorbe with his MP5 Submachine gun after he shot and killed him.

He didn't need to fight himself up through the ranks of a gang in the slums of Cité Soleil to become boss. His financial wealth and close relation to Aristide made him already one of their 'big chiefs.' Now in 2011, reports of violent incidents similar to 2004 emerged during the protests in Port au Prince against President Preval and his candidate Jude Celestin. The same tactics to suppress the demonstrators were applied, but this time it was not just a few photos. The new forms of social media platforms, blackberries, and other smartphones distributed videos of Jude Celestin supporters shooting and killing pro-Martelly demonstrators in broad daylight on Champs de Mars, close to the collapsed Presidential Palace. This was one of the main factors moving the US embassy to have a closer look at the voter fraud claim of the third candidate Michel Martelly.

Shortly after, the electoral council announced that the recount of the votes of the first round showed that Michel Martelly came second, and the deciding run-off on 20 March 2011 was held between Mirlande Manigat and Michel Martelly. President Preval and Jude Celestin accepted and supported the decision of the CEP, the electoral council. A rumor that made a lot of sense to me suggested that the real reason for Preval giving in was 11 US visas. The US threatened to revoke the permits to enter US territory of 11 individuals who were known to be the financial supporters of Jude Celestin and President Preval. Most wealthy Haitians had properties in Miami, and their children enjoyed the education and life in the United States. It was easy to gain profits as a prosperous business person or politicians in a failed state when your family could live outside in safety and security, and they could escape Haitian reality every Thursday in the business class of American Airlines. If the rumors were correct that 11 Haitians changed the results of the Presidential elections of Haiti and the votes of millions of Haitians, it would be the best example of how small the group of people could be holding Haiti hostage. Before the run-off in March 2011, Preval came through with the promise he gave the people of the slums of Port au Prince before he was elected in 2006, the return of Aristide. Three days before the final round, former President Aristide came back to Haiti on a charter flight from South Africa. His arrival was announced several days before and on the charter flight with him came US Senators and the Hollywood legend Danny Glover. I understood that many believed Aristide had fought for social fairness in his past, but his methods were far away from progressive Democrats like Bernie Sanders.

Max Kail

Around 3000 to 5000 supporters gathered at the airport for his return. I knew from Rudolph that Cité Soleil was not very excited about his return since he left 7 years ago and didn't do much for his people. But still, I expected much more, especially since I witnessed the return of 'Baby Doc,' Jean Claude Duvalier two months earlier which was a well-kept secret until one hour before his arrival.

It was a Sunday in January, and I was just about to make myself comfortable on the couch when I received a phone call from a man in the shadow. 'Baby Doc' is on the Air France flight from Paris to Haiti. Within 5 minutes I was on the way to the airport. I was fast, but one Toyota four runner with a PRESS sign in the window was faster, and I knew the information was public. At the airport within minutes thousands of people gathered, but not the people who usually join demonstrations, most of them were older people and wealthier people who just wanted to see Duvalier. But the return of Aristide or Duvalier did not have much influence on the elections, and Michel Martelly's victory was announced on the evening of 21 April 2011. Our photojournalist and a camera team from MINUSTAH wanted to check the reaction of the people, and I brought them in an armored UN vehicle to Champs de Mars.

When I saw the masses gathering on the large open area, there were countless people, I was first a bit skeptic if it was safe to get closer. But we realized it was a joyful moment like a carnival and everybody was celebrating and gave us thumbs up. It was a very positive atmosphere; Michel Martelly gave them hope. Even the HNP felt encouraged and identified some of the shooters who killed pro-Martelly demonstrators and arrested them. But President Preval was still in charge, and Jude Celestin came to the commissariat of Port au Prince with vehicles from the National Palace and a written order from the President to release the killers. On the way out, the killers told the HNP officers that they would come back for them. They fulfilled their promise when four of the HNP officers assigned to the commissariat were ambushed and killed a few hundred meters away from their duty station a few days after.

President Martelly was inaugurated in May 2011. It was a very positive event and it felt very dynamic, it looked promising, Martelly and MINUSTAH working together for a better future of Haiti. The Security Officer in charge of the new Patrol Unit didn't feel the same way about my performance on his team. The former French Special Forces officer took over the 'temporary' Patrol Unit, Ray, our Firearms instructor, put together with Serbian and Swedish Swat officers who were deployed as UNPOLS in Port au Prince just after the earthquake. The chaotic situation needed an experienced strike force for money escorts, and emergency responses and Ray handled it.

But when things calmed down after 6 months, it was time for Ray to re-focus on his training unit and hand over the unit to my supervisor who had the task to redirect the priorities of the new Patrol Unit in the right direction, the UNDSS path. I knew he always had the best intentions for me and didn't set the priorities and the new tasks, but I just couldn't adapt very well to the UNDSS preferences. It turned out I was not very skilled in detecting staff members driving without their seatbelt or using their cell phone behind the wheel. I didn't have any more success with the radar gun for speeding staff members either. Some of my colleagues were very good at it and 'caught' many violators every morning. Still, it was great to be back in Haiti to see everyone again, the men in the shadow, my informants and other Haitian patriots. John Taylor had to retire already because he had reached the age limit of 62. He was still around since he worked for VDI Global, an intelligence-based Security Company from the United States which maintained high profile security consulting for International Organizations in Haiti. It couldn't have been more perfect for me, and I was glad and thankful to return. But in the Security Section in Port au Prince I was alone with my interest in gangs and the dynamics of Cité Soleil and its politics. Even in MINUSTAH itself, only my Brazilian and Italian colleagues from Civil Affairs were left who worked for many years in the ganglands and still maintained meetings inside these zones. They were the only ones left of the civilian part within MINUSTAH who had still personal experiences inside these areas. For the rest of MINUSTAH, it was the UN Military or UN police which didn't seem to transmit much of their expertise to the non-military staff. The Chief and Deputy Chief JMAC, both civilian staff members and the principal advisors on security developments in Haiti, haven't been to Cité Soleil ever. They knew it from aerial photos or flying into Port au Prince coming from vacation. One of the main lessons learned from the US Military Intelligence Operations in Iraq was that no analyst could analyze or predict scenarios without knowing and learning the terrain and environment during field trips, JMAC could.

Nobody ever confronted them JMAC about their errors, and they themselves never looked back on any of their analyses and forecasts and tried to check how credible it was or what went wrong. It was like they created and reported about a virtual world outside the premises of MINUSTAH which had nothing to do with the reality of Haiti. Everything made so much more sense to me when I realized that the assumptions for JMAC analyses were taken from social media, this was so funny because I knew Haitians who were maintaining several 'facebook' sites or later twitter accounts with fake names to influence international community opinion. All of them had JMAC as a follower. In some of their briefings, I could even tell from who the information came and what was the intent behind. It was the same for the blackberry and later WhatsApp chats of security professionals. Security professionals of today didn't need to adopt critical thinking anymore. They all had one Haitian, who knew everything and was advising them on developments. Unfortunately, many of these Haitians had a political agenda and might have twisted the information a bit. The Security professionals didn't sit back for a second to think about whether it made sense at all and posted the report without any critical thought. Because the best security professional was the one who could post it first, other Security experts multiplied the data, and it looked like confirmed information, even though it all started with one post. This situation had a significant influence on the perception of international decision makers and granted Haitian politicians' power and popularity they never actually had within the Haitian population. Changes had to be made, and changes were about to come, but not as I expected.

First, in my personal life, I managed not to have the first cigarette in the morning and got rid of a habit which controlled much more of my life than I realized before I stopped smoking cigarettes. Shortly after was a 2 week training course which was about to change my life. The UNDSS Analyst training course was scheduled to be organized in Haiti. Many UN staff members from offices in Latin America were expected to participate. Adam, the Security Chief of Operations at the time insisted that I attend the training since he figured that I was the only one with interest and previous experience with intelligence information and analysis.

I was lucky he had a good relationship with the CSA and was pushing it because such training courses were privileges that could offer future career possibilities, even in the New York HQ. Jack who was still the IT-expert with a gun in SICU had completed the first analyst training course created by a former Colonel of the South African Army a few years ago. Since then the course found growing importance and acceptance, and Jack assisted the Colonel during the training in Haiti. He also assisted my future when he placed the name tags on the tables, and a colleague from the UNDSS office in South America came to my right. She was not just gorgeous but also a former National Intelligence Officer and had similar experiences like me in our past lives. She had a unique and interesting effect on me, and she made me study during the course and for the final exam. The first time I have ever studied for an exam in my 12 years with the United Nations. I usually applied a minimum effort strategy to pass the exams with the lowest score needed, which was generally more than enough. But this time I was going for the top score, that never happened to me. This lady made me want to be better, we finished with outstanding scores, and we met after the training course again on my leave. Not just my private life made a great turn; also, Haiti became exciting again when a man in the shadow called me:" We need to meet at Reggie's place, he just got appointed Secretary of State for Public Security'. One of the men in the shadow stepped into the light, Reginald Delva.

CHAPTER 15
Zombie Hunters' Re-Union

"*The only thing necessary for the triumph of evil is for good men to do nothing*", Edmund Burke.

Haiti, Port au Prince, May 2011

Reginald Delva was one of the men in the shadow I met years ago with John Taylor. He was our absolute expert when it came to kidnapping gangs and was the only one in the country gathering information about kidnapping incidents, phone numbers, vehicle license plates, locations, and aliases of kidnappers in a database. While most of us were focused on the criminal gangs in Cité Soleil, Reginald, 'Reggie,' focused on all gangs involved in kidnappings, many of them outside the gang strongholds. He was the choice of Michel Martelly for the position of Secretary of State for Public Security. We always felt in the past years that we operated behind enemy lines in the shadows of the walls and houses of Port au Prince since we worked gangs that were always protected by politics and the government. This time we could come to the light, one of us became the authority, it was time for a Zombie Hunters' Re-Union.

Reggie's house survived the earthquake without damages and was for the time being the office of the new Secretary of State for Public Security; the meeting point for the Zombie Hunters' Union. He took over the position from Aramick Louis, former high ranking HNP officer and trusted man for the Preval administration. The job description of the Secretary of State for Public Security in the past was focused on the 'share for the country' related to the transiting drug operations. It all started with Bob Manuel and his oversight over Guy Phillippe, the Ecuador Boys, and the other high ranking HNP officers. But with Reggie, the wind was coming from a different direction.

At first, Reggie was inquiring about the Inspector of the Anti-Kidnapping Unit, AKU of the HNP since this was the first significant type of crime he wanted to target. The unit had no funding, no support and was forgotten somewhere in a small room in the halls of DCPJ, the HNP Department in charge of significant investigations, close to the airport. Kidnappings were handled by the Joint Anti-Kidnapping Unit, JAKU, of HNP and MINUSTAH which contributed successfully to a high level of kidnappings for several years, between 25 and 30 each month. Reggie didn't even try to influence the Joint AKU and wanted to empower the Haitian AKU. As most violent crimes, most kidnappings were concentrated in the metropolitan area of Port au Prince and kept the logistics and information gathering reasonably localized. He established personal contact with the Inspector of the Anti-Kidnapping Unit and got them involved first, once a victim reported such a crime at DCPJ. He debriefed the victims together with the Inspector.

There was a significant spike of such incidents affecting the population of Croix-des-Bouquet. Croix-des-Bouquet was a quiet city north-east of Port au Prince with charming houses and a rustic touch with some agriculture in between. The kidnappers usually broke at night into homes, ransacked everything and took either the youngest or oldest member of the family with them for ransom. They left the incident scene usually with the vehicle of the victims. The gang or gangs operating were very brutal and sexual violence was always involved. The home invasions could last for 1 or 2 hours until they left with the stolen items and a kidnapped victim. It was ridiculous because it took the bandits in many cases more than 45 minutes to penetrate the iron gates and bars of the houses. The victims tried to call the commissariat in the area, but their calls were never answered. The HNP never responded to these incidents which usually indicated that the gang had political back up and the HNP did not dare to engage or received a financial kickback from the crime. Reggie figured in the debriefings that the kidnapped victims were not transported with the vehicle to their place of captivity. One bandit just brought the stolen items to an unknown location and left the car far away as a decoy, to distract. The victims were actually walking by foot in the area for 10 to 30 minutes until they reached their final destination in the neighborhood. The victims had a good idea about the surroundings, and the structure of the houses since most of them were unfinished constructions. It seemed that different gangs were operating using many different locations. The first step was to identify the locations which the victims described. We needed aerial photos.

The MINUSTAH helicopter was no option, I would have to request such photos through the CSA office, and it would have raised too many red flags, but Cege had a solution. Security Logistics requested drones 2 years before because they realized soon after my departure to Chad that UNPOL reporting was much too delayed to ensure timely restrictions of movement for UN staff members due to demonstrations. The idea was, to do it from the air with drones to keep everybody at a safe distance. The drones were delivered one and a half years later and didn't have the operational flying time and radius needed to comply with the requirements. They were an earlier generation and could not be used in winds above 15 Km/h or rain. The drones were just laying around in Ray's training center. I couldn't operate them, but 'Doc' did. 'Doc' was not a real doctor, he was one of us, a shooter with an academic touch. He was injured during the earthquake, and the UN offered him an assignment in New York where he could live together with his family. They all loved it, but after one-year was up. Doc was sent back to the country where he almost lost his life and was separated again from his family since Haiti was a non-family duty station. The UN had a very special way of dealing with staff who faced traumatic experiences. For us, it was great to have him back because we needed him to fly the drones.

The best time without wind in Haiti was early morning and the camera on the drone had difficulty focusing from high altitude, so out of 5 shots, one was ok. We had to wait for enough sun and not yet too much wind, which called for a very early wake up to be just in time in Croix des Bouquets. A UN vehicle in Croix-des-Bouquet after sunrise with some Security Officers and a little flying object was big news in Croix des Bouquet. We tried to limit our time as much as possible and hoped the photo quality was sufficient, so we didn't have to come back. It was not a gang-controlled territory, and the first visit was never a problem. People were curious, 'Abuelo' always said we were their 'Cable TV,' the particular event the population didn't see yet. To come back might have been a different story, especially if the kidnapping gangs in the area figured out what we were doing.

We had enough firepower to counter a potential threat but needed a cover for the UN Security Section if anything happened. One of the two Deputy Chief Security Officers was from the 'old' days, and he was our cover. He was in charge of Administration and Logistics, even though we all wanted him to be our Operation Chief. He was a former fighter pilot with combat experience, and we trusted him. Since Cege in Logistics, the drones and the training unit of Ray were under his command, he could give us the official authorization 'retroactively,' if needed. The photos were sufficient, Reggie identified several locations, and we didn't wait long for results. The Inspector with his small team of AKU hit the first hostage locations, and several victims were freed. These operations were the first successful hostage rescues since 2005. In the old days before President Preval was in elected, Brazilian UN troops acted on information from the men in the shadow, John Taylor, Gus, and other Zombie Hunters freeing kidnapped victims in Bel Air. 8 years later the Zombie Hunters were back in business. The information stayed strictly within Reggie and the Inspector of AKU with the approval of the head of DCPJ, the Central Directorate of the Judicial Police. Reggie's position was so strong because he had the full support of the RSO, the Regional Security Officer of the US embassy. He was not just a Diplomatic Security Officer in the rank of a Colonel, he was also a Zombie Hunter, alias 'The Dude'. With the backing of the US Ambassador herself, Reggie and the AKU had no limits or obstacles from Haitian authorities, and the Zombie Hunters were growing. The advisory functions of the hundreds of UNPOL officers made it almost impossible for any motivated UNPOL officer to have an actual impact on the security situation. Most of them were doomed to earn the title of 'Facebook Operators.' But two UNPOL officers found a way, they joined the Zombie Hunters' as well.

Both officers had US police background with extensive experience in organized crime. Bobby was an expert on violence and crime related to Mexican drug cartels and worked hundreds of kidnapping cases. Jose was our statistic and incident man; he received all reports from any commissariat unfiltered with complete information and analyzed them. Also, his Dominican background was gold in our future cooperation with Dominican authorities. It has to be noted that their function as UNPOL and the insight they had, made me realize that many UNPOL officers were absolute professionals and knew the dynamics of the country as well but were paralyzed by the system in place. Bobby and Jose were bypassing the system, and together we combined all available information, and it started to show connections between my gangs in the slums of Port au Prince, politicians and kidnapping gangs in Croix des Bouquet. Bobby made me understand and see that this was much more than separated criminal groups, he expected a well-coordinated system from street level to kidnapping and drugs, it had to be interconnected, and also told me, at some point we would see it. He was sure it was a considerable syndicate. But for now, our success and focus were Croix-des-Bouquet.

The gangs in Croix-des-Bouquets consisted mainly of 'deportees,' Haitian criminal offenders who were sent back from the United States, and 'escapees,' prisoners who escaped after the earthquake in 2010. These 'escapees' were usually the caretakers of the locations since they had their pictures distributed within the HNP and couldn't move around much. We knew about some cases in which 'escapees' got arrested by HNP officers and worked in their houses like slaves, still better conditions than dying slowly in a Haitian jail. The victims of these gangs were mid-level targets who could afford traveling to the US or even worked in the US. The gangs had outstanding intelligence about the financial situation of the victims, and in many cases, the gangs knew that they wanted to buy land or a car and had a certain amount of money available. In some cases, the victims were ambushed outside their gate when they arrived from the United States, especially when the bandits knew there was a gun in the house. Due to the high level of crime in the country, Haitians were usually very careful with the disclosure of financial information or transactions in Haiti but not in the United States. Friends and family members often knew about their financial plans, and the information made it all the way to the gangs in Croix-des-Bouquets. Many of the victims were even US citizens, which made the success of the HNP Anti Kidnapping Unit so much more critical for the RSO and his Ambassador. Once the AKU started to arrest kidnappers we were faced with the real problem of Haiti, the Haitian Justice.

We were faced with the real Rule of Law issue in Haiti, not the Haitian Police, Haitian Justice. HNP did their job, finding judges who did their job as well was difficult. If anybody questions the corruption in the Haitian justice system, just wonder why no judges were killed in Haiti. In any other country with severe organized crime issues, the most threatened profession was not the policeman, it was the prosecutor. The US Ambassador tried to address this issue. In the meantime, we analyzed our arrest statistics. The AKU operations resulted in freed victims and arrested the caretaker, the 'escapee,' but didn't impact the gang itself. It was a speed issue; many incidents could even be avoided if the victims could call a 24/7 hotline and HNP responded. But to rescue kidnapped victims faster and put more pressure on the kidnappers we needed not just a faster information flow, we needed somebody to track them, we needed dogs.

During my special forces training a lifetime ago we were hunted by National Police dogs to make our exercises more enjoyable. Even in a challenging environment, a dog could work for an hour before needing replacement or a break. We knew that they were walking less time than that and the number of people walking should have made it easy and fast for a good dog and his handler to track them. Reggie arranged a meeting with Scott, an experienced K9 handler from Florida who wanted to establish a business in Haiti. The world was small, when Reggie introduced Bobby, Jose and me to Scott, Jose and Scott broke out in laughter. They worked together on some cases back in the states. We were starting to plan for a future strategy when he had his first dogs in the country. Reggie also arranged a meeting with a company that offered new military grade drones. The company was based in Guatemala and had a Haitian business partner who had some connections to the government. Reggie asked a man who was still in the shadow and me to join the meeting. We met in a small conference room in a very private Hotel in the district of Paquot, Port au Prince. Two representatives of the international company and their Haitian partner waited inside the small conference room. Reggie entered first, and the Haitian partner started welcoming him but abruptly stopped talking when he saw us come in as well. I could see in their faces that they had expected an easy deal, a corrupt Haitian politician who could be financially satisfied for giving them an over-charged state contract, it was just written in their faces. I believed Reggie realized it as well and felt insulted. He did not even introduce us to them, he just told the three men that we were the people who had to be convinced about their product. The financial negotiations for the purchase were subject to the Office of Prime Minister Lamothe if Reggie selected their product. This was not what they wanted to hear.

One of the internationals looked familiar, and when I looked at his business card, I remembered that we met in the year 2000 in Jerusalem on protective detail for a visit of the Secretary-General Kofi Anan. He was a Security Close Protection Officer from New York and had a very controversial career after we met. I only knew rumors and couldn't evaluate if it was true, but still, I had no reason to change the uncertainty. He was struggling because he also thought we knew each other. He made some wild guesses but couldn't figure it out. I left him hanging because the situation was just too complicated. Their product was actually excellent, and we recommended it. Reggie was interested as well in a camera surveillance system for main roads to gather faster credible information on criminal incidents, especially kidnappings. The procurement process for the Haitian government was hopefully quicker than the United Nations, especially since the new Prime Minister wanted to explore Haiti's potential for tourism. The kidnapping threat was one of the major factors preventing international investing or tourism coming to Haiti, and he guaranteed Reggie all support he needed. Laurent Lamothe, the new Prime Minister, actually sounded like a man with a vision for the country. Even though he was said to be very wealthy and was one of the main financiers of the campaign of his friend Martelly, the fact that I never heard of him was a good sign. I understood he didn't make his money in Haiti and was therefore not much involved in Haitian politics, business or gang dynamics. But this made him an unknown to the Haitian business community, and they expected him to have more interest in opening Haiti to international business or the regional market. To open Haiti as a regional market and compete with outsiders was an inconvenience and unnecessary complication for the Haitian business elite. It would have been a severe threat to the system in place which worked so well for them. It was somehow funny for me to hear all of them complaining about how corrupt he was after a short period in office. I had to admit I had no insight to judge the accusations, but I just thought, could anybody be more corrupt than the others? Usually, the opposition accused the group in power and the other way around after politics changed. I never heard all of them accusing one person of such an extent of corruption. I concluded that this could only mean that all of them were upset because none of the Haitian business families benefited from Lamothe's corruption and this was not how their Haiti worked. For our Haiti, the only relevant fact was that the Prime Minister and the President wanted to get rid of kidnapping, and we were tasked to make it happen.

It worked very well for us, I just had to be careful not to raise suspicion within my Security leadership about my unauthorized activities. I couldn't let the rescuing of kidnapped victims interfere in the Security Seatbelt and Speeding Operation of UNDSS. For MINUSTAH and the UN, we still operated in the shadow. The criminal gangs of Croix-des-Bouquets had close relations to the contraband operations between the Dominican Republic and Haiti at the border in Central Plateau and its regional capital Hinche. Niko was the RSO in Hinche, and we almost worked together like in the past. It was a known territory of Ex-Fadh members, and one morning Niko received reports of a group of Ex-Fadh occupying a former Haitian army base in 'Terre Rouge' on the border of West Department and Central Plateau. The group had already been there for a few days, and Niko told me that the UN military and UN police were talking with Port au Prince about it, but nobody was checking it out and knew what they wanted.

JMAC was assessing the situation from their offices in Port au Prince. We knew that such an appearance had a more significant underlying reason, so we checked it out. We met the next morning at 06:00 close to this base. We parked the car outside and honked the horn. When we realized that some were looking out to check, we went to the gate. After a short while, they opened the gate. It was evident that whoever told them to occupy this building did not prepare them for a visit from two UN Security Officers. They all were older respectful Haitians, we were polite as well, and saluted the man who seemed to be in charge, from former military to former military. He was trying to reach somebody with his cell phone, but it seemed too early for the receiving end. Most of them just adjusted their simple different greenish colored uniforms. The commander told us that President Martelly promised during his campaign to re-establish the army and they were here to remind the President of his promise and claim their old base and their former responsibilities. While I was talking with the commander, taking his name and cell phone number, Niko covered my flank and checked out the rest of the people and their equipment, which was very poor. Still, somebody tasked them to do it, but we knew we were not going to find the reason here today.

I made it back almost in time to do my morning seatbelt checks when I received a very serious phone call from my OIC, Officer in Charge to report immediately to him and to the Chief of Operations. After Niko sent his report to the Chief of Operations, he called him to ask with what back up forces, he went there. Niko mentioned it was just we two. We both received a disciplinary reprimand for endangering ourselves and the image of MINUSTAH. Such an operation needed planning and a tasking order. Wow, they called our trip to the few old men in a former Haitian military camp 'an operation,' I was just happy they had no idea what else we were involved in. My little meeting with Niko and the old men in the military base convinced the Security leadership I was a liability and was moved to SICU, the old posting of John Taylor. Jack was still our IT expert with a gun and maintained our Security Data Base. The new OIC of SICU, my future supervisor, had just arrived in the mission from Iraq. Pike, former Navy Intelligence Lt. Colonel, was selected for MINUSTAH. My chiefs figured that three people and only one car, a normal Nissan Patrol would restrict my movement enough to keep them safe from my actions. They didn't know that there was always a way in the 'old' security. Cege had, as usual, the solution. Our old patrol vehicles were parked at Transport Section because of missing spare parts and were forgotten. After the earthquake, the new Patrol received three new armored vehicles. Cege asked Transport Section to make one operational vehicle out of the two vehicles. I signed for the vehicle and kept it in the dark. Even though Jack was close to retirement, his database stayed with us for all MINUSTAH and was the most reliable source of threat information in the historical context. There were several attempts to create a modern version for a database, but as Pike always warned:" The enemy of the good, is better." Pike approved my outside activities and was my shield, my cover to continue and get even more involved than ever before. Haiti had a lot to offer to get involved in.

CHAPTER 16
The Fake-Fadh

Haiti, Port au Prince, March 2012

Reports of self-proclaimed new Haitian army camps like Niko and I visited in Terre Rouge on the way to Hinche emerged, with an unknown number of people in these camps at the beginning of 2012. For the general population and JMAC, it was evident that these camps were organized and controlled by Michel Martelly. It was part of his presidential campaign to reinstate the Haitian constitutional army. Nobody bothered to have a closer look. It would have been obvious that something didn't add up. None of the leaders inside these camps were former high-ranking Haitian army officers, and in fact, the amount of real Ex-Fadh in the fields was less than a dozen. The history of good relations of Martelly and the Haitian Army should have presented a different setup. We tried to alert the MINUSTAH leadership that there had to be some destabilizing or violent intent behind these camps, but since JMAC didn't consider it essential, our administration ignored it until some of these Haitians in green pants started moving in small groups, established sort of checkpoints or directed traffic. The Minister of Interior at the time tried to gain control or influence over these camps, rather than requesting MINUSTAH support for HNP operations to end it right from the beginning, he decided to gain power by buying their loyalty with water trucks and food. He just maintained this movement for unknown interests, and it looked like a confirmation that the Martelly government was involved. There were three main camps, we knew the one in Terre Rouge, one was in Bon Repons close to the National # 1, and the biggest one was in Carrefour, Lamanthine 54. Since these were former army bases, the locations were of strategic importance and covered the three main roads leading in and out of the capital, I wanted to see for myself. I asked our photojournalist if he wanted to come with me to take a look at the biggest camp, Lamanthine 54. I thought if he wanted to see it, it justified my presence as well.

I had information about 500 to 1000 people inside Lamanthine 54. Most of the recruits inside these camps were not staying overnight. The field had a small wall and was along the main road. Looking inside was easy. We were registered in a log book at the main entrance and were introduced to the commander. Most of the people were very young and in civilian clothes. The commander and a few around him were the only people old enough to claim Ex-Fadh status since anybody below 40 could not have been in the Haitian Armed Forces. The commander and his group were much less welcoming than the people in Terre Rouge. They were angry, blamed the internationals for stealing Haitian land and money, MINUSTAH was an occupying force, and Michel Martelly did not come through with his promise to reinstate the Haitian army. If they did not get what they wanted they would burn the streets and cut off the heads of the landowners and the foreigners as the Haitian hero Dessalines did in the Haitian revolution against the French. The commander gave us a pretty good idea about the ideology taught and discussed with the young men in the camps that reminded me of Aristide's propaganda. There were around 200 young men around us trying to listen and watch what happened. When it came to President Martelly, I had the impression that most of them thought they were recruited in the name of the President. Nothing pointed to serious military exercises except some marching up and down. Anybody wanting to create an army type of force needed to start with simple tactics in group formations, like setting up checkpoints. They had no training, and nobody had the intent to make an army out of them, they were stone-throwing material for violent demonstrations. I was also sure there were no weapons in the camp. Nobody would equip them with expensive tools or weapons. But the tension in the field in Lamanthine was high and aggressive towards the photojournalist and me. These people were placed there for future trouble. The commander was not in charge and lost on how to deal with us. But there was no next time for us in this camp, that was for sure.

The camp in Terre Rouge was a different crowd, not more than 20 but all in an age which could fit an Ex-Fadh. The third camp in Bon Repons had around 300 young men inside. They looked more professional and of higher education and had all similar green uniforms. I remembered, shortly after my return to Haiti, Rudolph mentioned a camp to train Presidential guards for Jude Celestin. The field was precisely in the same location and Rudolph confirmed; it was the same camp and the same recruits inside. That was interesting, they knew they were recruited initially to protect Jude Celestin as the future President in a time nobody would have thought Martelly could become President. They were still there. The crowd in Lamathine was recruited during Martelly Presidency with promises they believed were granted by President Martelly. So, if they were told in the future to protest against Martelly, they had a legitimate reason. The two biggest camps, Bon Repons, and Lamanthine had a very distinct difference, the recruits inside. These camps somehow must have a combined purpose and objective. The average number of young people reported in Lamathine was around 500. With the 200 to 300 in Bon Repons, it was already a significant number if they became violent; together with the gangs, which were still mostly controlled by the people around Preval and Jude Celestin, made it an explosive mixture. JMAC even identified and named the recruits inside the camps as Ex-Fadh and gave them a false justification. The former Haitian army members were widely supported and respected by the Haitian population and were most of the time a willing partner to negotiations with MINUSTAH and the international community. But the few Ex-Fadh in this movement were low ranking, many of whom were dismissed for disciplinary reasons or known Lavalas members who infiltrated the army in the last years. When JMAC finally acknowledged this fact, they created a new term. They didn't want to use our term Para-Military, they called them Fake-Fadh. They might have been fake Ex-Fadh, but there was nothing fake about the camps and the people inside and that they were placed there for a purpose.

Actually, JMAC should have known all along. Most of my detailed information about the camp in Bon Repons came from a JMAC report from January 2011. Niko sent it to me, but I didn't even look at it first since my arrogance dismissed JMAC information on principle. But my pride had its limits, and I realized that JMAC had a very good debrief of a recruit inside this camp. The chiefs of JMAC seemed unaware or didn't remember it, and the UNPOL who produced the report must have left the mission already since it was more than one year ago. I forgot the report until JMAC started to discredit not just our description of the history of this movement, but also their own information. The report stated that the camp was organized by Rene Monplaisir and the recruits were suggested by candidates of the political party of Jude Celestin for Senators and Deputies. Each Senator or Deputy candidate submitted 10 names in November 2010. 240 recruits were selected, ten formed one group, four groups formed one platoon. The total strength was 6 Platoons to be trained and integrated into the HNP as the Security detail for Jude Celestin, once he was President. This was a strike force under the command of Rene Monplaisir and with frequent visits of Senator Jean Rodolph Joazile who was also some form of campaign manager for Jude Celestin. He coordinated the financing of the gangs in Cité Soleil, and he was the new face for Aristide in Cité Soleil. They had a lovely painting of him at the water tower on the corner of Avenue Soleil and National # 1, the entrance to Cité Soleil.

There was one more link from the past between the camp in Terre Rouge and Bon Repons, Youri Latorture. The interesting detail of Niko's report was that this group of Terre Rouge had meetings with Youri Latorture in the summer of 2008. It was the time when information on uniforms was circulating, and a former military base in Cap Haitian was occupied in September 2008. We also knew at the time that Jean Rodolph Joazile and Rene Monplaisir were part of these meetings, which completed the link to the camp in Bon Repons. Only the camp in Lamathine remained a mystery, especially since many advisors of Martelly tried hard to gain influence in the field, it was difficult to look behind.

Martelly in the meantime was accused by the parliament of double nationality, which was against the constitution. He was believed to be also US citizen. I didn't understand the fuss about it, but the opposition saw a chance to get him out of office. There were Senators in the past who had to resign because of such issues. Martelly showed how well he knew his people, he mastered the situation in a genius manner. The tension concerning this issue was building up, and a press conference was announced for later in the day. The rumors were flying, he had resigned, he left the country, he was too drunk to talk and more. At lunchtime, opposition Senator Steven Benoit gave an urgent radio interview because he feared for his life. I received phone calls from people who knew the country longer than me who were convinced that there was a coup d'état coming. I didn't see it, my informants in Martissant, Cité Soleil said all was quiet. Besides, coup d'états or riots usually came as a surprise, not when the whole country was waiting for them. The effect was amazing, there was already almost a coup d'état based solely on a rumor. The Haitians were convinced, even supermarkets closed before 15:00 in the afternoon. Not a car was on the street. Everybody was waiting near a radio or tv for the press conference.

The new CSA had discussed how to react to the crisis with his operational advisors. If Haitians believed it, UN staff members were even more panicked. The question was whether the staff should have been allowed to go home or should have stayed at the UN premises overnight. There were no indicators of trouble and since the streets were empty and the gangs were quiet, I advised them to send the staff home. Late in the afternoon, the press conference was held by President Martelly with US Ambassador Merten as the main speaker. He was fluent in Creole and told every Haitian in their mother tongue that Martelly was not US citizen. Any further accusation by parliament would have been an insult to the US Ambassador and the United States, and nobody seriously wanted this. The issue was resolved.

After this press conference on 20. March 2012 tension in the camp in Lamanthine was rising. Deputy Arnel Belizaire visited the camp with Guy Phillippe and showed support for their demands. Now there were two notable names involved in this movement, and a name like Guy Phillippe made this movement a serious threat from one second to the other. JMAC made a 180-degree turn and saw a very well equipped and armed fighting force with brand new assault rifles distributed to the recruits. It was scary how far they were from reality. Nothing changed, except Guy Phillippe showed up. He and Deputy Arnel Belizaire were usually accompanied with two or three pickups with loyal men with 'long guns', just in case the US DEA office wanted to pay Guy a visit. Arnel Belizaire was a well-known member of parliament and a great example of an elected Haitian official. He was in jail for car theft and other crimes and escaped during the earthquake. He campaigned, was elected and inaugurated as an escapee. The United States influenced the outcome of the Presidential elections, not the parliamentary elections even though the level of voter fraud was no different. Preval lost the Presidency but kept the parliament. Arnel Belizaire, like Guy Phillippe, had very close ties to Youri Latorture and Joseph Lambert. He was one of the hundreds of names in the Haitian cocaine family. The Guy Phillippe and Arnel Belizaire show went on for a few weeks and they started moving around the country in convoys. The government was watching it together with MINUSTAH. MINUSTAH Brabat could have ended it in a second but had to wait for host government authorization. It was a joke.

MINUSTAH let these 'Fake-Fadh-Clowns' wander around as though they were hundreds of Taliban fighters. MINUSTAH's lack of response had the rumors circulating, and it just got too ridiculous. I had a cell phone number for Guy Phillippe, and had an idea. I had to admit it was a bit controversial since the Nazis started the second world war this way, but it could work for a good reason this time. A false flag operation. I took a deep breath and called Guy. He knew who I was and my message was short and simple. I told him not to worry anymore about the DEA; he should worry about the US Navy Seals and the prison in Guantanamo Bay because I would make him a terrorist. I would organize drive-by shootings and other attacks on international community bases and write in my reports to MINUSTAH and the US embassy that he was behind it. He was not publicly seen with the paramilitaries after that day. If he took me seriously, I didn't know, but it was very possible he didn't want to take the risk. I was convinced it would have worked, even JMAC would have immediately identified any attack on a UN base as a master plan of Guy Phillippe. JMAC had already reported a development that would have included such a scenario. But it still didn't show me the real organizers behind the movement. Arnel Belizaire and Guy Phillippe pointed in the direction of the usual suspects, the members of the Haitian Parliament led by Youri Latorture. I was convinced we would soon know what the purpose was of these paramilitaries.

On the 8 of May 2012, 10 Senators were about to lose their mandate and immunity until new elections were scheduled and organized. Youri Latorture, Joseph Lambert and Jean Rodolph Joazile were three of these 10 Senators. On 8. May 2012, Youri Latorture and Joseph Lambert were announced as Special Presidential Advisors to President Martelly and Jean Rodolph Joazile was declared the new Minister of Defense. All three positions granted the individuals immunity and protection from prosecution. Even though it should have been a surprise that President Martelly brought former political opponents into his cabinet, it might have been the reason why two days later the camp in Lamanthine 54 was cleared by HNP and the other camps disappeared. Even without violence, the paramilitary movement achieved its task. My theory from 2008 to have civil unrest by a group of people and a new military force saving everybody could have been a possible scenario. The group in Lamathine 54 with the gangs would have been the rioting part, and the 300 well-dressed recruits in Bon Repons would have been the military force saving everybody after a few days. But for now, it was just a crazy theory.

CHAPTER 17

The JAKWG, The Joint Anti-Kidnapping Working Group

"As long as we live, we fight. As long as we fight, we know we didn't surrender, and the good spirit is still within us. And if death doesn't meet us as the winner, it shall meet us as a fighter." (Augustin of Hippo, 354 – 430 AD) In Memoriam of James Kfouri and John Taylor. Both met death too early, and after all the risks we took together, it seemed Cancer was our most deadly enemy. Knowing James, it made no difference how he met death, but death met somebody with great humor and spirit. John's knowledge and passion for Haiti lived on within us in the fight against evil, a fight which had only just begun.

Haiti, Port au Prince, October 2012

On 16. October 2012, Nicolas Moscoso was on the way to a party in Bourdon. His sister Coralie was with him because she didn't want to wait for their parents who were running late. It was a party of elite Haitian families close to the ruins of the Christopher Hotel in Bourdon. Almost at the entrance road to the French and US Ambassador's residences, they were stopped by a group of masked policemen. The HNP officers didn't say much, one officer made a phone call and told the other end that Nicolas was not alone in the car, he was with his sister. The other end answered:" Even better, take them both." The siblings didn't resist when they were asked to step out and enter the Toyota Land Cruiser specialized HNP units were using. They also didn't ask for a warrant, what was necessary for an arrest, they assumed they were now in custody of the Haitian National Police. Sort of, they were kidnapped. They realized it when the police officers blindfolded them once they were inside the HNP vehicle. Their parents were contacted shortly by the kidnappers. Reggie was in downtown Port au Prince checking arrangements for the official celebration of National hero Dessalines on 17 October 1806 when he received the call about the Moscoso abduction. He met the Inspector of the Anti-kidnapping unit at the crime scene in Bourdon. Some people witnessed it from an apartment complex close to the location and described a regular police operation of a specialized unit. We knew about kidnapping incidents with this modus operandi, and it was always very high-value targets. A similar kidnapping occurred April last year when a ransom of 800 000 US dollars was paid to release the victim. The victim was brave because he made an official police report against his kidnappers and identified them by their names. He named several ex-HNP and active HNP officers including an Inspector, Yves Michel Bellefleur, as his kidnappers. His heroic action didn't have any follow up by Haitian Justice or by the HNP leadership. HNP did not go after HNP or Ex-HNP, this was just taboo. Their past activities and duties from the time they were Aristide's loyal enforcers for the share of the country kept them faithful to each other until today. There was no follow up or consequence from the HNP leadership under Director General Andresol. Inspector Bellefleur remained in charge of the commissariat in Pernier, a neighborhood close to the Police academy on Route Freres.

There were several high-profile kidnapping cases in which victims were held hostage in Pernier or the surrounding area. I was chasing a ghost for years in this area. A hardcore killer related to kidnapping and drug trafficking with the alias 'Kilo' was working for a gang called 'Base Galil.' This gang seemed to be well connected and very powerful. Up to now our success in Croix-de-Bouquets had affected low-level criminals and mid-level victims, this case was on a different level, it was the most important case we ever worked on together. We knew there must have been Ex and active HNP officers involved, and even though Andresol's term as Director General had ended, we didn't expect a different approach from the newly appointed DG. It was the ultimate test for the Inspector of the Anti-Kidnapping Unit to decide where he stood, with them or with us. Reggie knew he was walking on thin ice and he had to be a hundred percent sure about his evidence to bring this to a successful conclusion. The first lead was the vehicle used by the kidnappers. Video surveillance footage from private enterprises along the way helped us to reconstruct their route and identify the vehicle. It was basic police work in other countries, not in Haiti. Reggie needed to make sure the collected information was safe, and he controlled it. Also, it helped when UN guys or internationals knocked at the doors of private enterprises instead of the HNP since the level of trust towards the HNP was still below zero. We had the possible Pernier connection in the back of our minds but couldn't find the link. We had hunters' luck, we identified the vehicle, and it led us to the Delmas 2 area. Delmas 2 was a gang territory mixed with large businesses and under partial HNP control. It was a tradition in Haiti that companies had close contact with the gangs surrounding them and maintained these relations with financial support for the gangs. It kept the businesses from troubles and safe, and it could come in handy for other particular tasks as well. But the vehicle didn't lead us to a gang in Delmas 2, it led us to a car dealership; actually, it led us there before the kidnapping even occurred.

On 30. September, a little bit more than two weeks before the kidnapping, an opposition demonstration was scheduled. Every year Aristide supporters organized a march to commemorate when he was overthrown by the Haitian Military in his first term as President. This time the political opposition joined the 'Lavalas' movement. It was the usual number of 3000 to 5000 demonstrators, an insignificant percentage of the Haitian population but enough for the opposition to demand the President's resignation. Our scouts within the demonstration reported that money was handed out from a white Mitsubishi to the demonstrators just before the protest turned violent and had a clash with the HNP. We tried to identify the vehicle or people inside who instigated the violence. One Reggie' scouts tracked a white car to the Mazda dealership in Delmas 2 and sent him a photo. It was the wrong vehicle, not the Mitsubishi we were looking for but a white Toyota Land Cruiser. It later turned out to be a vehicle used in the Moscoso kidnapping case. From this dealership, Reggie could identify a connection with the Inspector in Pernier, but command and control of the kidnapping were at Mazda, not in Pernier. While the ransom negotiations agreed on 2,5 million US dollars, Reggie got a name for the man who seemed to be the one in command. He just couldn't believe it, Clifford Brandt from the well-known elite family Brandt. Many United Nations Agencies and other internationals rented several buildings or residences from his father Fritz or his uncle Gregory Brandt. I always heard about 12 or 13 families who controlled most of the wealth in Haiti and Brandt was named as one of them. The Brandt was a Haitian institution and powerhouse, also personal friends to Ambassadors.

The method and form of kidnappers' communications during the negotiations and ransom exchange raised Reggie's suspicion about the will of the kidnappers to release the victims alive. He experienced cases in the past in which the victims were killed even after the ransom was paid. The pattern was the same. Reggie was convinced they planned to kill the Moscoso siblings. Reggie had worked too many cases, if he had this feeling, we had to act now. Reggie rushed directly to the President to get authorization for the arrest. President Martelly was as surprised as we were. He just asked if Reggie was positive because his wife came from a wealthy background and grew up with the Brandt's. Even the victims' father couldn't believe it, although the Brandt's were Moscoso family competitors in many business affairs. Reggie convinced the President, and the Inspector of the Anti-Kidnapping Unit rushed with his team to the Mazda dealership in Delmas 2 to arrest Brandt. When Clifford Brandt realized the police came for him, he left his 'blackberry' telephone on his desk and on the way out of his office advised one of his drivers to destroy his phone. He was arrested, and a few hours later after consultation with his lawyer, he admitted the kidnapping and gave Nicolas and Coralie's location. He brought the police to an empty house in Pernier where both children were locked inside a bathroom, blindfolded but alive.

This was big news, and the media went wild. Clifford Brandt stated via his lawyer that years ago, under the Preval administration, the Moscoso's were granted a multimillion dollar government contract against the Brandt's bid. Clifford Brandt still felt that his father and uncle were treated unfairly and the Moscoso's humiliated his family. When his chief of security told him he knew some kidnappers, Clifford Brandt decided to recover some of the money his father and uncle lost and ordered the kidnapping of Nicolas and Coralie. It sounded reasonable, given the history of crimes in the country and that wealthy families also used such types of negotiations to achieve preferred outcomes of business deals or state contracts. But his chief security made us suspicious; Edner Come was an Ex-HNP officer of the specialized 'UDMO' unit. 'UDMO' units were deployed in all regions as an effective strike force but were also the choice Senators and Deputies to protect and move their loads of illegal drugs or weapons. Edner Come was more than just an Ex-HNP officer with a criminal history, he was a hardcore version, and one of the few who served jail time after Aristide left. More than a hundred other high ranking HNP officers were dismissed for irregularities. But it was normal for rich families to hire these Ex-HNP officers, even from jail, for their security details because of their connection and access to HNP and criminal elements. 'Come,' before he started working with the Brandt family, had a known history with 'Kakos,' a gang that operated in Jacmel under the control of the Senators Lambert and Eddy Zenny. 'Edner Come' had at least two Haitian National passports, one with the name 'Jackson Travellino.' His connections to Pernier suggested that he didn't just know kidnappers, but was deeply involved in their operations. He seemed to have been the coordinator for several high-profile kidnapping incidents in the past. When I read the profile of Edner Come, I was sure we were not far away from my ghost 'Kilo' and 'Base Galil.'

While we were looking at the evidence collected from Pernier where the Moscoso children were found and the background and relations around 'Edner Come,' Reggie's technician worked his magic on the broken pieces of Clifford's 'blackberry.' The AKU Inspector collected it from the garbage bin and brought it to Reggie. Clifford's driver did what he was told, smashed it with a hammer and threw it into the garbage bin, he destroyed the phone, not the data. The conversations between 'Come' and Clifford regarding the Moscoso kidnapping showed that Clifford never intended to release the children, the plan was to wait for the night and execute them just outside Port au Prince. Besides the loss of 2.5 million US dollar ransom, Clifford wanted the parents to bury their children. Reggie saved their lives and without the coincidence that his scout tracked the wrong vehicle at the demonstration on 30 September, he would have never identified Clifford Brandt so quickly. As it turned out, our luck in getting to Mazda via the Toyota Land Cruiser was even better than we thought. We knew that the Toyota Landcruiser was stolen at the time of the kidnapping and I always wondered why it led us to Mazda even before it was stolen. It turned out that the gang stole the Toyota from a a relative of Clifford Brandt's wife who happened to visit Clifford in Delmas 2 on the day of the demonstration. Brandt's cell phone also made it clear that he was calling the shots. 'Edner Come' had the experience and the connections to the HNP, Ex-HNP and other criminal elements and coordinated the operations, but Clifford selected the targets. Clifford had the knowledge and inside information on the wealthy and beautiful of Haiti, selected the targets and decided on their life and death. Besides the kidnapping, they also were trafficking weapons related to Jacmel and 'Guns for Ganja.' The phone data also showed that they were planning to kill a public official, Secretary of State for Public Security, Reginald Delva.

Reggie realized that in another chat Clifford had received pictures of his own residence, his vehicle and the HNP officers selected and trained by a man in the shadow to protect him. The chat revealed that they decided Reggie was becoming an obstacle to their operation and planned to kill him. Reggie's recent success of against kidnappings in Croix-de-Bouquets and his plan to install camera systems in the Port au Prince metropolitan area of to combat the kidnapping threat made him compelling and dangerous. Neither Reggie nor his detail icked up on the surveillance and showed us we were now playing in a different league. While Reggie tried to connect previous kidnappings with information on the phone to identify more victims, we were informed of the assassination of Inspector Bellfleur. On the morning of the 9 November, 17 days after the arrest of Clifford Brandt, Inspector Bellfleur from Pernier was shot and killed after he dropped his kids at school. Reggie was just about to request his arrest to seal the other kidnapping cases and more. But four armed men with automatic rifles in a Toyota Landcruiser with Haitian official state license plates were one step ahead when they riddled the vehicle and the Inspector with bullets. Maybe Clifford Brandt and his lawyer realized that the strategy of a 'one-time' event, a mental break down over family shame was on thin ice. Inspector Bellfleur could have named the victims of other kidnappings as well. But it was surprising and unusual that the gang started to turn on each other so fast, not for Brandt, in the end, he was a rich kid, not one of them. Nobody knew how much insight Reggie had from the Blackberry information. There were already 15 other suspects identified and arrested, including high ranking HNP officers assigned to the Security of President Martelly. Something was special about Bellfleur. There must have been more at stake, some higher invisible force was involved. I had a suspicion it was my ghost 'Kilo' and the myth of 'Base Galil.'

This invisible force continued to cut ties, it tried to kidnap Clifford's psychic, advisor and lover, a beautiful Mambo, a female Voodoo priest. She contacted the spirits to select the targets and the best time for the kidnappings. The Mambo could identify several victims that she helped to select for Clifford but also had a broader knowledge of his criminal connections. The unknown force kidnapped her sister by mistake and Clifford was able to arrange her release. The sister was not happy about almost getting killed for her sister's boyfriend and contacted Reggie. Clifford was still in touch with his Mambo from prison and was convinced she could get him out with the help of the spirit world. The material world tried to counter this effort and the vision of the RSO of the US embassy came through.

The Joint Anti Kidnapping Working Group was created. The US Ambassador preferred the less dramatic name working group instead of task force. President Martelly and she agreed to an informal group led by Reggie and the Diplomatic Security Service under the protection of the US Embassy. We more or less continued our different individual efforts as before with semiofficial status and weekly meeting at the house of 'the Dude'. Jose, Bobby and I had the continuing support from the 'old' Security Section, other than that, MINUSTAH had no knowledge of JAKWG's existence. There was always a potential threat from criminals and gangs we were working on, but mostly we couldn't risk gossip about us, and the UN was all about gossip. It was also essential that our group and connection to AKU stayed secret to the rest of the HNP. HNP was not just deeply connected to the criminal elements but also to MINUSTAH and would have known very shortly of our existence. The UN Police Commissioner would have wanted to have a leading role in such a group, and the egos of the rest of the UN leadership would have destroyed our effort in a heartbeat. We were only effective as long as the bad guys did know what hit them and from where the punches came. We felt like the 'Gangster Squad' in the movie of Sean Penn. The Ambassador made sure we had support from the FBI or any other US Agency we needed. We even received support from a US prosecutor who was sent from the United States to oversee the ongoing criminal investigation by the Haitian judge. The US embassy was serious in its promise to support the efforts of the Haitian President and Prime Minister to battle kidnappings.

The arrest of Brandt had a fantastic effect on many HNP officers. How much more information I got from contacts I had already worked for years. The fact that Clifford Brandt was arrested and stayed in jail made people believe something was changing in Haiti. HNP officers had an excellent idea of what was going on but learned to live with situations beyond their control, and some were above the law. Many of my HNP contacts were the same generation as the police chief or other high-ranking officers, but never had the privilege or the will to work with or for the ones above the law. When I asked my contacts whether a senior police officer was 'clean,' most of the time I just got the answer: "He has a house in Vivy Michel, in Kenskoff and in Bel Ville." All these areas were costly and the houses worth a few hundred thousand US dollars each while my police contacts struggled every year to pay their small rents and maintain their families. The more information we received, the more we started to realize inter-connections between all these gangs like tentacles linked with each other. As Bobby predicted, it seemed to be a considerable syndicate.

Reggie happened to come across an alias, 'Kilo.' After all the years I had been chasing this ghost, one of my HNP contacts brought me a piece of paper, a National Identification printout of 'Kilo,' 'Jaques Lerwins Mathurin.' He even knew the vehicle he was using at the moment and wrote the license plate number of the green Toyota Landcruiser on the paper. He also knew how long I had been working on the case of who killed the five young men in Fontamara 47. Ex-HNP officer Gerry, arrested in 2008 related to a kidnapping case and escaped from jail during the earthquake. Like Come he worked for Brandt, 'Base Galil' and the gang of the Senators Lambert and Zenny in Jacmel, it was all connected. More than once I had showed my HNP contacts a picture of the HNP officers who killed the five young men in Fontamara 47 and never gotten an answer. But now, I didn't just have a photo, my contact even showed me the house of one of the killers in Jacmel. He knew it all the time.

He also told me that 'Kilo' led the kill squad that ended Bellfleur's life and career as a potential witness. I had no reason to question any of his information. That 'Kilo' led the kill team made sense, he was not Ex-HNP, he started his criminal career in Florida and was deported many years ago. He was one of Ketant's cartel killers in Miami, a professional who didn't rat on anybody. He would remove any threat for the 'boss', even an HNP officer. The question was, who was the 'boss' at the moment. In the past, my HNP contacts were convinced that none of my efforts could lead to significant results since they worked for people and organizations above the law. The arrest of Clifford Brandt and related HNP officers changed this perception, and we looked like we were on the stronger end. Shortly thereafter 'Kilo' was stopped and arrested in his green Toyota Landcruiser at the Dominican border. It always helped when one of us took the lead in collecting important evidence or even arresting key suspects since it gave the HNP officers some form of excuse and justification for doing their job. I had seen the eyes of a few killers, but when I looked into 'Kilo's' eyes, I was happy to have some reliable Haitian police officers with me. A fight with this guy was over when either he or I stopped breathing, and I could feel he took the last breath from many men, women and maybe even children.

Our success was mostly based on simple investigative techniques, just the effort to get up and go to look or check something brought us one or more steps closer to our targets. The AKU existed for many years on paper without support. It was separated from the joint MINUSTAH HNP Anti Kidnapping Unit, which was good news since they couldn't be trusted. They considered a kidnapping case successful when ransom negotiations were successful, ransom delivered and hostages released. Ransom was usually exactly the amount available from the victim's family. We knew there was a direct link from the joint UN/HNP AKU to the kidnapping organizations. The pieces of evidence collected showed us even how strong, it was scary but essential to know and deal with. I had to question not just the vetting of the HNP officers in this unit, but even of some UN police officers. Somehow the ignorance of the pure HNP Anti Kidnapping Unit for all these years kept the officers assigned to it away from the dirty business. They were not relevant for the kidnapping organizations. But since they had the attention of the US embassy and our support, it started to shine like a diamond. It just needed a vehicle sometimes. A young boy, the latest victim released, received food in a paper bag from his kidnappers before they let him go. He still had the paper bag with him when we debriefed him. Inside the paper bag was an invoice with the time, date and location of the purchase. The kidnappers bought the food at a new minimarket at a gas station that had a small restaurant attached and a camera recording the cashier area. Bobby took some HNP in his vehicle, went to the gas station and was able to recover video of two kidnappers who purchased the food. It didn't take long for the HNP to find them and follow up. Our information jumpstarted the HNP Anti-Kidnapping Unit and the wheels of kept turning. The HNP officers could finally do their job, and they did a great job.

Many times, we provided logistical support or paid from our own pockets to speed up the investigation or arrests. It was not a large amount of money, to rent a motorbike for HNP officers to follow vehicles or just to get food and water to keep up morale. It was a little money spent with an enormous impact after all those years and millions of dollars spent in UN troops and police officers without a single kidnapping gang arrested. It showed us that we didn't need to deploy this amount of UN police or military to get results, the right HNP officers just needed to be protected from the Haitian system to do the job. Of course, to have a real impact, the judges and justice system would have to be under special protection and supervision as well. But for now, it was already great and was about to get even better. The new PDSRSG for MINUSTAH came from the US Justice Department, he was a prosecutor a professional used to criminal cases. But even better was that he had Haitian roots and spoke Creole. The first meeting Carl Alexandre attended in Haiti in January 2013 was as the new member of the JAKWG. Eight months later in August 2013, we celebrated the first month without one reported kidnapping since 2004. It should be noted that with more arrests of kidnappers, victims and their families gained confidence in the HNP and reported more kidnappings. So, we were actually working against the numbers for a few months, but still, it went to zero. We didn't get them all, but since the gangs and most of the HNP didn't know where the punches came from, it became too risky. The key was control and protection of the information.

I was sitting next to the JMAC chief in the Senior Management Meeting with all heads of UN Agencies hosted by Carl Alexandre; my supervisor was on vacation, and I had to fill in. The JMAC chief presented the weekly statistics and numbers of incidents over more extended periods. They never analyzed the trends, they just made graphs and showed numbers. It was September, and he outlined how the number of kidnappings had gone down down since January 2013 to zero in August, and he said: "There were zero kidnappings reported in August, it shows our strategy worked, we identified a problem, dealt with it and eliminated it." If I hadn't been so stunned hearing the words coming out of his mouth, I would have fallen from my chair laughing, I could see Carl also had to bite his lip not to ask how JMAC did it and maybe we could apply such a successful strategy on other issues. Nobody asked JMAC how the hell they suddenly applied a successful strategy after MINUSTAH, with JMAC and their Joint Anti Kidnapping Unit, were flying blind for more than 9 years without any impact on kidnappings. Anyway, in the end, MINUSTAH and JMAC was my best protection for my outside activities. Freaking amazing, but on a positive note, JMAC was somehow part of my security. As long as JMAC took the credit, nobody was looking for the people responsible, and it kept me, my family, and my silent support in the shade. For the Haitians outside the UN, I was just another 'MINUSTAH Tourista,' stupid and blind.

CHAPTER 18
US Marshals Most Wanted, Wesnel Isaac

Haiti, Port au Prince, January 2014

Wesnel Issac was wanted in the United States for kidnapping and triple murder. The Haitian-born suspect was believed to have escaped to Haiti shortly after the bodies of the three murder victims were found in September 2007. The case resurfaced in US media in 2013, and in November 2013 the Federal Marshals placed him on the list of the 15 Most Wanted US Fugitives. Southwest Florida Crime Stoppers declared him one of the most violent men to ever walk the streets of Southwest Florida. In January of 2014 the newly arrived Diplomatic Security Officer of the US Embassy, call sign 'Charly' was part of our JAKWG to fill in for 'the Dude' until the new RSO arrived. Charly was the contact for all US Marshal matters in the RSO office of the embassy. He asked me if I could meet with him and two US Marshals who came to Port au Prince on the Wesnel Isaac case. He thought that maybe I could track the Most Wanted down with my contacts in the ganglands. We met in the Serv-Hotel close to the airport. It was built after the earthquake with solid steel construction and was the safest and nicest hotel in the area. The Marshals gave me a brief history of Wesnel Isaac. He was a career criminal, 34 arrests before he escaped arrest in 2007 when he was just 27 years old. He was recruited at a very young age by Zoe Pound, the infamous Haitian gang in Florida. His baby face didn't stop him from becoming one of the most feared Zoe Pound executioners. The US Marshals didn't have much on his possible life in Haiti, except that his parents had a brick making factory in Gressier. The US Marshals told me that there was a 25 000 dollar reward available for essential information which led to his arrest. This was great, but I could not mention this amount to anybody at first. My contacts would have brought me 5 different Wesnel Isaacs. I told the Marshals that I would say a reward was possible but not be specific. Such an amount was only useful if it was a great surprise in the end. I estimated around 2 weeks to know if I could locate him. If yes, I would have to check how to grab him, that was the tricky part.

I had scheduled a meeting with my informant in Martissant, the 'Favela' type gangland to the south of Port au Prince. All Haitians I worked with were my friends, but my contacts, informants or CI's were like my stepchildren. This one in Martissant, 'Vicky' was special, not just because he was the only one speaking very good English, he was a hunter himself, a vigilante. He worked with the Sri Lanka Battalion at times when it was actively pursuing bandits and worked with any trusted HNP officer in the area as well. He also had his own informant network in the gang areas and gathered great details on the gangs. Everybody knew him, and 'Vicky' had no political preference, which made all bandits his enemies, but he was armed and used his gun who knows how many times to bring final judgment to his declared targets. He was as lawless as Haiti could make anybody who didn't like criminals and had to be very careful about his movements since he was a marked man for all the gangs. If he could help get Wesnel, he could move out of the area with the reward money. We usually met in a small bar close to the seaside that was open already at 10:00 but whose guests came only later for lunchtime. In this area, he was well known and respected since he kept the bandits away. We discussed the Wesnel Isaac case, and he knew an HNP officer who lived and worked in the possible target area. He trusted him, and if this Wesnel was in Gressier, he would know. 'Vicky' planned to visit him at home later in the day. He complained about an intense headache and heavy pressure in his head. I usually felt this way before heavy rainstorms.

It didn't rain that evening, and when Vicky called me around 18:00 completely drunk, I guess his headache was also gone. I didn't understand much of what he said and waited for the next day. The next day was no contact, but I was luckier the following day. He told me that the HNP officer knew the address in Gressier, it was a brick production site along the main road, and he was supposed to get more from the HNP in the evening. Vicky was not reachable for another 2 days, and I started to get worried. His behavior changed, he acted weird. He seemed more careless and made cryptic comments about night clubs and other places he would have stayed far away from in the past. This was either a woman or drugs. His next phone call was not regarding our US Most Wanted, but money, he needed it now. It was the first time he had asked me like this, and I told him I couldn't get to Martissant before the next morning. He said no problem, he would come with a moto-taxi, a hired motorbike driver, to my office in Delta Camp, next to the US embassy. Now I got worried, some lady was making him really nuts. He never exposed himself this way. He came, and I gave him around 50 US dollars in Haitian Gourdes. I asked him, what her name was, but he denied it. He told me it was something higher, which I didn't understand. He had to go to his home town in the region to pay for the perfect prayer to solve this issue. I had no idea what he was talking about. I thought he was full of shit and just crazy in love. I told him I wanted to meet his HNP contact as soon as possible to deal directly with the HNP officer until Vicky came to his senses. It took me until Friday morning the following week to get in touch with Vicky; actually, he called me from a different number because he lost his cell phone. I asked him where he was and if we could meet right now at the usual spot. I needed a minimum of 45 minutes to get to our usual place, but I needed to get in touch with the HNP officer. I was close to the 2-week period I mentioned to the US Marshals to know if I could locate Wesnel and I didn't want to look like an 'all talk – no action' guy. Up to now, I couldn't even find my own informant. I found Vicky one hour later at the bar and without wasting time I left with him to his contact's workplace. Vicky still rejected my theory of him being crazy in love and always talked about a higher problem, something spiritual I didn't understand. He did not go to his home town for the prayer yet, so I begged him to do it after our meeting today. I just wanted the old Vicky back again. Once I could deal directly with the HNP officer, he could go and take his time.

Vicky introduced me to 'Dinero,' his HNP contact. He was very reserved and cold, he seemed upset. If he was pissed off at Vicky, I could understand. 'Dinero' wanted to know what was in it and I gave him a 1000 US dollar reward as a realistic amount. I could see in his eyes it was a good amount, he wanted it. He must have already had an extra income from all the drugs passing through Route National # 2, the only road connecting the South with Port au Prince. Even though the drugs were all linked to parliamentarians and their business partners, the HNP still got a share for their passive cooperation. Maybe it was true what I was told, that Haitian drug dealers were very 'cheap' and therefore 1000 US dollars was still a good motivation for 'Dinero.' We left together to visit the brick-making business, it was an open land with a small building and some bricks outside. It didn't look like a bustling place, but at least we knew it existed. There was a worker present who told us to deal for any business directly with the owner. We got a number and an address not far, a house next to Route National # 2. We heard from neighbors that the owner had two sons, one of them lived in the area and had a little depot, a small shop for daily products in Carrefour. 'Dinero' had a task for the weekend. We exchanged numbers and dropped him back at work. On the way back Vicky talked more mysteriously than ever, I started to believe it was not a woman, he sounded severely depressed. I gave him 100 US dollars in Haitian Gourdes and begged him to go to his mother in the region and do his prayer. He was standing on the street, and before he closed the car door, he said:" I don't know if I will live or die." I answered him he should take it easy and take a break in the countryside. It was past lunchtime, and I was rushing back to Port au Prince. I took advantage of my armored vehicle and took the shortest route through Cité Soleil. Until Monday I left the gangs and most wanted fugitives behind me, my daughter was turning one year old tomorrow.

I had a long list of things my wife needed for the birthday. Haiti was a non-family duty station because of the risk and bad infrastructure including lack of medical facilities and schools. My girlfriend could visit me anytime, but as soon as I married her, she was not allowed anymore in the mission area. Since life of Field Service Officers was in the mission area, it was pretty much the only place possible to establish a new relationship. The moment it became a legal family it was supposed to get separated again according to United Nations regulations, preparing for another impending divorce or encouraging maintaining a mistress on the side. This kind of system explained the high probability of separations of DPKO staff members. My wife and I made it work in Haiti and kept a very low profile. We lived in a tiny apartment close to my office, Niko and Abuelo lived in the same compound which made it safer and more comfortable. We had planned a small party on Saturday with some Zombie Hunters. This was pretty much the social life of my daughter in Haiti since a 'Kindergarten' was no option, and my wife started homeschooling according to the Montessori philosophy. If I had known that Maria Montessori made all her school materials in wood and we had to bring it in our suitcases via airplane, I would have at least tried to argue against it. We also brought on our last trip the table decorations, things for cupcakes, piñata and many other supplies, all in the Minnie Mouse theme. My daughter and all of us had a nice event. It was still dark when my cell phone was ringing in the kitchen, I forgot to switch it to silent mode for the night. I rushed there as fast as I could and saw Vicky's new number on display. I checked the time, it was 03:00, I just hung it up. I was sure he didn't go to his mother; he just came out of a night club completely wasted.

'Dinero' called me Monday morning, he was excited and screamed into the cell phone. I didn't understand anything about his French. It took me some time to get the message that Vicky was killed by bandits of Grande Ravine and Ti-Bois. They didn't kill him in the street, it seemed they took Vicky inside gang territory and tortured him. In the end, they cut his head off and dumped his body in some public toilet. My mind picked up on the public toilet, I never saw one in Haiti, and one in Grande Ravine must have been really messy. He said it happened Saturday. I remembered Vickys phone call and was rechecking the time on the call log on my phone. It was 03:01, maybe 'Ti-Keken' or 'Krisla' the gang leaders of Ti-Bois and Grande Ravine wanted to talk to me and not Vicky. I called a friend and asked him about it, he called me back and said the Inspector in charge of the commissariat in the area confirmed it. I left the office to go to this commissariat. It was built before the earthquake just below the high-school which was used by the Sri Lanka Battalion in Martissant in the past as a small base. The high-school today is actually a public high-school.

The Inspector was at the station, and he showed me the report he made on the killing of Vicky. He told me he knew Vicky and was very shocked about his death. Also, the Inspector had very detailed information because Ti-Keken and Chrisla made his torture a public event. How he was captured was unclear, he was not sure, as he heard two versions. One version claimed Vicky was going on a motorbike to Ti-Bois to hand himself over to the bandits. This version didn't make sense at all, but Vicky didn't make much sense the last two weeks either. The other version was more plausible that he was drinking in one of the night clubs he mentioned to me, and some bandits of Ti-Bois with the help of an unknown HNP officer managed to grab him and bring him into the Favelas of Ti-Bois. His torture started at around 19:00 when 'Ti-Keken' took a machete and chopped off his right hand. Vicky was tortured and questioned by 'Krisla' and 'Ti-Keken.' They went through his phone and asked him about all the numbers he called. His pain and suffering ended at 03:00 when they cut off his head and his body was dumped in a public toilet; his head and right hand were kept by the bandits.

Many of his informants living in Grande Ravine and Ti-Bois were lucky that Vicky had lost his phone and didn't have many numbers saved. Most likely, my contact number was one of very few. The Inspector didn't know if they called me before or after they decapitated Vicky. He offered to ask his informants, but it didn't make a difference anymore, and I told the Inspector I wished he would have told them everything right away to have a faster death. The Inspector replied that it wouldn't have made a difference and explained further that it was not just punishment and torture, Vicky was a sacrifice for an evil spirit. He must have read my face correctly because he insisted, Vicky's torture and death were a gift, a blood sacrifice to an evil spirit. He told me all these gangs are into black magic and the ritual was performed before the new moon and ended precisely with the new moon. At least this was what the Inspector believed. I googled it and 03:02 was the time of the new moon, the Inspector was right, spooky. I knew that farmers cut the grass in the week after a new moon, because the fresh grass grew faster, and even some women cut their hair according to the moon calendar but cutting off a human head, what the hell? I was not sure how much of it was really Voodoo or just a message to all the people of Martissant since Vicky was a vigilante, a hunter of the bandits and his terrible death should have been a warning for the people. In the end, fear was instrumental in controlling people, and even religion usually gets hijacked by power that uses fear to serve the same purpose. I guess cutting up Vicky for Voodoo and evil spirits worked very well.

I wanted to know more about his abduction. Somebody must have sold him out. Vicky behaved very strangely the past two weeks, but I couldn't imagine he surrendered himself to the gangs. I had his last sentence in mind if he would live or die, it was so strange, I went to the bar where we usually met next to the Royal Haitian Hotel. Twenty years ago, it must have been a very nice hotel. At the turn into the parking lot, there was usually a man with a red Digicel t-shirt, he sold telephone credit time. He was there, but something was wrong.

I knew he flinched. I didn't know if I saw it or just felt it, but I knew he was watching out for me. I couldn't explain, but it was not the first time it happened. Maybe it was my experience as a shadow of people in my past life, tapping telephone lines, observing them while always watching out for counter surveillance. Perhaps it was just pure intuition, and I was lucky and born with it, but I knew I had to be quick. I parked my car; I didn't even switch off the engine and went to ask the two ladies working behind the bar. I could see they were already shocked before I even asked them; it was a waste of time, this was burnt ground. I got back in the car, and on the way out I could see a 'Rasta' on a motorbike talking to the Digicel man looking in my direction. The 'Rasta' came for me. I didn't show any reaction and turned into National # 2 towards downtown Port au Prince, with the 'rasta' on my tail.

I couldn't lose him by speeding, not in Port au Prince traffic and a controlled threat was better than an uncontrolled risk. I kept him in sight. He didn't make phone calls or seem to have more guys on motorbikes around him. It didn't look like they planned an ambush right now. This guy was just checking me out, where I worked or lived. The different gang territories in Port au Prince came in handy because even though these gangs were inter-connected, the guy on the motorbike behind me could not just drive through the different 'bases' of Cité Soleil. He might have made it through the first but for sure not the second 'base' and would have risked his life trying it. It was the best way to lose him for now. If they wanted to know who I was and pass it on to their political contacts, or if they already had authorization from the politicians to do me harm was not critical, I had to reassess my surroundings and routine, especially around my family.

I was already careful and had specific procedures as a routine to keep us safe. Before I went into the street of our residence, I always turned into another street to park for 1 minute around a corner so that anybody following had to make a turn into this street as well. This didn't take long. I never used the armored vehicle for my family, I always had another car with tinted windows available. Still, we were cautious and checked for tails. It could be 2 or 3 guys on a motorbike behind the vehicle, or when stopped in traffic or parking the car, the bandits would have approached from the blind spot of the side mirrors. Whenever the vehicle came to a halt, regardless of the reason, it was essential to do a shoulder check to the left and right. In the time of smartphones, it was necessary to pay attention to the surroundings, not the phone. My one-year old daughter already pointed out the motorbikes driving behind us. At home, our apartment seemed from outside not well protected and was actually a small little house inside a compound with high walls and barbed wire. There was a storage area, but the landlord made a small kitchen and bathroom with one big bedroom out of it when he heard we were pregnant. I had a chicken wire fence inside the window to prevent Molotov cocktail or gas grenades. The door was reinforced from the inside with reliable but straightforward metal latches. There were several pepper sprays placed in the small apartment not visible or reachable for our daughter, just in case somebody surprised my wife before she got to her automatic assault rifle. She knew how to handle the gun, and she had seventeen loaded 30-round magazines ready to engage. Whoever wanted to come to do evil had to face an evil mother. I concluded that our measures and procedures were still sufficient. I also never shared personal business or details with my informants, they never knew where I was living or with whom. The most important security measure was to control the information about you and your surroundings. We didn't live like other Internationals in a big house with nannies, gardener, and cook, we had one person helping us in the household and never went out for dinner. I usually had lunch at home as well since it was close to my office.

I told my wife about the death of Vicky and that they tried to follow me, so she was also more alert.

Vicky's abduction stayed in the dark, and I refocused with 'Dinero' on Wesnel. 'Dinero' told me it was Voodoo that made Vicky so crazy in the past two weeks. He was convinced the bandits got to Vicky with an Ougan or Mambo, a male or female Voodoo who cursed him. But he also told me that a spirit so powerful had to be in physical form with him or close to a place where he was frequently. It was said it could be anything, a doll, a little ball, or just powder close to the bed of a person or inside the car. I remembered once one of our national staff members found some items inside the drawer of his desk which didn't belong to him. He was scared to death and brought a

Voodoo priest to clean the office, himself, his family and made a trip to some hot spring to heal. Years ago, I once told my informant Moses from Martissant who was always smoking pot with the gangs that I didn't have money at the moment because of some issues with my apartment in Miami. I made it up. I had no apartment in Miami, but his Marijuana consumption was getting a bit too expensive at the time. He asked me who caused the issues because he could help me to get rid of that problem.

I was thinking he meant his contacts to Haitian gangs in Florida and I told him no violence needed, but he said he could send a Voodoo curse to the guy. When I asked how he said they could send Voodoo curses with pigeons to anybody anywhere and he was absolutely serious about it. I was wondering about the real history of pigeons as messengers, did they first deliver Voodoo spells? Immediately the two pigeon houses in a small park opposite the residence of Aristide came into my mind, on the wall of the small park were paintings of pigeons with short branchlets in the beaks that I always perceived as a sign for peace. Now I was wondering if these pigeons had maybe a completely different purpose since it was said Aristide was deep into the dark side of Voodoo. It seemed 'Dinero' was also deeply into the power of Voodoo, so I wanted to get going before the spirits got to him as well.

Within a few days, he had the address of the little depot in Carrefour. He believed he saw Wesnel Isaac and almost arrested him. He couldn't tell from the pictures I showed him if it was really him which made me suspicious. I asked him about tattoos on the forearm, and he believed no tattoos. Wesnel had praying hands tattooed on his forearm. I was just happy 'Dinero' did not know about the 25 000 US dollars, he would have brought me one possible suspect a day. We went to the depot, and it turned out that two small depots next to each other looked like one. Wesnel Isaac's was closed, according to a person with several weeks in the area.

I asked 'Dinero' to check with people around and other businesses if they had some details. He did very well and gathered that Wesnel's father gave him the depot to make some money, but he was not really into the sales business. Somebody knew that Wesnel lived close by in Carrefour, he had no exact address but saw him with his red Toyota 4Runner turning into a side street of the Route #2 in Carrefour. We had a car and a street, now we were getting somewhere. I told 'Dinero' to take it easy and slowly and check first if he knew anybody in this street well enough to talk to him since 'Dinero' also lived not too far away. We were lucky, he had a cousin in the same street. The cousin didn't know the name of Wesnel but identified him by one of the US Marshals pictures Marshaland knew his house. But he 'hadn't stayed there for a while because it was under some reconstruction inside. His wife was pregnant with their second child. Sometimes, the red Toyota was parked outside the house or outside the hardware store with basic construction material in another street nearby. 'Dinero' was checking the hardware store if we could get an idea of how far the construction progressed. 'Dinero' passed Wesnel's parent's house on his way to work every morning and evening and he never saw the red Toyota parked there. We could rule this location out for being the temporary home. I reminded 'Dinero' to be patient because I could feel him becoming desperate for the 1000 US dollars and he wanted to push it. Wesnel had been on the run for six years, a few more weeks wouldn't matter.

The next few days 'Dinero' seemed to pressure the owner of the hardware store more than he should, maybe he even threatened him. He got copies of the receipts of items Wesnel bought in the past. 'Dinero' made waves and I got worried that the current would sweep away our most wanted. I went to Carrefour early morning to slow things down. "Dinero' claimed he didn't push.

We went together to check on Wesnel's house in Carrefour to see if we could see any construction still ongoing. According to the hardware store owner, he hadn't bought any material for the past two weeks. When we got close to his house, we saw the red Toyota 4 Runner parked in front. I told 'Dinero' I was going to pass his house and turn and check if we could stay somewhere close enough to see him coming out and grab him. My mind went lucky, lucky, lucky until I saw them. Two, four, at least six shooters were between the car and the house, and they all appeared focused on us. Everybody had their hand in the back or in front of the t-shirt. I was flying blind into this one, I forgot who we were chasing. These guys didn't give a shit about law enforcement or a white guy with a gun who might be freaking 'Terminator.' They faced specialized police strike force units in Florida before they were jailed and deported back to Haiti, they were hardcore Zoe Pound veterans. Breathe, I told myself, it could be worse. I could be in a Saharan riverbed called a 'wadi' filled with rainwater with no idea before I had to cross it back by foott that there were crocodiles inside.

But I neglected any safety rules and the street was a dead end and I had to get back the same way. My armored vehicle mitigated my arrogance and ignorance, thank you Cege. We passed the Zoe Pound gangsters pretending not to be impressed at all. I turned fast and went back before they could block us in. I almost thought of waving them goodbye, they knew why we were here. Wesnel felt the current but didn't consider it necessary to run, he was prepared to pick a fight. We passed them, and I told 'Dinero' to stay away from now on. Soon or later they would have identified him and would have ended his life faster than any Voodoo spirit could. I told 'Dinero' to check with his cousin in the area if he heard about Wesnel's wife pregnancy and if we had a possible hospital for the due date. We had to let Wesnel loose to get him in an unexpected location and moment. It was already the end of April, and we figured we had to be close to the due date. We identified the hospital in Carrefour to be the delivery location, at least the first child was born there. I was about to go on leave for two weeks which might have been exactly the time for the birth of Wesnel's child and made sure 'Dinero' had the contact and connection to Charly in the US embassy. 'Dinero' had

a look out at the hospital and on 07 May 2014, Wesnel brought his wife to this clinic. They were accompanied by his parents who stayed with her, and he left again. 'Dinero' had some HNP with him for support on the first night but stayed alone until morning. Wesnel's wife had some complications which kept her in the hospital for longer than expected. Wesnel must have figured after three days that it was safe to pick her up himself and see his child. 'Dinero' was there, but alone, so was Wesnel. Both were in an empty corridor. 'Dinero' made his move.

He sat down next to him and had his 9 mm Beretta pistole in his right hand covered with a t-shirt. Wesnel hadn't noticed the gun yet when 'Dinero' said:" Mackenson, I got you, you are under arrest." Wesnel, looked at him and said, who? 'Dinero' continued:" Somebody identified you as Mackenson from Ti-Bois, don't make any trouble and come with me to the commissariat or I kill you right here." Wesnel denied being Mackenson, and 'Dinero' showed confusion, and they both agreed that they could figure it out at the commissariat if he was Mackenson or not. 'Dinero's' move was genius. Once at the commissariat in temporary custody as Mackenson, Charly sent a vetted HNP unit to pick him up and bring him to DCPJ, before a judge could free him.

The red notice of Interpol wouldn't have made a difference. It worked perfectly, and I received an email from Charly while on leave about the arrest, and he asked me to contact 'Dinero.' When I called him, I heard loud background music, and he was screaming into the telephone. I didn't understand much but something about US money, and the US Marshals. He was partying hard, and I had to expect the US Marshals told him the full amount he was supposed to receive, I just hoped he kept a low profile for his own security. I was back a few days later, and Charly told me that he went nuts when he heard that he was about to receive 20 000 US dollars. I wondered why not the full 25 000 US dollars since he didn't just provide information which led to the arrest, he arrested him and delivered him. But 20 000 was still a lot.

'Dinero' already had all 20 000 US dollars planned out, including a trip to Miami with his family. I was not sure how long it would take until he received the payment, so I tried hard to bring his expectations down and bring his focus on the gangs who killed Vicky, but it was a waste of time. And as I expected, such an amount was not quick money. The weeks passed by, and he kept on calling and asking for it. I understood his desperation and Charly tried to do his best to speed up the process.

In the meantime, everybody who helped 'Dinero' in this case wanted a piece of the pie since it was in the Haitian news. The worst was that all media reported a 25 000 US dollar reward since it was stated by the US Marshals on their website. At some point, the US Marshals got upset about the constant pressure from the embassy in Haiti and started to argue that since he was a law enforcement officer, it was his duty and he shouldn't get anything. Luckily this was not the last word, he received his payment and made his trip to Miami with his family. I tried to continue working with him on Vicky's killers. Anything I asked him to check about the gangs who killed Vicky, he answered with questions like:" Is this for the US embassy, because I would need a new car, mine is getting old." My final visit was when he told me that I had excellent contacts in the US embassy, and we could make money with it. When I asked him how he told me, people pay for US visas. 'Dinero' got too greedy, he was infected by the need and greed for more money. This was burned ground, I left Carrefour and 'Dinero' behind.

CHAPTER 19

Too close to 'La Familia'

Haiti, Port au Prince, February 2014

The news of the arrest of a US Marshal most wanted was nothing in Haiti compared to the news about the arrest of the head of the notorious gang of 'Base Galil.' The "Dude" had already left Haiti, but his vision, the JAKWG was still operating and together with the AKU we were about to hit our biggest target. The beautiful thing was that we could actually sit back and watch the magic of the Inspector and his AKU team under Reggie's guidance and the supervision of the Chief of DCPJ. It was running very well and smoothly, and our meetings could focus on other important topics, like good cigars, single malt whiskeys, and beer. There were very few new kidnapping cases, we could actually look at old cases with all the information we gathered. The kidnapping of the Haitian businessman Sami El Azzi on 17 February 2014 was a rare event. The modus operandi with official state license plates, white Toyota Land Cruiser with tinted windows and a few masked policemen as kidnappers pointed at 'Base Galil.' It was almost an insult to us. Especially since we had already identified vehicles and cell phone numbers Base Galil was using in prior kidnappings. While the ransom negotiations went down from 1,200,000- to 800,000- US dollars, one of the kidnappers, alias 'Commander Jeff' was stopped and arrested in his green Nissan Patrol with several official license plates, sim cards, money, and weapons. He led the Inspector to the house where Sami El Azzi was held and watched by three other members of 'Base Galil'. AKU's swift and professional actions were beautiful to watch. Four members of 'Base Galil' were arrested, and the hostage freed. It couldn't be better, this was our chance to finally take this gang apart piece by piece. We knew this gang was not just about kidnapping, it was about drug trafficking and money laundering as well. And we were about to stop it. A careful estimate suggested that the gang received a minimum of 2 million dollars just in ransom for reported kidnappings over the past three years. The sim cards and other pieces of information started to show the extent of their drug trafficking and money laundering operation, and in short order it brought Reggie and the AKU to the top of 'Base Galil.' AKU identified 'Son Son La Familia.'

It took me some time to understand 'Son Son La Familia' was one person and not a group, and his real name was Woodly Etheart. It didn't tell us anything, at least Jose and Bobby were as clueless as I was. But our friends in the shadow got really quiet when Reggie told them the name. I didn't know much about President Martelly's past life and career other than that he was a famous Haitian singer. Had I known, I would have become quiet as well. Whoever knew Martelly and his wife's family and friends knew one of his oldest and closest friends, Woodly Etheart. The President was a frequent guest in his expensive restaurant 'La Souvenance' in Petion Ville, which also had catering contracts with the National Palace and many other Ministries. He was running this restaurant together with the President's brother in law, Charles St. Remy, who everybody called 'Kiko.' Oh boy, I thought, but Haiti was too small to avoid such contacts, and I was convinced the President was one of us, screw his friend. The head of DCPJ must have thought exactly the same when he rushed with Swat and AKU to the house of 'Son Son La Familia' in Delmas 83. Unfortunately, it was an old location, and the suspect had moved some time ago. The premature raid alerted him and he went on the run. It was regrettable, there was no time pressure like in the Brandt case, and all evidence and connections should have been investigated more deeply before such a move. Even though the head of DCPJ never gave us the reason to question his actions, it was a bit suspicious. Reggie was convinced it was just a mistake and we never got any other reason to assume the opposite. The investigating judge issued a warrant for 'Son Son La Familia' and even ordered the arrest of his wife for suspected money laundering. She was jailed in the Petion Ville women's prison. We were on it, and nobody was above the law under this administration.

The wife of 'Son Son La Familia' joined female prisoners who most likely never saw a judge for several months if not years. The acting Government Commissioner ordered her release and stated just before he resigned from his position immediately afterwards that he released her on humanitarian principles. The release was illegal, and I realized that some were above the law as well in the Martelly administration, , I just didn't know yet how many. My positive spirit sometimes refused to see the truth if it didn't fit the image my mind created, it could lead to blind loyalty. I guess this could explain the political preferences of many Haitian patriots who had the right intent and were just played by their idols. Things started to get complicated for the AKU Inspector and us. Reggie told us there were rumors about a reshuffling of government positions and he knew his position was menaced as well. 'Son Son La Familia' was in hiding but not deep under the surface. It was pretty much common knowledge that he moved in palace vehicles and stayed at houses and apartments of the President's family.

It was time for me to take some history lessons and a man in the shadow brought me back to Lieutenant Colonel Michel Francois, where it all began with Pablo Escobar. Michel Francois and President Martelly shared the same nickname, 'Sweet Micky' and were good friends.

My immediate question of who got the nickname first was ignored, and he continued. It was the time when the Ketant brothers became the number one organization providing not just the logistics to facilitate transit in country, but also distribution in the United States. This package deal made the Ketant cartel successful and influential. They ensured their control in Haiti and the United States with young, ruthless men, the Lieutenants, the hands-on guys in their cartel. One of them was 'Kiko,' Charles Saint-Remy, the President's brother in law, who was in charge of the planeloads landing on Soleil 9 close to Port au Prince. 'Kiko' was not the black sheep in the family, his father operated on a higher level in the organization, in charge of moving money for the Ketant cartel. I always heard that Martelly's wife came from a rich family and that she was crazy for money, I just didn't know it was easy money she was crazy for. 'Son Son La Familia', like 'Kiko' a hands-on guy in the same organization, was leading a kill squad, the 'Base Galil,' named after their favorite Israeli assault rifle. Ketant might have been in jail, but 'Kiko' and 'Son Son La Familia' never stopped their activities. I started wondering how much the old cocaine connection was still controlling everything in the country. Bobby always saw patterns and the different mafia-like structures, and claimed it was a professionally organized narco-cartel. I started to understand what he was talking about. We didn't hit a kidnapping gang, we hit the cocaine family or at least a part of it.

It was not over yet, there was still hope, Reggie was promoted to the Minister of Interior. We were all surprised about Reggie's promotion in the government reshuffle the beginning of April, and my confidence in Martelly's good intentions was renewed. Reggie became Mr. Law Enforcement, and we grew even stronger. Just before his being officially inaugurated, we had another JAKWG meeting. The drones, which the Haitian government ordered finally arrived and Reggie wanted to test one of them with us, on a Sunday morning. These were the moments that really tested the never-ending support of my wife and daughter. I had a time-consuming hobby of, chasing kidnappers in addition to my UN-job, while my wife was homeschooling and entertaining our daughter 24/7. At night we also studied for my master's degree. It was in the final stage, and each evening my wife reviewed my writings from the night before, and in this manner we worked forward day by day. It was sometimes a painful process for both of us.

Reggie selected the Police Academy football field for the event. It was a good location that offered a large open area without buildings and trees and on a Sunday, we shouldn't have many people around. I didn't want to miss it, mainly because these drones were supposed to be idiot proof, anybody could fly one. When we met at the football field, we had to wait some time for Reggie's tech guy. Reggie had already started checking into his new office, and it seemed to be such a mess that no minister before him even tried to sort it out. While talking, he almost fell asleep in front of us. Once the tech guy was here, he introduced the drone to us, mostly to me since I was the one who wanted to use it as much as possible in the field. I already imagined myself stalking the killers of Vicky in Grande Ravine and Ti-Bois from the air. It was effortless, just the touch of the fingertip on a tablet made the drone go up, down, left and right. It was after 10:00 and the heat made us hide in the shadow next to our parked vehicles. Learning by doing, that was it. I was ready with the tablet to operate the drone, the tech guy placed it a few meters away from us. At first, he was warming it up until suddenly, he lifted it up in the air two meters where it remained, just hovering. It looked so cool, the tech guy said "Bring it up to 30 meters", and showed me how to drag the point on the vertical line up to 30 meters. I looked at the drone, then at the tablet and moved it all the way up to 30. My finger and my eyes were faster than the drone. When I looked up, I saw trees and thought, you idiot. I tried to drag the little point down back with my finger, but the drone had a slight delay and was going straight for the tree. The next second, we saw leaves flying and the drone coming down in two or three parts. I just crashed the Haitian Air Force. I never saw my partners of the JAKWG moving so fast, like receivers trying to catch a quarterback's terrible throw. The parts were supposed to handle such impacts, but we couldn't make it fly again. I looked at the vast open football field in front of us and at our little spot under the tree. That was really smart I thought. Even though I didn't place the drone under the tree, I guess I could have looked up. I destroyed the Haitian Air Force and thought I better not ruin the whole Sunday for my family as well and left. We never tested any of the drones again, and I doubt any of the drones were ever used, at least not for the purpose intended. It was the last meeting of the JAKWG.

Reggie's new position kept him so busy that he never made it to another meeting. We started to understand that his promotion was not a move to make our efforts stronger, it was a move to paralyze Reggie. Martelly knew how to counter the obstruction of justice rumors and demonstrated his good intentions to combat kidnapping to the US embassy by promoting Reggie. But getting a grip on the ministry and his office was impossible and too complicated. Whenever I met Reggie, he was just exhausted. We all remained in contact and assisted him with ideas or information as well as we could, but we had minimal impact.

Prime Minister Laurent Lamothe never changed his objective of promoting tourism and was not friends with 'Kiko' or 'Son Son La Familia', whose arrest he authorized. Reggie and Lamothe were in hot water, and the parliament-supported opposition demonstrations against Lamothe intensified. Since the business community already accused Lamothe of being the most corrupt politician ever, parliament joined in and formed a powerful smear campaign. The demonstrations never exceeded the usual insignificant number of 3000 participants, but the business community used their contacts and social events with the international community to destroy Lamothe's reputation. As the Haitian saying goes: "If you want to kill a dog, just tell everybody it has rabies". Even 'Kiko' joined the opposition demonstrations against the Martelly government. We also noticed some Latin American elements around the events that seemed to have financial influence. We could never figure out their exact role in support of these demonstrations, but we could track their vehicle to an NGO from Venezuela. Considering that most of the cocaine from Colombia comes via Venezuela, it was not a surprise that an organization from this country helped to get rid of Laurent Lamothe and his cabinet, including Reginald Delva. We got a feeling this was not just about Martelly's family or friends but something more significant.

What many internationals did not realize at the time was that Laurent Lamothe implemented several social programs for the poorest people in Haiti and for students. One program was running public kitchens in all the slums of Port au Prince and the countryside. Students received monthly financial support based on their progress. These programs might not have been sustainable because they were funded with foreign donor money, but I never heard of any politician who had implemented such programs before, not even Aristide. I knew from Rudolph that it had a considerable impact on the people of Cité Soleil. At the time a meal that cost 25 Haitian Gourdes in a public kitchen would have cost 100 Haitian Gourdes elsewhere. I had no doubt that this administration had corruption issues similar to previous administrations, but at least the poorest people of Haiti had their share as well. I didn't know if Martelly was given a choice of La Familia or the Haitian people and didn't believe he decided in favor of La Familia; Martelly most likely was just a tool of the Haitian cocaine family. Laurent Lamothe and Reggie resigned in early December 2014. They knew they couldn't compete with 'Kiko' and the 'La Familia' business. This was not Martelly's call, this was above him, and he had no control. With 'Base Galil' we hit something more powerful, his past and his drug trading family members and friends. They couldn't risk exposure and had to get rid of Lamothe and Reggie. The people in need lost programs that made their lives easier, and it exposed what Haiti really was, a cocaine country.

This time I expected the people to rise up, to say enough is enough and initiate real food riots because of the immediate tripling of the cost of living after Lamothe's resignation. Every meal went back up to 100 Haitian Gourdes or more for several hundred thousand Haitians. But there was nothing, no reaction at all. The Haitian people did not know that their elected representatives were supposed to serve them and not the other way around. The people in Cité Soleil must have thought Lamothe was crazy when he provided this to them almost free. As the Haitian saying goes: "Anybody who gives something for free is an idiot, and the one who doesn't take it is stupid". It was also an excellent indicator for past and future riots that were always claimed by politicians to be a social uprising of the Haitian people. It was never the population, there was always somebody paying and organizing it, and unlikely for a greater good. If there were no riots after the resignation of Lamothe, there would be no riots in the years to come without somebody financing them. I had hope that Lamothe could run for President, but he needed a 'discharge' from parliament. This was a process that approved and declared his time and actions as Prime Minister as just and legal and was needed for him to be able to run for President. The parliament controlled it, and since Lamothe was not a big supporter of the drug trade, it was pure science fiction he would ever receive this discharge.

'Kiko' and the rest of the narco-traffickers won, Haiti lost, and we had to consider payback. It was time to take a step back, look for shade and listen to the winds of change. We all exposed ourselves at some point, but Reggie and the Inspector of AKU faced the most significant threats. While Reggie tried to step out of the light back into the shadow, the AKU Inspector couldn't resign from the HNP fast enough. After having brought kidnappings down from an average of 30 to 2 per month, he should have been a rising star in any police force, just not in the Haitian, he had to get out. The US embassy hired him in a position in which he had the best possible protection and was not involved anymore in law enforcement, he had to give up his childhood dream and became a civilian. The new Prime Minister appointed by the President was Evens Paul, the former mayor of Port au Prince under Aristide. The justification I heard for his choice was that he had excellent contacts with the demonstrating mobs, only in Haiti could this be a necessary competence for the Prime Minister. Just to be clear, none of the opposition demonstrations exceeded 5000 participants and represented an absolutlye insignificant percentage of the Haitian population. The appointment of a Prime Minister was usually a very lengthy, painful and expensive progress to achieve enough votes in the parliament. It often took 2 or 3 candidates. It was a terrible sign when the parliament agreed on the first suggestion of the President in the voting. The International community always wondered why Haiti never changed, but they still watched the same people getting back into public offices. Was this only because of their past political experience? I always wondered how the international community expected the same people who were part of creating the mess could suddenly become the solution. As Einstein said:" We cannot solve our problems with the same thinking we used when we created them."

In April 2015, against the will of the investigating judge, a speedy trial was organized in which the ruling judge decided there was no case of the country against the suspect Woodly Etheart and released him. It was not just an illegal procedure but also an absolute slap in the face to the international community's efforts to reform the pre-trial detention and justice system in general. MINUSTAH had not been able to improve this situation within the last 11 years. More than 80 percent of the thousands of prisoners were still in jail for years without ever being brought in front of a judge. The US state department human rights report described the situation in Haitian prisons as overcrowded, poorly maintained and unsanitary. This could also be the description of a toilet in a soccer stadium at half time. Even the comment that in some prisons, detainees slept in shifts because of lack of space, could not in any way describe the circumstances these people lived in. An HNP officer working in prison once mentioned that his human rights were violated because he had to watch this every day. The cost of hundreds of UN police officers and civilians assigned to sections tasked with modernizing the system was wasted money. The fact that MINUSTAH helped Haitian governments to power and kept them there without any improvement for thousands of people living and slowly dying made MINUSTAH complicit in these human rights violations and deaths.

It was not that there weren't attempts. Carl Alexandre visited the prisons and was shocked at the conditions and how disconnected MINUSTAH correction officers were. In their defense, they most likely gave up trying at some point. Carl ordered them to go examine each case for the crime charged and the time spent in pre-trial detention. The aim was to create some form of a priority list and select all petty criminals or unknown offenders to be released as quickly as possible. The file was established, and about 300 detainees were identified as either being jailed for nothing or very minor offenses. The list of the 300 detainees had to go through the Ministry of Justice.

I did not know about this list until I requested an urgent meeting with Carl Alexandre. My cell phone was running hot because my contacts warned me about hardcore criminals getting out of jail. I was also worried about Clifford Brandt and that maybe the rumor was related to another planned prison break as had happened in August 2014. At that time Clifford's family invested around 500,000 US dollars to get him out of the new prison in Croix des Bouquets. According to the plan, Clifford was supposed to get a head start to reach the Dominican Republic before the rest of the inmates caused chaos and havoc. The doors of the prison were just opened, and more than 300 criminals escaped. The planted rumors of the coming days about an assault team, helicopters and Colombian drug traffickers who were freed were all bogus. The prison could have withheld a company of soldiers long enough for UN Military troops to arrive. I had the details about it since my HNP contact was recently arrested and placed in Croix des Bouquets. Clifford Brandt was captured three days later by the Dominican authorities at the border. My contact did not escape and died a few weeks later of an unknown sickness. None of the HNP leadership considered it a reason to resign, and nobody demanded any resignation. Maybe because it was not incompetence, just business.

When I met Carl about the rumors of hardcore criminals being freed, he confirmed to me that it had almost happened. He told me that 300 innocent inmates were identified by MINUSTAH and presented to the Minister of Justice to be processed and the detainees officially released. Processing in the Haitian Justice Department was a very flexible term. The list was prepared, and the detainees were about to be released, the only issue was that names on the list had nothing to do with the names MINUSTAH presented. Carl did not know who was responsible or at what stage the names were changed. I suspected a joint effort all the way up to the President since a get out of jail free card initiated by MINUSTAH and authorized by the Minister of Justice was a lucrative business. It became a pay to play list to get out of jail. Since Carl pulled the emergency brake, the whole project was dropped by the Martelly administration. If their friends couldn't get out, neither would the innocent people rotting in jail. They had just one way left out of jail, in a coffin.

Usually, MINUSTAH was guilty by association with the Haitian government or by doing nothing about it. But in some cases, MINUSTAH was the offender itself.

The aftermath of the Cholera epidemic most likely caused by Nepalese UN soldiers based in the Central Plateau was a sad example. In Nepal, Cholera outbreaks were relatively common and could be dealt with, but in Haiti it had deadly consequences for more than 7000 Haitians, many of them children. Haitian lawyers immediately formed a group to represent the victim's families and sue MINUSTAH and organized a demonstration in front of the UN Log Base for a Saturday. Pike had to cancel his weekend trip to Miami to meet his wife because JMAC expected severe violence against MINUSTAH. Our threat assessment predicted a quiet weekend. Of course, after thousands of Haitian deaths caused by MINUSTAH, our threat assessment must have sounded insane to any rational mind. But TIH, this is Haiti, we knew nothing was going to happen. Secretary-General Ban Ki-Moon stated a few days before the scheduled demonstration that the United Nations had no liability due to international agreements and would not pay a dollar. This statement showed that a substantial investment by the lawyers in any kind of demonstration was very unlikely. The lawyers never had the intention to bring justice to the Cholera victim's families, they just wanted to make money off a tragic event. Otherwise, they would have been traveling to Central Plateau to engage with the population or even bring them to UN Log Base in busloads. We knew nothing of the sort was in progress, so it was easy to predict. The demonstration consisted of a few international journalists who wasted their money on the flight.

It was the right decision not to negotiate with the Haitian lawyers, but still, the UN had to take responsibility for the tragic deaths. The UN Agency UNICEF was tasked to build sanitary installations for the populations in the affected areas and received millions of US dollars to do so. It was the right intent, but Pike and I had to witness the unbelievable implementation of this program. When the Secretary-General announced a visit to see the result of the program, Security was tasked to visit the installations with UNICEF representatives and select the best possible locations for the Secretary-General to see. A few days before the SG visit, several joint MINUSTAH Security and UNICEF teams moved out of Port au Prince to do their assessments. Pike and I were tasked to go to Jacmel. I was surprised, I didn't know there was Cholera in Jacmel. We picked up the UNICEF staff member in Petion Ville and drove to Jacmel. UNICEF implemented these programs with Haitian partners, national NGO's. The UNICEF representative didn't know where the office of the Haitian NGO was located in Jacmel, so he arranged a meeting point on the main road in the center of Jacmel. One man came with a Toyota Landcruiser marked with the NGO and UNICEF logo. This told us that UNICEF bought the vehicle for the NGO. Although this was a great initiative to provide them with needed mobility, I just saw a perfect smuggling vehicle that wouldn't be stopped by HNP. The Haitian UNICEF partner explained to us that we were going towards Kay Jacmel, a few kilometers outside town, and we would meet their national contractor on the main road to guide us to the project. That the UNICEF representative had never been to the office of their local partner in Jacmel was worrisome. But that the local partner did not know where the project was and contracted it out to somebody else was scary, unless the objective of the project was delegation or outsourcing of tasks.

We reached a small village in the mountains above Jacmel. It was a very calm and peaceful place. Not even the cell phones could disturb since the cell network didn't reach this far. Women were washing clothes; some children and men were gathering and watching us. As usual, they all were very interested but respectful. I asked one of the ladies if she heard about Cholera, she said yes. When I asked her if they had Cholera here, she was laughing and told me no, that was far away in Central Plateau. The contractor of the local UNICEF partner showed the UNICEF representatives the UNICEF project, the sanitation installation preventing any future Cholera outbreak.

The public toilet was in between the trees and the simple mud houses of the village. It was a hole in the ground surrounded by three old metal roofing sheets. The metal sheets formed three sides of a square, the open direction faced bushes and trees for privacy. It was a typical village toilet but for sure not new. I didn't have to ask anybody to know that this toilet had existed for many years. Where ever the money for this project went, it didn't go down this toilet. Actually, there was an almost full roll of toilet paper next to the hole, which must have been placed there just before we arrived. The best of all was the UNICEF staff was asking us seriously if a helicopter could land here close to the village and if the area would have been safe enough for the SG to visit this location. Any aircraft would have not just blown away the UNICEF project itself, most likely most of the houses as well, but we couldn't believe the man seriously considered this as a potential location. How bad must the other projects have been. Still, for Pike and me it was a pleasure to escape the sadness of Port au Prince and see the beauty of the Haitian countryside.

CHAPTER 20
Fishing boats worth millions of dollars

Haiti, Port au Prince, April 2015

Cité Soleil also had its beautiful views next to the Caribbean Sea when the eyes caught only the fishing boats hanging on single ropes in the sea. If the wind blew in the right direction and plastic bottles were not covering the water around the ships, it looked beautiful and peaceful. In April 2015 I was on leave and far away. I still followed up with my contacts and monitored the most important headlines. I read about a sugar boat that arrived in Haiti and was busted by a DEA-BLTS-HNP operation that seized around 100 kg of cocaine and a few kilograms of heroin hidden on the boat. I didn't pay much attention to it and just wondered which idiot puts only a hundred kilos of illegal narcotics on a ship full of sugar, it should have been 100 kilos of sugar and the rest cocaine. I was about to return to Haiti when Rudolph sent me a message that 'Ysca,' the gang leader from 'Belekou', had become a major drug dealer. I was sure Rudolph exaggerated because it would have been much too complicated and expensive to transit drugs through the different gang territories of Cité Soleil. These gangs were used by the drug dealers and or politicians to inflict violence, insecurity or organize demonstrations, but not to move drugs. Especially with regard to the upcoming parliamentary and presidential elections. Even though Cité Soleil was going through the most peaceful period since I knew the place, 'Ysca' had a different political alliance than 'Ougan' or 'Gabriel.' The drugs were the main financial resource for the electoral campaigns of all these political alliances. There would have been serious fighting over the control of these financial resources. So far it was still quiet in Cité Soleil. Since our JAKWG abrupt ended and we all needed to look for shade, I thought Cité Soleil was the perfect spot to hide. Due to my contacts within these areas I had unique access for a 'blanc,' a foreigner. It became a bit of a hobby, I turned from hunter to humanitarian, though only in Cité Soleil. I had frequent meetings with representatives of different 'bases' or even with the gang leaders themselves to develop a strategy or projects which could bring maybe some form of income without a gun in hand. I met 'Ysca' a few days before my departure, and I didn't see a Bentley or Ferrari parked in front of his little house in the former stronghold of Amaral. I planned to follow up and clarify the information with Rudolph, upon my return.

When I met Rudolph a few days later, he ensured me that 'Ysca' was sitting on hundreds of kilos of cocaine and heroin. I knew his quality of reporting, so I listened to the winds coming from 'Belekou.' And yes, there were drugs, a lot, Rudolph was right. I finally made the connection to the sugar boat bust that happened next to Ysca's stronghold. In the old days when Cité Soleil was the root of all evil, the DEA and HNP would never have made it to Terminal Varreux, since it was located between Belekou and Wharf Jeremie, two gang strongholds controlled by Amaral in the past and now by 'Ysca.' Nowadays, with a strong Brazilian UN military presence, they could reach the location and enter the premises without being openly attacked by criminal gangs. The terminal always had arrangements with the gang leaders of Belekou since the terminal was operating through the years next to the root of all evil in Cité Soleil. They didn't need a UN peacekeeping force to keep their business running. The sugar boat was a delivery for the enterprise of Marc Antoine and Sebastian Francois Xavier Acra, two brothers who inherited the family business built up by the grandfather. The Varreux Terminal, the private port, was owned by the brothers Gregory and Fritz Bernhard Mevs who inherited their business from father and grandfather as well. The Mevs and Acra families maintained good relations with every president from Aristide to Preval and Martelly and had it all covered over the years, from the gangs next to their port to the politicians in charge. Like most wealthy families they hired security personnel who could offer intensive experience and relations to criminal elements and the HNP. Even though MINUSTAH troops were stationed in the Cité Soleil, it was still important to keep a good relationship with Ysca in his territories. He could easily interrupt or even close their business by placing burning tires and having the population demonstrate in front of their gates, besides robbing trucks or visitors to the terminal. Ysca's contact was the security chief of the terminal, and on some occasions, the big chief of the terminal, 'Bernie' Mevs, paid his respects to Ysca in person. The terminal had a permanent arrangement with Ysca to keep visitors and their trucks safe aside from the strict security set up of the terminal itself. This time Ysca provided an extraordinary form of protection.

I learned later that the security chief of the Acra brothers received a phone call about the DEA/BLTS team on route to the port. Whether the mole was within HNP, the government or justice department was never revealed to me, it was even possible that he received several phone calls from different entities since such a tip paid very well. Ysca was called by the terminal security to send as many fishing boats as possible. That was an unusual task, but his territories surrounding the terminal could provide a small Armada within a few minutes. Years later in August 2018, the Miami Herald ran a news article by Jaqueline Charles about it and a related investigation into DEA wrongdoing. The report was based on DEA agent complaints that accused their own organization and the Haitian BLTS-HNP unit of corruption and incompetence. When I read the article, I realized they must have felt in the DEA like I felt in the UN. No doubt they joined with the best intentions and were disgusted by the incompetence of their agency in Haiti. In this news article, a Haitian police report described that the workers of the port surprisingly discovered the load of cocaine and heroin between the sugar. Then suddenly, out of nowhere, people came in vehicles with tinted windows to pick up most of the drugs before the DEA and BLTS-HNP arrived on the scene.

Like every port in Haiti, it was well secured and owned by one or more business families, Senators or other well-to-do individuals, not the government. In most of these ports, called 'Free-Trade-Zones', neither customs officers nor HNP were present. Free trade was a very flexible term in Haiti. The DEA prepared to take down this sugar boat with their HNP partners from BLTS, they had a confidential tip and not a phone call from the terminal about a discovery on the sugar boat. Also, these ports wouldn't just open the terminal gates when they stumbled across cocaine on a sugar boat and offer it for free to anyone who could be faster than the DEA. Of course, anybody more trustworthy than the neighboring gang leader would have been preferable, but time was short, and there might only have been a few who could make it. That day, things only got complicated because the DEA was about to hit the boat. The information about the DEA operation was leaked as soon as the target was officially made known to the Haitian government, HNP and the 'justice of the peace' who had to be present for such an operation. The DEA most likely knew the risk of a leak and tried to shorten the proper procedure to get the go-ahead as fast as possible, 2 hours was a good time since the location was in Port au Prince. No wonder they never busted anybody outside

Port au Prince. This time it was close, but most of the cocaine and heroin packages were safe on the fishing boats. The DEA must have seen an unusually high amount of fishing boats sailing toward Belekou. Of course, they couldn't know how many were there on normal days since it was not the normal hangout location for US embassy international staff. I wished somebody would have told the fishermen how many million dollars' worth of cocaine they had in their boats, they would have set course for Miami.

I wasn't surprised anymore about such families involved in drug trafficking. Why not, they had the logistics and the status to be above the law. It was now up to Mevs and Acra lawyers of to work on the cover story and let Haitian justice do its magic. The generation in charge of these businesses today didn't grow up with the same disciplined and hardworking mentality of their grandfathers, they were used to pass school with financial help and the rest of their lives as well. Additionally, the deteriorating economy must have hurt the businesses of the elite families as well over the past 20 years and they needed to find alternatives to maintain their status. Cocaine was just too easy. Their names and enterprises were big and well known enough that nobody would have questioned the permanent source of their wealth in US dollars, even the IRS. The business community offered this service to the drug dealing political elite that could not explain their US dollar income. It was convenient that there was no functional taxation or any form of law and order in the country. It made it just so easy. I was convinced that even some UN staff members made a lot of money on the side transporting cocaine from the South to Port au Prince, their UN vehicles were untouchable by the HNP. It was just such easy money.

The DEA estimate of the size of the drug load was 800 kg of cocaine and 300 kg of heroin with a US street value of 100 million US dollars. 'Ysca' had an easy catch, he was suddenly sitting on hundreds of kilos of cocaine packages and even some heroin. There was as usual in Haiti an ironic part to it, it was pre-election time, and Ysca was aligned with different politicians than the Acra brothers. The parliamentary elections were supposed to take place concurrent with the Presidential elections in October 2015. The Acra brothers supported the political party of Michel Martelly. 'Ysca' was aligned with the political opposition. He was sitting on drugs worth millions of dollars which could make a significant difference in campaign finances for the elections. This made the negotiations complicated and were far beyond Ysca's authority. While negotiations were ongoing Ysca' was trading one kilo of cocaine in exchange for one new HNP Galil rifle and ammunition to the HNP-UDMO base recently built in the center of Cité Soleil. The people of Cité Soleil called it the UDMO prison because they never left their base. Even if an injured civilian or victim of an incident knocked on their gate, they didn't open. They opened for Ysca though, who collected firepower to contribute to the success of his political partners in the upcoming elections. For the HNP officers, it was a great deal as well because the usual buyers were the politicians and they paid much less. I was just worried about the impact on the peace treaty among the gangs that had kept Cité Soleil a safer place than Petion Ville for the past two years.

In the meantime, the investigative judge actually suspected several people including the Mevs and Acra brothers, which resulted in temporary indictments. But this was not done to serve justice, it was done to serve the judge. The judge, as usual, declared in furious radio interviews that he was about to arrest all of them and bring them to justice. The posturing was simply done to raise the bar for financial negotiations with the suspects. It was Haitian Justice in its best. Most of the charges were dropped, and the man who was identified as the 'Kaiser Soze' was a low-level longshoreman, a worker from the terminal who was arrested and jailed. According to the Miami

Herald article, three years later he still awaited his trial for smuggling cocaine and heroin. As if all this wasn't enough, Martelly had to put a cherry on top of it. I had to give it to him, it was actually a symbolic decision. In January 2016, shortly before Martelly handed over his presidency to an Interim President because of the continuing election delay, Martelly appointed Marc Antoine Acra as Goodwill Ambassador of Haiti and granted him diplomatic status and immunity while he was still a suspect. The choice couldn't have been better since Goodwill Ambassadors, according to Wikipedia promote ideals from one entity to the other, or the population. Marc Antoine was not the first appointed Haitian diplomate with a questionable background. It was a presidential tool to protect friends by designating them as Ambassadors. Rene Preval appointed the former Secretary of State for Public Security under Aristide, Robert Manuel as Ambassador to Mexico before he was hired by the United Nations in their mission in Colombia. Nobody could blame the Haitian people for their distrust towards the International Community. They knew that the same evening the sugar boat was busted, or maybe one before or after, the Acra brothers were sitting down to dinner with Ambassadors, including the US.

CHAPTER 21
The Price for the Hope of Cité Soleil

Haiti, Port au Prince, May 2015

The three foremost gang leaders were not sitting at a lovely dinner table in a fancy restaurant when they agreed on no criminal activities inside their territories and safe passage for the population of the different areas within. They all agreed on a truce among themselves and with the government. The public kitchens financed by the programs of Prime Minister Lamothe were under the gang leader's supervision, and the people in Cité Soleil lived and slept in peace. It was actually amazing to watch how the gang leaders Ougan, Gabriel and Ysca were in the process of moving from community controller to community leader. Even though Lamothe's programs stopped after his resignation, the truce remained in place. Carl Alexandre visited Cité Soleil frequently, and since he spoke Creole, he held town hall meetings in the Hands Together high school with mostly parents, but later with broader audiences as well. He saw after his first visit what impact it had when 'the big chief' of MINUSTAH showed the people of Cité Soleil the respect to come and talk to them. At first, he needed a little bit of a push since he was a busy man. After Carl met Father Tom at some official ceremony, he was invited to the graduation of the Hands Together high school students in Cité Soleil. I became the relay communicating between him and Father Tom. Even though Carl was not yet long in the country, he was already sitting on the 'Haitian Carousel.' It was the process in place which kept every international decision maker with good intentions busy but also ineffective. Every rich Haitian liked to present himself as the one rich Haitian who wanted to change the country for more fairness for the poor. Every rich business person or politician had a project or a problem he was developing and liked to show to international decision makers to seek their help and support. None of the issues seemed very difficult to fix, except that there were so many of such small problems that the international decision maker just went from looking at one problem to another. When two years had passed, this international decision-maker was still looking at issues, and not one problem was fixed. Carl had to delay and delay until I finally wrote to him that the people of Cité Soleil were used to be on the bottom of the priority list of international or national politicians, but I would not ask Father Tom to further delay his graduation.

Carl didn't delay anymore. I coordinated with the Close Protection Unit and moved the actual location of the high-school a bit out of the red zone, so security measures didn't need to be too tight. I knew Carl wanted to come in low profile and not escorted by two jeeps full of soldiers of the Brazilian UN contingent. It was a fantastic event; the town hall was almost full. Some parents did not come because they did not have dresses which they considered appropriate for such a VIP. Carl Alexandre was the first MINUSTAH VIP who talked directly to the people of Cité Soleil. The word must have gotten out that he was there because suddenly the mayor of Cité Soleil arrived at the end of the ceremony. He was invited every year out of courtesy but couldn't give 'a rats ass,' as Jimmy Dutch would have said. Carl stayed focused on the people and not on the mayor. His time in

MINUSTAH left behind a Computer Center run by Hands Together named after Carl Alexandre as a thank you for his efforts and support. The center contained more than 75 computers with an electronic library of more than 50,000 e-books donated by a Canadian charity. The computer center had internet access, and the University of Los Angeles offered scholarships for online university degrees for the best graduates of the Hands Together high school. He also left behind the most modern soccer field on the island of Hispaniola. Carl Alexandre, the Brazilian Force Commander and the heavy machinery of the Brazilian UN contingent set the foundation for an artificial grass soccer field donated by Jones Day, a large US law firm. Since the soccer field was inside the premises of a Hands Together school in the heart of Cité Soleil, rules about its usage were strict, and it was not a recruitment center for the criminal gangs.

The first game on this field was a selection of the Brazilian UN contingent against a team from Cité Soleil chosen by Gabriel, Ougan, and Ysca. It was fantastic, and I hoped that all VIPs, US, Brazilian, other Ambassadors, and Carl Alexandre realized the symbolic of this event in the heart of Cité Soleil. Brazilian soldiers were playing with gang members of Cité Soleil. The gang leaders kept Cité Soleil safe. They were still criminals, and I knew about their criminal activities outside their territories. They had the mobility and left their strongholds on hundreds of motorbikes donated by friendly politicians and the business sector with their handguns to conduct their criminal activities in Petion Ville, around the airport or in other wealthy residential areas. But it was a first step in the right direction. Sometimes there were small issues inside Cité Soleil like two rival gang members were drunk and had a fight. It could always end up at the cemetery, but if such incidents happened, I received messages from the gang leaders to tell Carl Alexandre that it was just an accident, there was no war. Sometimes I could resolve issues in meetings with the representatives of all 'bases' of Cité Soleil. There was peace in Cité Soleil but no jobs. One of my visions was to exchange the charcoal used for cooking with briquets made out of banana leaves, paper, or anything that was not plastic. Haiti had almost no natural forest anymore, the deforestation was so extreme that it formed a visible natural border between Haiti and the Dominican Republic. Anybody flying from Santo Domingo to Port au Prince could identify immediately Haitian territory, the trees disappeared. 95 percent of cooking was done with charcoal, and nothing was in place to stop it. Father Tom's schools in Gonaives were already cooking with natural waste briquets. It was not complicated to produce. It needed a simple press and a different metal oven than the charcoal oven. All could be produced locally, and Haitians were very good with metal work and metal recycling, so this was no issue at all. The only real investment was a wood shredder that could have been rotated within the bases of Cité Soleil.

The plan was to provide each base with one or two presses and, the material for the briquets in the first stage was available in the garbage around. The plastic could have been separated, and the bottles could have been sold to an NGO that was already in Haiti buying plastic bottles. It had to be noted that depending on the wind, Caribbean beaches in Cuba and many other islands around Haiti suffered from garbage pollution, mostly plastic bottles coming from Haiti. Hands Together would have bought the briquets and the briquets ovens from the different bases. There were already studies made showing that besides the environmental benefits, natural briquets could be sold at least 35 percent cheaper than charcoal on the Haitian market. The first step to introduce the new ovens and briquets would have been to give it for free to the ladies in the markets who were cooking food for sale. Next would have been the households in Cité Soleil.

We would have had to compensate the shipments of charcoal arriving at the 'wharf,' the small port of Cité Soleil as well. Charcoal was brought to Port au Prince from the regions mainly on trucks, but Cité Soleil received it from Jeremie on boats. These boats could deliver fruits or other goods from Jeremie, but it would have been an important issue to resolve at an early stage. The man in charge of briquets production in Gonaives for Hands Together came to Port au Prince with an example of a wooden press and a metal oven to discuss a training schedule for the bases of Cité Soleil. I could see the fear in his face when he realized we wanted him to go to Cité Soleil. He had all the reasons; it was important not to forget where we operated. Even I still had Rudolph watching over me and my activities in secret. He updated me with inside stories so I could control my moves. I sat down sometimes in the middle of Belekou talking with Ysca or in Boston talking to Ougan, and my Glock 19 wouldn't have helped much if they wanted to set me up. I had to remind myself I was in ganglands, when they were at war with each other they barbequed rival gang members and ate them.

The pre-election period came closer, and there was already growing tension in Cité Soleil because of the different political candidates seeking the gang support. Rudolph warned me that in the Boston area, Ougan received money to start a war. He knew I had a meeting scheduled with all the bases. Rudolph advised me to be cautious because the wind was changing in Boston. The meeting started as usual until 'the twins,' two real twin brothers and gang members representing Boston began to bad mouth me and all other foreigners in Haiti. Rudolph was right again. I could see in the faces of the others that they knew it was coming. They didn't look disappointed or surprised, maybe a little sad. It seemed they just took it as the natural cause and effect of elections in Cité Soleil. I had to face the fact that Ougan was not yet a community leader, he was still a controller, a tool for somebody outside Cité Soleil. To gain political support, he had to start a war. The peace was about to be over, and as long as the elections didn't have a winner, this was going to get worse. I knew it was our last meeting. I just had one more message for them and for their gang leaders: "If you all want to know how much it costs to keep Cité Soleil the way it is and take away the hope from your people and children. Exactly the amount of money that Boston received to start the war is what its costs". I always had a Hands Together teacher with me to make sure my important messages were translated. I didn't even wait until he finished his translation. My car was parked inside the compound of the high school where we held the meetings, and I could get in my armored vehicle without issues. The school was on Soleil 9 not far from National # 1 not deep inside of Cité Soleil. Still, Rudolph visited a friend in the area and would have warned me during the meeting about any threat. The following night, the soldiers of Ougan attacked Gabriel's territory.

Gabriel controlled the largest population of Cite Soleil, and his cousin was expected to run as Deputy for an opposition party. This area held the majority of voters and was crucial for successful elections. Reginald Boulos and other businesses on the airport road wanted to replace Gabriel to ensure the majority of Cité Soleil supported the candidate of Martelly's political party. I saw several videos made by Brazilian soldiers of the fighting. They were not allowed to interfere without a request from the Haitian authorities. According to the evaluations from the MINUSTAH Police Commissioner to New York, the HNP had developed so well that they could handle any situation. They didn't consider the politics that prevented the HNP from doing their job if the gang conflict was related to political causes. According to the long-term plans, MINUSTAH had already started downsizing Military contingents since the mission was to come to an end within the next two years. MINUSTAH military only acted on the demand of the host government in support of HNP. The population of Cité Soleil suffered again while HNP and MINUSTAH were watching. It showed the people that even MINUSTAH accepted the natural cause and effect of elections in Cité Soleil. The fighting stopped when Gabriel and Ougan found a solution, Gabriel's cousin ran for the position of Deputy under the banner of Martelly's political party PHTK.

This made Ysca the next target whose childhood friend Junior, planned to run for Deputy from Cité Soleil as well. Unfortunately, the pre-election period went on until November 2016. The longer pre-election periods took the more damage they did. More weapons, motorbikes and ammunition was given to the gangs and caused more fighting and suffering for the population in the gang strongholds. MINUSTAH and the HNP kept on watching. Not just in Cité Soleil, in the entire metropolitan area, HNP officers couldn't arrest anybody before checking with the commissaire whether they were allowed to bring the criminal to the police station or should let him go on the spot. First, the commissaire had to check the political connections of the bandit, he might have been connected with an influential political player and the future Deputy, Senator or even President. The safer choice was always, let the bandit go. Ysca withstood the pressure from Gabriel and Ougan for a long time. He bought a lot of firepower with the Acra 'sugar,' but at some point, he had to decide. He could stay loyal to his friend, Junior and his political alliance or end the suffering of his people and look for a truce. He lived among his population and saw them suffering, maybe this made the difference to Martelly. But most likely Ysca was really in charge and could decide. He agreed to a truce and to not interfere in the election of Deputy Lemaire, the Senator or the Martelly's presidential candidate. But he also didn't support or allow politics to interfere with him or Belekou anymore. He cut ties to all politicians, even to his friend Junior and his political alliance. He did not allow any candidate or politician to campaign or place any poster in his controlled territories. This was a huge step because as a consequence, he removed all the voters in his areas from the upcoming elections as well which was a significant number of votes. Ysca declared Belekou independent from politics and became the biggest threat to a system that kept a small percentage of people in paradise and the majority of Haitians in hell.

Life outside Cité Soleil did not yet face many changes. An older woman could still go safely with the tap-taptap-tap from Delmas 31 to the 'Station Gonaives' where the buses leave Port au Prince to the North of the country. One old lady wanted to go to Cap Haitian to see a Voodoo priest to seek protection for her son from the spirits. She came from Cap Haitian with her husband and their young son many years ago when the sugar plantation in their region closed. They moved to Belekou in hope of work. Her husband became a lawyer, at least everybody in Belekou believed he was a lawyer because he could get birth certificates. It was not complicated, he just needed to go to the courthouse, write the name in a book that was laid open in a room and pay the fee to get the paper. But he could write so he could get the paper. He could make the children of illiterate, undocumented and unregistered people official citizens. For the people of Belekou, he was an advocate.

The bus went the shortest way through Cité Soleil on Soleil 9 or as this new part was called, 'American Boulevard.' She could even see her house in Belekou, her son still lived there. He moved her out of Cité Soleil some time ago because of the violence. Just after Bois Neuf at the North end of Cité Soleil, the bus was stopped by armed men. Gang members from Bois Neuf stopped the bus, and some of Gabriel's soldiers entered it. They didn't want to rob the bus; they were looking for somebody. They took the old lady outside. One of them made a video call and showed the other end of the conversation the face of the old woman, he turned the screen back and just nodded his head towards one of Gabriel's soldiers, then pointed his gun at the woman's head and pulled the trigger. The old woman was the only person Ysca ever allowed to hit him, his mother.

The trigger was pulled by Gabriel's man, but the order came from politicians. The information about the mother, where she lived, where she was going or how she looked like must have come from somebody close to Ysca. Maybe even his childhood friend Junior since Ysca became useless to his political ambitions. Ysca stopped being a tool for politics and this was his punishment. But it was also expected that Ysca would make a mistake, expose himself and could be killed. The mother's body was never recovered; this was done so that Ysca could not get back at the killers with a Voodoo spell. In his rage, Ysca's initial reaction was to stop a 'tap-tap' coming from Gabriel's territory and force it into Belekou. All 'tap-tap's' have a metal construction to provide shade on top and on the sides, just the back was open for people to get on and off. They forced the driver to park the car with the back against a wall so nobody could get out. After his soldier shot the driver, they poured gasoline over the 'tap-tap' and burned the passengers alive. The neighboring territories of Gabriel could hear their screams. Ysca was left behind alone in this world full of hatred. He stated that he was dead inside and the only thing that kept his body breathing was the hope of making Gabriel feel his suffering. As long as Ysca and Gabriel were in charge, there would never be peace again. I thought to myself that in the future Gabriel better keep a cyanide capsule in his teeth, just in case he falls in Ysca's hands alive. To date, Ysca has withstood all attacks and remained the first independent gang leader I have ever heard of in Haiti.

CHAPTER 22

Blood Sacrifice

Haiti, Port au Prince, September 2015

It was said to be a super moon and a blood moon, never seen by any generation in this lifetime and was occurring on the night of 27 to 28 September 2015. I didn't know that there was more than just a full moon and read about it a few days before. On Monday morning just before the last turn to my office, I saw the moon almost in front of me. It really looked amazing, orange and much bigger than usual. I saw the moon there frequently in the morning, but never like this, it looked beautiful. My office was now in Charly Camp, the UN camp for military contingents based in Port au Prince. It also included the Regional UNPOL headquarters and UN clinic. The only two security offices here were Ray's training unit and SICU with Pike and me. Niko had joined Ray as a firearms instructor some time ago and since most of the Security containers were also in Charly Camp, our Logistics officer Cege had a great reason to maintain a satellite office in Ray's unit. It was the third training center Ray had built in his MINUSTAH time since all Security Units moved after the earthquake from the UN Log Base to Delta Camp next to the US embassy, and it was the best. When Ray was offered a spot in Charly camp next to his shooting range, Pike, my supervisor explained to the CSA that it was necessary for us to be close to our UNPOL colleagues and we moved with Ray. We had a small compound separated from the rest with our gym, the classroom and a briefing room for SICU with a fridge. The shooting range was 50 steps from our offices, it was a perfect set up. We had absolute peace and could work out or do some shooting exercises every morning before we had our coffee. We were so isolated that even Ray could sometimes give training sessions to HNP officers who worked in secret with me. Since Pike was my constant shield when he was here and attended all meetings, nobody in the Security Section actually knew if I was in the mission area or not. If I needed to go someplace with back up, I had the best shooters right there with me. With the constant support from Cege in Logistics, I always had an armored vehicle and an alternative vehicle with tinted windows for my family since a child seat didn't fit very well in a non-family duty station.

Occasionally we had beer and cigars after work, it was like a support group meeting to keep us sane in the MINUSTAH circus. We had frequent outside visitors who had clearance from the Brazilian Military checkpoint to enter and exit without special procedures. Walter, alias 'The Motomedic' from the US embassy was always happy to join. He was reserved about his skills but was a true professional. He was not just the medical emergency plan for the US embassy, also for the Zombie Hunters since we tried to avoid the UN clinic. Past experience taught us to use alternative resources for medical care. Since I had my family as well in the country, I needed an emergency solution before we could reach good medical care in Miami and Moto-Medic provided it for all of us. It was Monday morning, and we had a few days until our next support group meeting on Thursday. When I finished my morning workout with Ray, I quickly went through the reports from the weekend to brief Pike on his arrival while Ray prepared the morning coffee. It was paradise and the best'

UN presence environment' I ever had. I stopped calling it 'UN work environment' ever since I met Bill in Chad and when I asked him what he did before he joined the UN his answer was:" I worked." To receive our salary, we just had to be present.

This Monday morning, I skipped coffee. I was looking at the Daily UNPOL report from yesterday and a kidnapping incident in Jeremie. A newborn baby was kidnapped from the hospital in Jeremie, so far, no contact was made with the kidnappers. I remembered talking with Reggie a while back about a kidnapping case in which the victim was never found again. Reggie told me that sometimes these kidnappings were Voodoo related, and the victims were selected and killed as sacrifices for black magic. I didn't know why my mind always neglected such stories but not this morning. It really hit me; I was shocked. When I read the UNPOL report, I thought of the particular full moon, and I knew it was real, this baby was not taken for ransom, it was chosen to become a blood sacrifice in a ritual. There were always stories about the black magic and many times people accused of such witchcraft were lynched by the population. My rational mind considered the black magic of Voodoo to be related to the use of poison to harm people or lower somebody's breathing to a point near death to have him resurrected as a zombie. But human sacrifices? I could never grasp or acknowledge the existence of any form of belief that justified sacrificing a baby. Later that day I managed to reach a UNPOL officer in Jeremie, and he confirmed to me that everybody suspected the baby was stolen to be slaughtered because of the full moon. It was a particular full moon, and the baby was the first-born son of a young mother. Somebody powerful paid a lot of money to an Ougan, the male, or a Mambo, the female Voodoo priests to gain more power from an evil spirit. Maybe one of the candidates running for the parliament or presidency wanted to get a head start with black magic. I knew already that all the drug dealing politicians were very superstitious and deep into the Voodoo power. This was not just in Haiti, when I talked to policemen from Colombia or Mexico, they told me the same thing. They all had their 'bruja' or 'brujo,' the female or male witch in Spanish to use the spiritual world in their favor. But I never considered the evil of it as it became so real for me this morning.

I knew from history that the Celts, Incas, Aztecs, and many other cultures used sacrifices and in extreme cases human sacrifices to please their gods, but we live in the time of the Internet and interactive cyberworlds. That this still existed today was just nuts. I heard the stories that Aristide had babies stolen out of the general hospital to be slaughtered in sacrificial rituals by his Voodoo priests or that he bathed in human blood. One of my colleagues who arrived in the first days of MINUSTAH in Haiti was at Aristide's looted residence and saw skulls of babies in some creepy room. But I always brushed it off as propaganda or misinterpretation, and of course, it was still possible there was a reasonable explanation for it. Who didn't have a human baby skull in his home? Even when I came across UNPOL reports from Jacmel over the past two years that recorded dead bodies without head or right hand in a seemingly regular frequency, I didn't make the connection, like something in my mind blocked me or protected me from seeing it. But this was real and thinking back, it would have been interesting if these dead bodies in Jacmel without head or right hand were related to the moon calendar. I realized I had found a great topic for our next support group meeting on Thursday with beer and cigars and did some research.

I consulted a Voodoo priest, an Ougan with healing force. He explained to me that a male Voodoo priest can either connect with the light only, or the dark only. An Ougan heals and a Bokor does black magic. Only Mambos can connect with both the evil and the healing force. It was fascinating to see the Haitian's reaction when I asked about these sacrifices. Some told me what they heard or even experienced, and some were just laughing about it and told me it was just nonsense. They must have known it existed, maybe they were deep into this themselves? The black magic of Voodoo was a sensitive topic, and most people were frightened by it. Francois Duvalier, 'Papa Doc' was also called the Voodoo Dictator and built his power based on the African roots and its Voodoo religion mixed with Catholic beliefs. He ended the ruling power of the mulatto minority and catholic church that suppressed the African roots with the support of Haitians in the countryside and their religion, Voodoo. 'Papa Doc' was a US-educated doctor who gained popularity in his fight against malaria and other diseases. Once he declared himself as president for life his title was not enough anymore to keep power, he transformed the spiritual power of Voodoo into the material world and created his militia, the 'Ton Ton Macoute.' It was a Stasi, Gestapo type of paramilitary secret police. 'Ton Ton Macoute,' was a mythical figure that stole unruly children and ate them for breakfast, and this gave a hint about their tolerance. Many 'Ton Ton Macoute' were Voodoo priests and had spiritual and material power over the population. I read that 'Papa Doc' even dressed as the image of 'Baron Samedi' the most powerful Voodoo spirit, the spirit of the dead. Duvalier knew very well the power of Voodoo since he published in 1944 an academic research paper about Voodoo's influence in the successful slave revolt against the French. The real interesting question now would be, did he actually believe in the spirits, or did he just use it and master its power over the Haitian mind?

The violence of the Voodoo priests against international Catholic priests after his election resulted in the formal excommunication of 'Papa-Doc' by the Vatican and all foreign priests left the country. The Voodoo priests took their place since Haitian Voodoo had many Catholic aspects. Years later, the Vatican returned to Haiti and granted Duvalier even the right to appoint his own Vatican officials, which was a unique power and could maintain the intense mix of Voodoo. It would be interesting to know how much the teaching of exorcism of the Vatican differs from the Voodoo version of liberating a possessed person. His son 'Baby Doc' inherited at age 19 the spiritual and material Haiti from 'Papa Doc' and watched it until his departure with 34 years of age. When the Duvalier regime ended, many Ton Ton Macoutes or Voodoo priests faced retaliation from the population and went into hiding until Aristide gave them a legal status as an official Haitian religion.

I always understood Aristide as the political opposition to Duvalier, but on the spiritual level, they agreed very much on how to rule and control the population. Aristide might have been a priest, but the young 'chimères' in his orphanage grew up with Voodoo to become Aristide's version of the 'Ton Ton Macoute.' Aristide had a deep-rooted connection with Duvalier's form of control actually. His father was a 'Ton Ton Macoute.' A Voodoo priest told me that his father was also an Ougan and lynched by the population for witchcraft. Maybe he created the 'chimères' as a punishment for the people who killed his father, the Haitian population. Duvalier created the 'Ton Ton Macoute' to compensate for the power of the Haitian Army, and Aristide created the 'Chimères' to compensate for the power of the Haitian Police. Both groups ruled by the fear they spread within the population. The Voodoo priest explained further that it all came down to light and darkness, love and fear, low and high frequencies. The low vibration of hate, fear, and greed was the frequency of evil. The Voodoo drums just had to beat to these frequencies to awake and connect with these evil spirits. In Haiti, the power of the darkness was extreme because the dark side controlled the environment.

This was a scary thought because if an elite believed in maintaining their power with the force of darkness, and this force was only strong as long people were suffering, they would never let Haiti change its frequency and rise out of the ashes. They had to keep Haiti precisely as it was. If greed and egoism were aligned with the dark force, it was a simple way to see it and was actually the in-depth underlying explanation for many Haitians why their country was cursed. Somehow, I couldn't blame them since nothing changed after billions of US dollars were donated to the Haitians. Even the most powerful couple the world ever experienced, at least since Cleopatra and Julius Cesar, the Clintons loved and enjoyed visiting and influencing Haiti since 1975, and yet the country and its people were still on the bottom. The Voodoo priest also told me it all came with a price to pay. The spirit would grant you your wish, but the bad energy would get to you as well at some point, like in Goethe's Faust, when Faust sold his soul to the devil for power and knowledge until it bit him in the ass. Many Voodoo priests in Haiti believed that Aristide's mental and health issues were a result of the black magic he used to stay in power catching up with him. I have no idea if Aristide has mental or health issues, but this would in general make sense to me. I was never much into religion but always believed in the principle of what comes around, goes around. Whatever I did bad, it will hunt me and catch up with me one day.

I got to know of a young man from a wealthy family in Haiti. His aunt was a voodoo priest with the talent to connect with the light, but also the dark. The family had some issues and reached out to the spiritual world, the spirit demanded a sacrifice, the first-born son of the family. The young man, the chosen sacrifice, realized that his family was going to mourn his sad, sudden death in wealth and luxury. He got on the next plane to the US and never returned. It could be an ordinary homeless person, as were the cases with the dead bodies in Jacmel. These dead bodies had the head or the right hand cut off. According to the Voodoo priest, the right side is the connection to the spiritual world, somehow the spirit cannot do much with the left hand. If a person demands something extremely powerful from the spirit, it requires a sacrifice of a newborn, a first-born son or even from one's own blood family. At first it sounded crazy, but on the other hand, I didn't have to look back in history, just to the wars or civil wars of today that were so predictable it suggested they were intentionally created for money and power of a small elite. If so, this elite didn't care about the fear and suffering it causes. The principle is the same just the sacrifice is on a much larger scale. The trouble of connecting with the dark side was that it couldn't bring happiness. That's why Darth Vader was never laughing in Star Wars. It's like an angry man trying to get happy by applying more anger. Greed and power always demand more. The desire for more is a bitch, it is infinite.

Our thoughts and feelings are energy and create the world we live in. It is said that if we focus hard enough, we can achieve anything we want, some maybe just don't believe it without dark spirits or a drastic event like a sacrifice. I started to see it relatively simplistically, it starts with small steps such as telling a child to grab something to be safe, instead of telling the child, not to fall. The second way already indicates a negative result and makes a fall more likely. I understood the fear factor in the system and its power, not just in Haiti. It exists in everybody's life and has an enormous influence. How many people make an important decision in their lives based on fear? They didn't follow their dreams because they were afraid of giving up their job, their safety, and their comfort zone. Decisions or actions based on fear were unlikely to produce happiness. I was never into Fengshui or anything similar, but I looked at the yin yang symbol differently since the Voodoo priest explained to me that we all have the dark and the light in us. I understood we could do evil things; the difference was the intent to use the evil force. For example, self-defense requires a violent action with a justified purpose. I wished Luc Skywalker would have met this Voodoo priest, he was always afraid of the dark side in him, instead of acknowledging it and keep using it for the right intent against the baby eating Darth Vader's.

It was a spooky subject, somehow scary and I remembered one sentence got into my mind over and over: Don't be afraid. I remembered it from childhood and that I heard it in church and wondered if this was the main message in the bible, not to let fear, the evil, control me. Not to give in these low frequencies to overcome me and my actions. I never gave praying much thought, but if all our thoughts are energy, praying actually made sense. It's like focusing on a goal. Some studies claim that mass meditation for peace could avoid several deaths in conflict zones. This would be an entirely new concept for peacekeeping operation missions, 10,000 meditating soldiers with a Guru in the middle, it would be worth a try. I actually realized that there were many quotes in the bible which were trying to protect us from our natural enemy and also our closest friend, our ego, which is the portal for the evil to get to us. We are so egocentric that we consider the world we see and feel is our outside experience, but it is just what we believe we see, it is the interpretation of the information our eyes and other senses send to our brain, and in fact, it is our inside experience. Depending on how our brain is wired it interprets the world. Our outside experience is the cause and effect of our actions, how our environment and people react to our actions and our thoughts. This is what connects all of us and defines the frequency of the vibration around us, it represents our world.

In the end, the use of Voodoo comes down to power like many religions or systems designed to control the masses. Unfortunately, I developed the suspicion that black magic had a much more significant impact on incidents and events in Haiti than expected and would be worth a closer look, because there are certain days that the connection between the spiritual world and the material world is stronger, and Voodoo spell or ritual has more power. Full moons, new moons, days with the numbers 13, 31, or days which occur only every four years like 29 February are used a lot. I assume that many incidents in Haiti correlated to these special energetic Voodoo days and could shed some light on the possible extension of its influence in Haiti. Max Beauvoir was elected supreme leader of all Haitian Voodoo priests in 2008. He held the Voodoo ceremony in 1975 that ignited Bill Clinton's interest in Voodoo culture. He didn't mention in his book if it was the woman who bit of the head off a chicken or the man who walked on hot coals, but he was so inspired that he gave his political career another try.

I wonder if he was asking the spirits for help. Bill Clinton also mentioned in his book the secret of zombification that was studied by Harvard researchers and that Max Beauvoir helped to encounter. It was a powder made out of poison extracted from the puffer fish. With the right dose, it could lower a person's breathing to a level close to death. Max Beauvoir also explained in an interview after the earthquake that Haitians were much less fearful of death than other cultures because according to Voodoo culture, everybody lived 18 times. The statement almost suggested that a Haitian life could be easily spared since most likely there were many more to come and was a dangerous viewpoint with regard to human sacrifices. It was his belief, and one wonders how many times he tried it until he died at the age of 79 in 2015. It sounded to me like the underlying reasoning and justification for sacrifices. I heard a similar rationale behind the broader acceptance of homosexual practices in the Voodoo religion because it is more liberal, not homophobic. But it is never mentioned that anal sex has significant meaning in black magic rituals, especially involuntary and the rape victims in such ceremonies can be very young. The religious aspect of some of these rituals seems to be just a cover up for sick criminal offenses. Max Beauvoir was a western-educated man and was too smart to talk about the black magic of Voodoo, but as the supreme leader, he must have been a black magic master as well.

The general population is deeply rooted in Voodoo without sacrificing anything or anyone. When anyone identifies somebody who did, they meet a violent end. I couldn't blame the population since I didn't believe that many justice systems in the world were prepared for ritual baby murders, definitely not the Haitian justice system. I would hope that black magic does not have power over Haitian politics and life as it seems, but the indicators raise suspicion. Even in the election of Martelly, an outspoken opponent of Aristide received a significant and maybe deciding support in his campaign when Aristide's Voodoo priestess 'So-Ann' surprisingly endorsed him. She was the soul of Aristide's 'Lavalas' movement and endorsed Martelly. From one moment to the next 'So-Ann' was cheered by both pro- and anti-Aristide Haitians. 'So-Ann' was said to have prepared a unique bath with human blood for Aristide, maybe she did the same for Martelly. My supervisor Pike always said:" Divide and rule. Let the masses believe they support two different causes while their leaders sit together and sip champagne."

Listen to the person who is seeking the truth but be cautious about the one who claimed he found it.

CHAPTER 23
Narcos-Re-Union

Haiti, Port au Prince, March 2015

In March 2015, while the election campaigns slowly started to kick off and 'Son Son La Familia' was in hiding, the manager of the Claude Construction company based in Delmas 33 went to the bank to withdraw money for his workers payroll. He was accompanied by a Dominican colleague and not far away from his office when a motorbike struck his vehicle. He stepped out of the vehicle to assess the damage and was shot dead by three armed criminals on the motorbike', one of many violent crimes in the capital of Haiti. It was common modus operandi of the criminal gangs to observe banks to select their targets and follow them to a convenient ambush location. Many times, they received detailed information from inside the bank about the exact amount of the transactions. It looked like a normal violent armed robbery in Port au Prince, except that anybody coming from the bank would have been very suspicious of a motorbike with three men on it and even more so if this motorbike hit their car. Definitely, the person wouldn't have just gotten out of the car. It turned out later that no money was stolen. It was not an armed robbery; it was an assassination. The fact that he stepped out of the car could indicate that he actually knew somebody he wanted to greet or even knew the killers. But still, it would have been just another victim of a violent crime, if the victim hadn't been Oriel Jean. Oriel Jean was the security chief of the National Palace for Aristide from 2001 to 2003. He was also a key witness against other suspected Haitian drug traffickers in a trial in Florida after his arrest in 2003. It was said his testimony was crucial to sending big fishes and junior partners of Jaques Ketant like Serge Eduard to jail. Like in Youri Latorture's days as palace security, Oriel Jean was the authority and had oversight and control over the financial contribution to the country from the drug transit operation throughout Haiti. He knew who delivered to the 'Palais National' and how much and spent just a few years in jail until 2006 due to his cooperation and worked after his release at the Miami airport. He returned to Haiti in 2012.

His murder immediately became political theater. One half of Haiti suspected Aristide was behind the killing, the other half accused the CIA or Martelly. I guessed somebody like Serge Eduard had several years of reasons more than the others since he received a life sentence. Serge Eduard was very creative, and Ketant loved to brainstorm with him at parties in Ketant's house about different ways to smuggle cocaine into the United States. I guess the list of possible enemies was long since more than 16 Haitians and one Colombian were arrested for serious drug charges between 2003 and 2005. Many of them were Haitian officials under Aristide who downplayed their role in the cocaine business and pointed at privateers like Jaques Ketant, Serge Eduard or 'Ed 1', Jean Eliobert Jasme. I also thought it interesting that many of these arrests and extraditions were authorized by Aristide in 2003. He must have tried to clean house and his refute image as President of a narco-state. I imagine he also hoped to improve relations with the Bush administration since the US started to question the support of a majority of the Haitians for him.

The arrests didn't save his presidency but might have helped to keep him away from US justice since he handed over all these suspects alive. There was not much information circulating about the killing. Jean didn't have political ambitions, and he seemed to be a private man working for a construction company. The construction company, Claude Construction, was located in a large building in Delmas 33. It was also a club, a casino, and a private lottery business. Claude Guillaume, a businessman from the South of Haiti, owned the building, the lottery, the casino, and the construction company. I couldn't get much on him or about him. It seemed to be unrelated to the murder.

Haiti forgot about it when Hillary Clinton announced her candidacy to run for President of the United States. Since her successful election was not questioned by anybody at the time, Haitians tried to prepare themselves for her as the next President of the United States. Even though, or maybe precisely because of the long history of Bill and Hillary Clinton with Haiti, many Haitians were very suspicious about this future. The Haitian population was already divided in the past about their close relationship with President Aristide, and since Bill Clinton was the face for the heavily criticized earthquake relief efforts, Haitians were extremely skeptic. The Haitians living in the United States might have been more supportive to her, but I saw in the 2008 primaries against Barack Obama that most Haitians preferred the first black President over Hillary Clinton. But I understood the argument from many internationals and wealthy Haitians that she was at least more involved and focused on Haiti than any other candidate and this could be only positive for Haiti, or at least favorable for the elite in Haiti. It was about one week after that, another news rocked Haitian radio and TV waves. A federal judge reduced the 27-year sentence of Jaques Ketant in half, and he was about to be released from prison. He was not the only one, 'Ed 1' former junior partner of Jaques Ketant had received the same news a few years before and was just about to finish his prison term as well. Both came on special flights with many other Haitian deportees back to Haiti. The Ibo Lele Hotel prepared for a big party in May 2015. 'Ed 1' arrived a few days earlier, and when Ketant arrived, he was welcomed at the airport by Garcia Delva and Roro Nelson. Garcia, or Gracia Delva, as he called himself as a popular 'konpa' singer was welcoming Ketant in the name of Youri Latorture. Roro Nelson was welcoming Jaques Ketant for President Martelly. There was a short hold up since the BLTS unit had to finish some formalities first but then was party time in Ibo Lele.

The hotel was empty as usual, and all rooms were available for the narco-family and their entourage. I knew about the party because I was told 'Flex,' one of the US DEA most wanted Haitians was with them. He was said to be ruthless; a former Aristide kill squad leader; he had a room in Ibo Lele next to 'Ed 1' and acted as his bodyguard. At the time the DEA seemed to have no interest in their most wanted. Actually, I believed they should have shown a bit more interest to the guest list in general. President Martelly hosted the party since he was a good friend with the owners of Ibo Lele and with 'Ed 1'. I picked up a few more pieces of the puzzle in the huge network of past and present Haitian drug trafficking; Martelly was a tool for this family until he became a member when he married Sophia. Her father, Charles "Bebe" Saint Remis was a business partner of 'Ed 1', they facilitated drug and money movements for the Ketant cartel between the United States and Haiti, and the young Martelly was moving money for Charles "Bebe" Saint Remis. At least now I knew how 'Kiko' Saint Remis, his son and bother in law to Martelly made it to mid-level management in Jaques Ketant's organization; he learned the business from his father. My question which was first, the relationship with the daughter or the business with the father in law, was ignored, but I learned further that Martelly and his concerts in the United States became a money laundering machine for the Ketant and Co. cartel. Many names from this evening I never heard about and didn't pay much attention to, except Claude Guillaume. The employer of Oriel Jean was at the Ibo Lele as well and seemed to be one of the big shots. He was Jaques Ketant's cousin.

It was awful timing for US justice to release drug lords Ketant and 'Ed 1' in this pre-election period. While the democratic primaries started in the US, Haiti was just a few months away from the parliamentary and presidential elections. It could only increase the amount of cocaine and the money resulting from it since elections were not only expensive in the United States, but also in Haiti. Ketant and 'Ed 1' just slipped back into their organization which never stopped trafficking. But according to the DEA, 'Ed 1' retired to Miragoane and Ketant retired to the South of Haiti. They visited Port au Prince from time to time to have a chat with the local DEA agents. It was not a secret, on the contrary, it was almost like a status symbol. 'Kiko' St. Remis more less had it in his CV that he was a DEA informant. For Haitians, this was like being granted immunity by the DEA since everybody knew they were still moving narcotics. These 'rehabilitated' criminals talking to the DEA were like the informants of JMAC in MINUSTAH sent and controlled by Haitian politicians and the business community. It gave them not only the opportunity to control their knowledge and information, they also learned what the DEA knew. Of course, I was not aware of all the obstacles DEA agents faced in Haiti, but some of these obstacles seemed pretty obvious. Drugs were no secret, and also the DEA presence and activities were no secret either. Even I knew their safe houses in different locations and when they met 'Kiko", Ketant or 'Ed 1'. Ketant traveled in a motorcade of a minimum three to four vehicles like a president.

The DEA seemed to be pretty much doomed in Haiti. Even if they signed up a serious informant, a real mole, the chance that this informant would be exposed was very high. Haiti was just too small to keep it a secret. Haitian drug dealers were smart enough to use such a snitch for their advantage instead of killing him, they turned the snitch. Of course, if I had the choice between becoming a chain saw 'chop chop' or a double informant, the answer was obvious. Only in cases when the individuals cooperating with the DEA were on a high level in the cartel and had the overall details of the joint drug operation, the cartel didn't hesitate to terminate the threat. Such a high-level threat was most likely Evinx Daniel who disappeared in January 2015. He was the owner of Dan's Creek in Port Salut, the favorite hotel for many internationals on the weekend and President Martelly until hurricane Mathew made an aquarium out of it. He was the drug lord controlling the shipments arriving in the South where most of the cocaine was transiting through Haiti. He was one of the main players in the cartel until his vehicle was found abandoned in Gonaives. His body was never recovered, and it was possible that it was for Voodoo spirit reasons, since the Haitian cocaine family was very superstitious and deeply into black magic Voodoo. There were all kinds of speculations. I could imagine Herve Foucard, the future Senator of the South and Daniel's wife had a good idea what happened to him since Foucard took over Dan's operation and according to friends, also the widow. Daniel might have just retired voluntarily to the Bahamas. But it was more likely he was marked and disposed of as a threat by the cartel, even though he was just an environmentalist.

Evinx Daniel was cleaning the sea in September 2014. He fished 50 bags of Marihuana out of the sea. It was actually dumped by a boat which was running aground and was stuck for some time. The local HNP units were not an issue, Daniel had them on the payroll. Only if Port au Prince heard about it, it got complicated, and the word was spreading fast. Usually, it was a regular event, a drug boat that couldn't move anymore and risked attracting too much attention just informed their contacts and dropped the bags, the fishermen picked it up and transported it individually inland in small portions to an agreed-upon meeting point. They would be part of the average population traveling on buses, motorbikes or other transportation and more or less untraceable. Far inland the fishermen received their price for the service, and the load was saved and regathered. This time something went wrong, and he was arrested. His arrest was big news since everybody knew of his friendship with Martelly and his rank in the cartel and everybody knew it could only happen because of US DEA involvement. His quick release was surprising and must have made his partners suspicious. Most likely they sacrificed him for the safety of the rest. Herve Foucard was already a junior partner and the perfect replacement since nobody questioned his successful election as Senator.

The list of candidates running for parliament looked like a who's who in the Haitian narcotic scene and bringing back Ketant and 'Ed 1' at a time when campaign finances were needed, could only mean more drugs and money moving between Haiti and the United States. Even Guy Phillippe was running for Senator, he finally watched and learned from the strategist Youri Latorture. At first, it was necessary to become a respected politician and Senator in the eyes of the international community before he aimed for the highest public office in the country, the presidency. This was the final goal for everybody who needed immunity for life, as it was perceived by some that Aristide had this privilege because he was a democratically elected President. Others claimed that Aristide's immunity was based on a book in which he described the details about his relations with US administrations, especially Bill and Hillary Clinton and that this book was safeguarded by an unknown number of people. I could imagine Aristide handed enough drug dealers including Jaques Ketant to the US authorities to gain his immunity, from 'country' to 'country.' When some of them testified against him, they didn't realize that Aristide had already sold them out. But for this election period, all candidates were safe from the long arm of US Justice. Every candidate running for parliament or president was granted immunity just for being a candidate.

Youri Latorture and his sidekick Garcia Delva were running for Artibonite Senate seats. Joseph Willot, who controlled landing strips (not the Federal Aviation Agency approved-type) for fixed-wing planes coming with cocaine from Venezuela in Central Plateau was seeking immunity again. Joseph Lambert aimed to continue representing the people of Jacmel. Ralph Féthière, another 'Ecuador Boy' aimed to keep control over the ports in the North of the country, and Hervé Foucard became the new drug lord in the South and was naturally selected Senator for this area. There were many more candidates than available immunities, but the above names were absolutely solid bets to have the majority for successful elections. They might have been running in the past for Lavalas or other political parties, this time most of them gathered under either Martelly's PHTK movement or Youri's AAA party. Money and drugs didn't know political colors or preferences, just the green of the US dollar bill. Negotiations were ongoing among the candidates and competition about who was entitled to win and what terms they could offer to the losers. The elections were canceled, annulled or delayed further and further and most negotiations found agreements, one way or the other. My supervisor Pike always said:" Don't worry about the Haitian elections, once the US elections are finished, Haiti will have a President as well." It seemed most candidates agreed already on the terms of losing and winning and it didn't look like many cases were leading to violent confrontations.

When I heard of the assassination of Jean-Marie Liphete, my first thought was that Acra wanted to cover their tracks. He was their security chief when the sugar boat was busted by the DEA-HNP operation. His name was never mentioned in the media, and I thought why kill him? And when I heard, Jean-Marie Liphete was shot and killed in broad daylight in front of an Acra office, I thought how stupid. I pre-judged the situation, it was not about the sugar boat anymore, Haitian justice took care of it. It was the final offer in negotiations with his political competition and settled the case. His competitor was Claude Guillaume, former employer of Oriel Jean and cousin of Jaques Ketant. Claude Guillaume was running for the political party of Jean Henry Ceant, presidential candidate and former Aristide notary. He was said to be the primary money launderer for most of the big drug traffickers in the country. Liphet and Guillaume were competitors in the race for the Deputy of Petit-Trou-de-Nippes/Plaisance in the Nippes department. It was a beautiful quiet place in the South of Haiti, the birthplace of Jaques Ketant.

During the negotiations, Ketant called Liphete and offered him a good deal if he let Claude Guillaume win the elections. It was fair from Ketant since I was told that the tip to the DEA about the Acra sugar boat came directly from the cell in which Jaques Ketant spent his last year in jail. Liphete didn't give in. He went a step further; he gave disturbing details about his competition during a radio interview in Petion Ville close to the Hotel El Rancho. He stated that Claude Guillaume was an American citizen, was arrested for drug trafficking in the states and a fugitive wanted in the United States. As a US citizen, if true, he was not eligible to run for a position in the Haitian parliament, as there were some examples of candidates taken off the list. Liphete left the radio station and drove to his office at the Acra building less than 20 minutes away. The killers took him out of his car, dragged him on the street in brought daylight, put a gun in his mouth and executed him. I never read any report about this radio interview or the information he stated. It showed me how and who controlled the Haitian media and how confidential and quiet the media and rumor machine of Haiti became when it was related to Ketant's affairs. But this was not even the best of the story.

Claude Guillaume was family, a cousin of Jaques Ketant and was running his business while Jaques was in jail in the US. Before that, Claude was overseeing the distribution of Ketant's cocaine in Florida. Claude Guillaume is a US citizen and was arrested in 2001 with 4 kg of cocaine in his vehicle, and the police seized 2,7 million US dollars in cash at his residence. He must have had a great lawyer since he pled guilty and didn't face much prison time. But since in the US even money gained from drug trafficking is subject to income tax, the IRS calculated almost one million US dollars income tax to be paid retroactively by Claude Guillaume to the United States of America. A flight to Port au Prince was much cheaper, and since the 'Pate' Jaques Ketant was arrested, he needed to take care of family business in Haiti anyway. Claude's family runs the Guillaume foundation, a charity organization which was a very well-known move by several drug traffickers to connect themselves with foreigners who actually wanted to help, and a donation was merely online. In Haitian reality, the Guillaume family ran Jaques Ketant's narco-trafficking operation, the biggest and most successful logistics operation in Haiti. The family was also the key to the rise of the Ketant brothers.

Claude distributed the cocaine in Florida, and his brother Luckner handled distribution in New York. Luckner's lawyer was less successful since Luckner spent several years in jail as the suspected chief of a criminal organization, but nobody ever made the family connection with Ketant. The rest of the Guillaume family was more fortunate and were never arrested since they mainly took care of business in Haiti. I saw once Claude Guillaume entering a room in which 'Kiko' and Martelly were present, and I knew who was chief, it was neither the President nor his brother in law. When Martelly ended his term as President in February 2016, and the parliament had to elect an interim President until the elections in November 2016, Jaques Ketant and his money appointed Jocelerme Privert, former Minister of Interior under Aristide and Senator from Nippes department as the Interim President. I just had to acknowledge the fact; Haiti was run by a drug cartel. I didn't know who was on top. It was like there was an authority part, like Youri Latorture, Oriel Jean, Guy Phillippe and the rest of the HNP who protected and controlled the trafficking and there was a logistic part, the civilian operation under the Ketant brothers. In the days from 1993 to 2004 it was pretty clear who was in charge, 'the country' was above all, and the country was President Aristide, maybe he still is.

CHAPTER 24
Mission complete

Haiti, Port au Prince, November 2016

The Haitian presidential and parliamentary elections finally ended in November 2016 and with some necessary second round run-offs in January 2017. As Pike predicted throughout the never-ending process, the USUS elections needed to be finalized before Haiti could succeed as well. Jovnel Moise was declared President-elect after the first round at the end of November 2016. There was no doubt that he was the most popular candidate. I would have voted for him as well since he was a complete unknown before being announced as a candidate and had no adverse public history. He might have had skeletons in his closet, but it was likely a tiny closet compared to all the others in the race for highest office. Even though the result seemed to reflect the Haitian people's wishes, there was no excitement about it on election day. It was like the population knew the elections were fixed and didn't need to make an effort to influence the result by casting a dissenting vote. The Haitians knew their democratic process and had lost confidence in it many years ago. But people identified themselves with Jovnel Moise. He was a skinny man, and his suit seemed too big. Even though he could articulate himself very well, he always looked a little bit nervous. Abuelo nailed it when he saw the President-elect in a speech the first time: "Meeen, he is a patsy, the fall guy. The moment our military troops leave this country, they throw him out of the palace". I agreed with Abuelo; he looked like a throw-away President, filling in for the time being. I couldn't say much about the opposition's accusations, but the fact that he was unknown gave him credit and made him look like the most honest of all of the candidates. He actually tried to bring a message to the people. Not that it mattered much since anybody seeking success in these elections just needed control over the voting centers and accurate national voting registration data. Political party representatives in the voting centers made sure that ballots with these names, dead or alive, voted. International observers had no idea who was who and were just glad that violent incidents were very isolated. Agreements were already settled before the elections and ensured a quiet process. It was a form of evolution in comparison with previous elections when bandits were openly intimidating voters in Port au Prince or the traditional rural method of gun-blazing bandits exchanging the original ballot boxes for ones with the winning ballots. It was smooth, and Haiti and the HNP passed the final test as though they were ready to take full control and let MINUSTAH leave in October 2017.

The winning Senators contributed their part to the theatre by arranging the outcome among themselves; everything went according to the plan. The positions in the lower chamber were also sorted out, and Claude Guillaume was Jaques Ketant's first family member to receive official Haitian credentials and can again travel to the United States on a Haitian diplomatic passport. Garcia Delva, Youri Latorture's right hand man, who was deported from the US a few years ago, can again perform concerts in Little Haiti in Miami. It was almost too good to be true, except for Guy Phillippe. Most candidates had a known criminal history in Haiti or the US, but Guy Phillippe was the most famous one. Like most of the winning Senators, he didn't have much of a challenge in this election. Guy just caused most of the headache during the campaign and fueled the rumors of a small well-equipped army protecting him in his stronghold close to Jeremie. He spread the word for safety in case the US DEA office ignored his immunity status as a senatorial candidate. The rumors strengthened when a group of armed men attacked two police stations in Les Cayes and killed one policeman. One attacker was killed as well, he was dressed in a perfect green uniform with Haitian badges, black military boots and an old army rifle next to him. When I saw pictures of the dead paramilitary, my first thought was that he was old. He also had cotton in his ears; this was the first armed Haitian who tried to protect his hearing. If one of the minibuses used by the attackers hadn't had an accident after the attack, most people would have bought the story of Guy's army. The minibus left several seriously injured gunmen behind and showed that it was just a group of thugs without uniforms. The old man was a plant to make the group look like a platoon of real soldiers. The old man didn't die that night; he was already dead. The cotton was put into his ears in a morgue.

I was told that in the past dead bodies taken from morgues were used to blame political opposition for human rights violations and massacres. We knew some of the injured bandits and could link them to Guy Phillippe and Arnel Belizaire, the parliamentarian elected as a prison escapee. The attack on the HNP stations in Les Cayes was not just to create the perception of a severe fighting force supporting Guy Phillippe. To hit the HNP in Les Cayes was like hitting the drug lord in Les Cayes. It must have been either money or a shipment of drugs Guy wanted. Somehow it looked like Guy went rogue and turned against his family members. But Guy Phillippe was definitely not a stabilizing factor in the country.

Our friends from the Diplomatic Security Service in the US embassy let us know that he was still marked. Even though the times of JAKWG were past, we still continued our cooperation and efforts. The current RSO, call sign 'Delta' and his team were reasonably young, but all combat approved operators and very much hands on. While I helped to catch one US Marshal's fugitive, the Deputy RSO, call sign 'Bravo', did it on a weekly basis. He understood the environment and proved how successful HNP officers could be when they were protected and working with a respected authority like the US embassy. But he also found his frustrating limits when targets were close to the cocaine family and only moved in official government vehicles. But Guy Phillippe was the most wanted, master fugitive who slipped so many times through the net and was now Senator-elect, but still a marked man.

We were enthused and reached out to our scouts and informants. I knew one of his safe houses in Port au Prince that he frequently used but didn't know we knew about. The elections were over, and the winners needed a legislative certification document from the election office, the CEP in Petion Ville, before the official inauguration on Monday, 09 January 2017. Jeantel Joseph, Deputy of Pestel, the Guy's hometown and a leading member of Guy's political party, went to the CEP to pick up the papers for the freshly elected Senator on Wednesday 04 January. He was refused because the document could only be handed over to Guy Phillippe himself. This message on our Zombie Hunter chat was electrifying; a man in the shadow had a tip that Guy had to come in person to the CEP But the CEP was not a good location for an arrest, too many people, police and armed security personnel for public officials; it would have been messy. Despite this, the RSO started preparing to get the authorizations needed for such an arrest and extradition since it looked like the only real hot spot. There was a short window for Guy to get his documents, only

Thursday and Friday before the inauguration on Monday. The short window was a grey zone; Guy was no longer a candidate, he was Senator-elect, but not yet inaugurated. Our interpretation was that he lost candidate immunity and hadn't gained immunity as a Senator yet. He didn't have legal protection, and it was our last chance for the next 6 years. Interim President Privert signed the arrest warrant and necessary extradition papers. He was not the first and most likely didn't expect to be the last to sign such papers. These documents were signed several times in the past years before unsuccessful arrest attempts. The man in the shadow placed a scout at the CEP. Guy was careful and didn't waste time; he was fast getting into the CEP and out again. When the scout called the man in the shadow that Guy arrived, he already saw him coming back out; this window was too short.

The shadow warrior referred the scout to SCOOP FM. He heard earlier on SCOOP FM, a Petion Ville radio station, that they would have a surprise guest. He was sure the surprise was Guy. The RSO and his men geared up and with a small vetted HNP unit headed towards the radio station. The scout confirmed that Guy's convoy of three vehicles and his security detail were parked in the street in front of the radio station. The interview started; it was Guy Phillippe. The RSO and his team were still around 10 minutes out. Guy seemed to be relaxed and happy and sounded cocky during the interview. The interview went on for several minutes until he stopped in mid-sentence; there were some background noises and then no words. It seemed to take forever. He must have been tipped off and run, again.

A few minutes later on another security chat, an international security officer reported shots fired in Petion Ville. Shortly thereafter, our Zombie Hunter chat lit up, they arrived just in time, Guy Phillippe received a text message during the interview about the HNP unit coming for him and got out. He ran directly into the strike force of HNP and Diplomatic Security Services who had just rolled up in front of the station. The Hunters came in, and Guy's security didn't put up much of a fight, only a few shots were fired.

It took a few minutes and the RSO gave Guy a ride to DCPJ next to the airport to finalize the paperwork and wait for the DEA plane to land. Now the time was crucial. Whenever I was asked what would happen if Guy was arrested, I always had the same answer. If he could be flown out shortly after the arrest, there wouldn't be much backlash. Once Guy left for the US, nobody would want to put himself too much into the spotlight after the fact. Also, the usual investment of money in demonstrations must have an objective or result and no such event would bring Guy back to Haiti once he left. My argument was based on the premise that the story about his popular support was a myth and people didn't care much about him. He was not Pablo Escobar who built schools and hospitals for the people. The real threat came from his partners in crime and the demonstrations they could organize. If they thought violence could prevent his extradition, it could trigger an April 2008 riot scenario. My assessment was immediately put to the test.

Shortly after Guy arrived with his new friends at DCPJ, the first Senators and Deputys came to demand Guy's immediate release. Youri Latorture was one of the first and loudest of all. I was surprised how openly they displayed their fear and anger about Guy Phillippe being in custody. It showed me how important and significant Guy was for the cocaine family. They were already making calls to mobilize their gangs and the estimated 2.5 hours for the DEA plane to land might be too long. By then the airport road in front of DCPJ was blocked and filled with gang members. The situation got tense, and the Diplomatic Security team didn't want to attract more attention than necessary. The RSO left it with the Haitian authorities and withdrew his Zombie Hunters.

It was the right decision since the crowd in front of DCPJ grew fast, and the airport road was just about to be made impassable. Nightfall might invite significant violence if the parliamentarians and their supporters believed it was necessary. The head of DCPJ and the vetted HNP unit remained behind and stood their ground. In the end, it was a Haitian affair.

Guy Phillippe knew that his buddies were there to back him up and wouldn't let him get out of the country, in the end, they were all family, and he was an elected Senator. The clutch made terrible noises when the US embassy vehicle left DCPJ; the junior RSO was not very comfortable with the manual transmission. Also not very pleased was Guy Phillippe. He was squeezed in behind the front seats and had the boots of the RSO and other Zombie Hunters in his face. Guy must have been pissed that nobody realized the US embassy team left DCPJ with him. They were cruising through a safe neighborhood until the DEA plane arrived. I went to UN Log Base that had an entrance gate to the runway of the International Airport to check a possible alternative. It was not needed. The group blocking DCPJ was still convinced that Guy was inside. It was almost unreal when I saw the plane taking off into the darkness; Guy Phillippe was on his way to Miami. He could have made this flight years ago without handcuffs.

Guy's arrest reminded me of our good times and the impact our JAKWG had on kidnappings that haunted the country since 2004, causing so much suffering and fear. For 9 years MINUSTAH had zero success against this threat with all their military and police forces. So many civilians died as collateral damage during the gun battles against the root of all evil in Cité Soleil. So many millions of MINUSTAH dollars were focused on the gangs in the poorest slums of Port au Prince without having any impact on kidnappings or other criminal statistics. The men and women who finally countered the kidnapping were Haitian HNP officers and the victims who trusted in the US embassy's protection. The oversight and selection of the investigating judges completed the success. Without significant UN military resources, respect, guidance and support under the umbrella of the US State Department made it happen. The HNP officers knew what was going on in their country but could never act on it. The HNP Anti Kidnapping Unit brought kidnapping in Port au Prince to zero in August 2013.

The sweeping condemnation of all people in Cité Soleil was proven wrong, and even the gangs and their leaders showed during the period of Prime Minister Lamothe they were willing to participate in more constructive roles within society rather than representing the monsters of darkness. They almost became community leaders instead of controllers. When the Haitian cocaine family removed Laurent Lamothe and Reginald Delva, they destroyed the progress made and the luxury of hope for most of the Haitian people. JAKWG didn't end abruptly because we attacked a gang in Cité Soleil, we were shut down because we touched a nerve of the Haitian Narco-Family. 'Son Son La Familia,' 'Kiko,' mid-level Lieutenants, we stepped on a tentacle of the preeminent Haitian drug cartel, and President Martelly happened to be married into it.

Our combined knowledge and the Dude's vision to combine it in a JAKWG proved that in the right environment Haitians can solve Haitian problems. They just had to be protected from the existing Haitian power structure. The real root of all evil was apparent, but we couldn't say it. The insecurity in the country is part of a strategy to keep international investment out and humanitarian aid in. Haiti's democratically elected officials maintain this system. Stating the obvious out loud would not be politically correct. This political correctness kept MINUSTAH leadership from identifying the real roots of all evil for all these years. This political correctness holds the UN itself hostage and prevents its original purpose of improving the lives of people in need. As a retired German General stated recently; the wall of political correctness has to crumble. Twice only I saw this wall of political correctness crumbling in the Senior Management Team meeting of all UN Agencies. Once, Carl Alexandre called MINUSTAH a 'do nothing mission' and faced an immediate indignant reaction of Section Chiefs acting like sulking children. The other time was when the Brazilian Force Commander called the root of all evil by its name.

General José Luiz Jaborandy summarized the Haitian reality in a few words on 28 August 2015. It was the Senior Management Team Meeting that discussed the latest cancellation of the presidential and parliamentary elections due to demonstrations claiming irregularities and gang violence. As usual, an insignificant number of 3000 Haitian demonstrators caused annulation of the polls. The General must have been upset about the theatre as well and stated that if Haitian politicians stopped providing guns to the poorest neighborhoods of Port au Prince, Haiti wouldn't have a gang or crime problem. He further argued that everybody in the international community knew how these politicians made their money and were complicit in allowing it. Haiti could never change without us (the internationals) addressing the real issues. The same Friday the General left Port au Prince for Miami to continue a flight to Brazil to see his family. He was much respected and suffered a fatal heart attack on the airplane to Brazil. I saw him running every morning in the Brazilian camp. He was another victim of the anger and frustration caused by the blatant injustice in Haiti.

I couldn't imagine the General would have been as satisfied and optimistic as the rest of the International Community about the November 2016 elections and the near future of Haiti. He knew the gangs were well maintained by the politicians and business community and could destabilize the country any time it was needed and convenient. He knew MINUSTAH was focused on gangs in the poorest neighborhoods that wouldn't have had a single bullet in their guns if the Haitian elite hadn't provided it to them. While President Moise prepared to take office in February 2017, MINUSTAH leadership summarized its achievements and patted each other on the back. It was time to start the drawdown process until MINUSTAH and its UN military contingents left in October 2017.

President Jovnel Moise presented himself as a willing partner to the IC Maybe he was a little bit too willing. A significant change in fuel prices that seemed to be ridiculously high, triggered barricades throughout Port au Prince for a few days in July 2018. There was no HNP response to the small violent groups at several roadblocks concentrated in international residential areas. Even though the HNP could have controlled the situation, Haitians and internationals were left alone. The only heavy HNP presence was at the parliament that was in session during these rough days. Other HNP officers were in civilian clothes as demonstrators and coordinated the simultaneous mounting of barricades and obstacles. Violent looters targeted businesses of the President's leading financial supporters like Reginald Boulos. Money was sent to the slums for the most influential opposition gang leaders, like the new root of all evil, 'Ti-Arnel' in Village de Dieu. Ysca also participated since Gabriel and Ougan remained loyal to the President. What was interpreted by the media as social unrest was, as usual, a well-orchestrated and coordinated violent rock-throwing operation. The men in the shadow identified Youri Latorture as the principal strategist of the scenario just before the violence paralyzed Port au Prince for a few days. The tip off was Garcia Delva delivering money from Youri to gang leader Arnel just a few days before it started; this gave the Zombie Hunters a hint just ahead of time, and unfolding events completed the puzzle.

The rise in fuel prices was the trigger, but there was much more at stake. The International Community wanted Jovnel Moise to reform state contracts with private businesses related to customs at the Dominican border and Haitian ports and cancel overpriced agreements with private electricity suppliers. In other words, the International Community wanted the President to cut the primary financial resources of some of the most powerful families in the country and the front for money laundering operations of the drug traffickers. The only legal money left would have been foreign aid money. Such changes would have been a challenging task with 8,000 UN troops in the country, but without any, it was a suicide mission. Most of the business community, parliament and a lot of money made sure the HNP had a very 'active' role in this attempted coup d'état. At the height of targeted looting and violence on Saturday, Senate President Joseph Lambert, tried to convince the Diplomatic Core Group that he had to take charge of the country since the President and Prime Minister had lost control. According to the constitution, he was third in line for the top seat since Youri Latorture recently handed over this position to him almost as though he knew elections might be forthcoming. It took 9 months for the first attempt to overthrow the President and the government. The Diplomatic Core Group's answer was, no, we won't accept a new President, and on Sunday things calmed down after severe damage had been done. The Core Group's answer might have been different had the planned prison break at the national penitentiary in downtown Port au Prince been successful.

A riot started in the 'Titanic,' the high-security block of the national penitentiary. The 'Raz Kabrit' gang had weapons and equipment smuggled into the 'Titanic' to break out of the cement block, which affected most of the prison. The UDMO unit permanently stationed outside the prison left for unknown reasons and destinations. The HNP officers inside the prison were not included in the coup d'état and stood their ground. They stopped the crowd at the last gate before the street with lethal force. The standoff lasted hours until the inmates decided it was not worth their lives. The prisoners in the 'Titanic' were all hard-core criminals and would have caused horrifying havoc and chaos among the population of Port au Prince. A few brave HNP officers changed the outcome of these riots and most likely prevented a coup d'état. The fact that gang leaders Ougan and Gabriel in Boston of Cité Soleil stayed loyal to the President was a significant factor since they were expected to switch sides. Joseph Lambert would have had to organize elections within 3 months, and everything would have been prepared for Youri Latorture to become President of Haiti.

Since this didn't work out, a new Prime Minister was negotiated with the parliament. The parliament immediately ratified Jean Henry Ceant. This was always a bad sign but no surprise since he had the blessing of Jaques Ketant. He was not only reputed to be a money launderer for the biggest narco-traffickers in the country but made it clear that his administration would have never agreed to Guy Phillippe's extradition. The parliament had a trusted Prime Minister and successor if the President resigned. I was told that the President had already resigned once or twice, but the Core Group ignored it. The President was still in charge because the International Community finally started to reject perception and look at reality. The group behind in this coup d'état was so powerful that nobody involved questioned the outcome and HNP leadership took success for granted. That it didn't work was just TIH, This Is Haiti.

The riots in April 2008 didn't target the Presidency, but the July 2018 riots did. In both scenarios, the parliament was in session, and sitting members were crucial organizers. The riots in July 2018 showed one significant change in the country that will dictate Haiti's security environment in the future. Control over drug trafficking switched from the Presidential Palace to the parliament with the election of Jovnel Moise, who seemed to be either too small or not a member of the Haitian cocaine family. So far, the Haitian cocaine family seems to be a happy family. But the limited number of immunity positions in parliament and many candidates make it unlikely that this family will stay peacefully together forever.

When I heard about the riots and the attempted prison break, I thought immediately of Clifford Brandt. It seemed he was not much involved. I learned that the Brandt family was actually arranging to have their son moved to prison in Gonaives, the Youri Latorture's kingdom and the mysterious ways of Haitian justice under Youri's control were reopening the Brandt case at the beginning of 2019. For a successful new trial, it was necessary for witness testimonies and pieces of evidence to change or disappear, and Youri could organize it. Most likely not too fast, since Youri will need Brandt family financial support for his presidential campaign. As President, he could pardon Clifford if justice was too slow or uncooperative. A not guilty verdict could be difficult for even a Haitian judge when Reginald Delva presents all the facts and evidence again during a trial.

But Haitian justice in its infinite wisdom found a way. Discredit Reggie. The same way a young motivated HNP officer was jailed for a crime that didn't exist and died, Reggie was implicated in an incident with which he had no connection. But Haitian justice's best friend, the Haitian media, could kill anybody's reputation. It was not about critical thinking or investigative journalism; the media transmitted the agenda of the people above the law. A September 2016 weapons seizure was reemerging in September 2018.

At the time of the seizure in 2016, Reggie was no longer part of the government. An investigative Judge from St. Marc, in Youri's kingdom, named several suspects in the case, including Reginald Delva. The investigating judge claimed that the weapons were related to a security company that was created during the time Reggie was Minister of Interior. The security company was never mentioned in any investigation by Haitian or US authorities. A security company needed a Notary declaration and signatures of the Ministers of Commerce and of Interior to become a licensed company. The judge claimed that the security company was just a front and not a legitimate company and with his signature, Reggie supported an illegal company. That was precisely why a notary first had to acknowledge legal intent. The notary was Jean Henry Ceant, the parliament's choice for Prime Minister. His name was never mentioned once in the media or by the judge. The weapons seized in St. Marc were hidden in a Mitsubishi Fuso coming on a ship from Orlando in the United States. The load was 156 shotguns, 5 AR15 military assault rifles, two Glocks and lots of ammunition.

ATF, the responsible US agency investigated the case, and the brothers Junior and Jimmy Josef were found guilty of exporting weapons illegally to Haiti. Junior Joseph was former US military and owner of a gun shop in Orlando. The phone records, WhatsApp and other communications showed clearly the primary receivers of the weapons were the drug lord in the South Herve Foucard and Aramick Louis, Secretary of State for Public Security under Rene Preval before the Martelly administration. At the time of the seizure, he was a special advisor to Interim President Privert and also a good friend of the Ketant family.

This is unsurprising since Louis started his career in this big family as a high ranking HNP officer and was Director of the West Department in 1997. He was Guy Phillippe's boss. Aramick Louis was the person paying for the weapons and Herve Foucard and his half-brother facilitated the incoming shipment. His half-brother Nicolas Pierre Louis, was a bit junior to 'Kiko' Saint Remis and lower in the Ketant organization but well known in the ports of Port au Prince and St. Marc.

He could facilitate an inspection-free delivery, except that this time, customs agents found the weapons. This case is typical because it shows how media and justice twist things on command and tried to destroy Reginald Delva. It was a bit ironic because Reggie helped the US authorities to get to the bottom of it. If anybody in the US embassy or ATF in Florida had previously never questioned the corruption of Haitian Justice until this day, this case finally opened their eyes. Even without evidence, Reggie could be placed under arrest for one year, a long and dangerous year. We all advised him to leave the country. He knew how the media would have twisted it, and he stayed, the last man standing in the light.

The dark side is dominant in Haiti, but its greed will never be satisfied. At some point, the group benefiting from this power will become smaller and smaller until they at last turn against each other. We tend to look with western industrialized arrogance on less developed countries without recognizing our own elites. What was once the political choice of the people is today an elite, disconnected and above the people and the law. I was not born in the United States, but I believe the USA is one of the most amazing creations in history. In a time when it would have been reasonable for George Washington to name himself king, he and the founding fathers wrote a declaration and constitution to protect the people from their government. The premises for these documents were that with absolute certainty, any government long enough in power would turn against its people. The founding fathers of the United States of America created a bill of rights to protect the people and prevent elites or single Presidents from becoming rulers for life and maintaining their power with 'Ton Ton Macoutes', or any other form of suppression. Even though many of these Presidents for life sought power to bring social justice for the masses, there was always the moment they got corrupted by power and greed. I wondered if this happened to the founding father of Haiti, Jean Jaques Dessalines when he became Emperor Jaques I of Haiti. Did he betray his people for the greed of unlimited power as Francois Duvalier did? I guess there is always the point when liberal becomes radical, and tolerance turns intolerant. The founding fathers of the United States knew it and also knew that it all starts with the freedom of the spiritual mind and to express it. Freedom of religion and freedom of speech and the individual right to bear arms as a guarantor.

MINUSTAH came to an end, and so did the last of MINUSTAH's Zombie Hunters. Abuelo returned into the jungles of South America where his career started. Ray and Cege went to other missions to complete one or two more years until their early retirement. Pike was undecided about two offers and was researching which mission was closest to the nearest cruise line harbor. Niko wanted to make a move to Iraq and had it all settled with brave colleagues serving in Iraq who needed somebody they could rely on. Our Chief Security Advisor had only to contact the CSA. in Iraq and DPKO could have made a quick lateral switch. The two CSA's came up with a better plan. A friend of the CSA in Haiti needed a job as well. Our CSA brought him to Haiti on a temporary contract, which was a loophole to get friends inside the system regardless of their experience. But to guarantee him a proper deal, the UNDSS CSA in Iraq took him instead of Niko. He was a good UN staff member, friendly but useless. Ray never qualified him for any weapon, I think he didn't even give him a pepper spray. Niko retired, and it turned out to be for the best since he was about to fight our deadliest enemy, cancer.

For us, my family and me, we couldn't continue this way. First, I was disgusted by my own organization, and this wouldn't have been the basis for a healthy 'presence environment.' Second, we had a miscarriage in 2016, we blamed it on the Zika virus that was at its height in February 2016 in Haiti. Today I believe it might have been the anti-mosquito spray which we used intensively, since

Max Kail

Zika didn't have any impact in Haiti at all, and reportedly in no country other than Brazil. The Zika virus was an epidemic during the carnival season in 2016 in Haiti, and since this was the time most Haitian babies were produced, all NGOs were frightened about the upcoming maternity seasons in September and October. The fact that there was no increase of congenital disabilities in Haiti in September and October made me wonder if maybe the accusations against Monsanto chemicals by the population in Brazil had merit. Notably, this was only mentioned in the first articles about a significant increase in congenital disabilities in a specific area in Brazil; that the affected population blamed Monsanto chemicals for it. A few weeks later, Zika warning signs were even at the Miami International airport. I remember that within a few weeks the WHO, CDC, UN, and US health agencies, declared the Zika virus responsible. It was amazing to see how the media was pushing the Zika threat, and it appeared to be a distraction tactic. There was no follow up on the impact anywhere else, except the fear and worries for many people first and the release with a healthy newborn after. In Haiti, nobody would question the possibility that a powerful enterprise can make a problem go away by financing studies and dictating the media focus on it; maybe Haiti is not so different after all.

I realized the fight against evil has a very significant spiritual part in all of us. The battle is much more spiritual than I ever considered because it is in us. 18 years of service with the United Nations made me meet incredible people and experience incredible moments. When I joined the UN, I thought I would help change the world and had to realize I just helped to maintain the status quo. Haiti was the most fantastic experience and the worst experience. I saw hope in the eyes of the HNP officers when Brandt was finally arrested and they thought they could help change their country. I also saw their resignation, that the people above the law were still in power and will remain there. We, the international community, actually claim we come to help the people, but never deal with the people, only with the elite. We want the same political and economic elite in the country who created the mess to fix it. Trump was a very controversial candidate because he buried political correctness 6 feet under. I believe 6 feet under is precisely where political correctness belongs. To change things for the better, we have to identify the real issues and call them out.

Also, we should admit, the approaches of the past 30 years have proven ineffective and new strategies are needed. Haiti is not a failed state, it just fails the majority of Haitians and works only for a small elite, a cabal. It seemed we operated behind enemy lines, but the Haitian population never treated us like an enemy. We operated in occupied territory; our enemy was the cabal occupying the country. The population has no say in elections, the elite controls the votes. Corruption within the Haitian Justice system allows drug money to maintain the system and the international aid keeps the rest of the country afloat and in check. So, we either change approaches or stop pretending we want change and stop giving false hope to people in need.

All this injustice made me angry and frustrated, but I didn't want to be angry and frustrated. I learned that this feeds the evil, I will not. An old friend made me realize what to do. I have to confess.

Numquam Retro

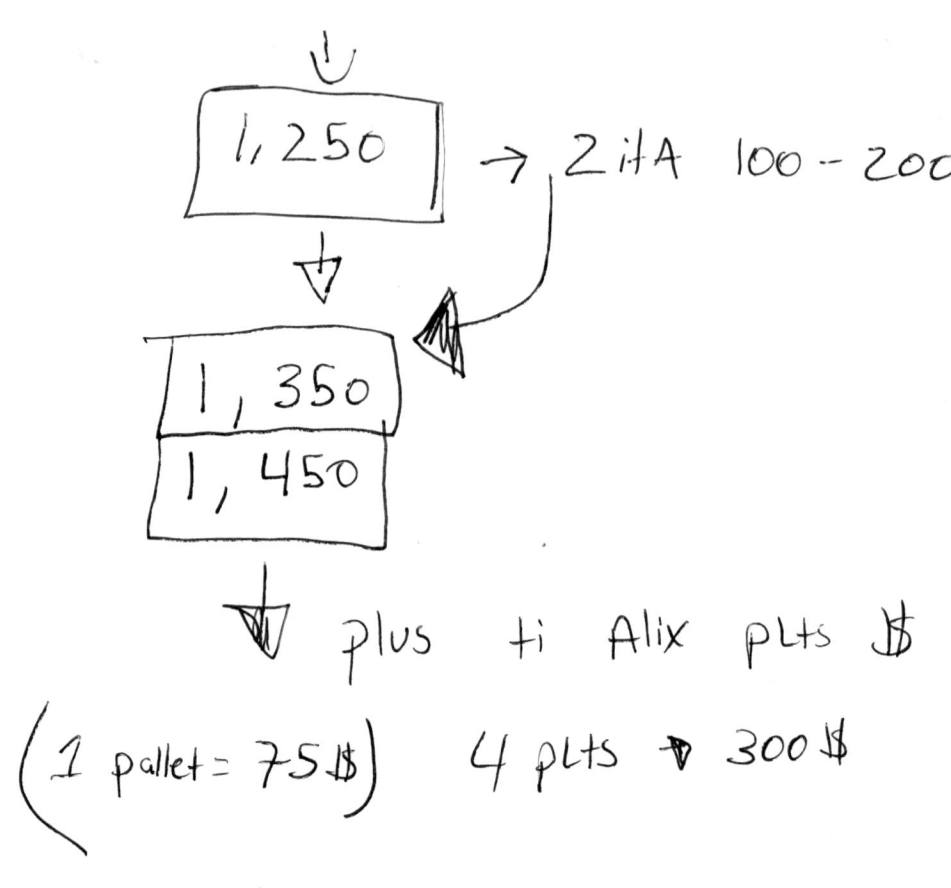

800
+ 300
[1,100] → Dider 150-200
        ↓
    [1,250] → ZitA 100-200
        ↓   ↰
    [1,350]
    [1,450]
        ↓
    plus ti Alix plts $

(1 pallet = 75$)   4 plts → 300$

Last week of Aug/sept
        Hopefully → 1,650